STUDIES ON VOLTAIRE AND THE EIGHTEENTH CENTURY

250

General editor

PROFESSOR H. T. MASON

Department of French
University of Bristol
Bristol BS8 1TE

MARTIN SMITH

Studies on Voltaire
and the eighteenth century:
summary index to volumes
1-249

THE VOLTAIRE FOUNDATION
AT THE TAYLOR INSTITUTION, OXFORD

1989

ISSN 0435-2866

ISBN 0 7294 0346 7

British Library cataloguing in publication data

Smith, Martin
Studies on Voltaire and the eighteenth century:
summary index to volumes 1-249
— (Studies on Voltaire and the eighteenth century,
ISSN 0435-2866; 250)
1. Europe, 1715-1815. Catalogues, indexes
I. Title   II. Series
016.9402'53

ISBN 0-7294-0346-7

Printed in England at The Alden Press, Oxford

Contents

Introductory note

THIS summary index is not intended to cover all subjects touched on in the 249 volumes that precede it in *Studies on Voltaire and the eighteenth century*. Its aim is to include all persons and major topics mentioned or implied in the titles of contributions to those volumes and the principal subjects treated in the main body of the works.

For ease of reference, titles of articles and monographs are given in full throughout. To reduce the number of places in the analytical index that a user might have to consult, the detailed subdivision of topics has usually been rejected in favour of a fairly broad and flexible interpretation of head-words; the presence of the full titles of contributions should quickly clarify any vagueness consequent on this arrangement. Very general terms, such as Enlightenment, have been avoided (but special senses, such as Aufklärung, are included). Similarly, France does not appear as a head because the great majority of contributions treat of French matters. The broadest head here, 'ideas', covers the history of ideas in a very wide sense. To reduce the amount of guess-work the user might need to exercise to find a given topic, and to avoid multiple '*see also*' directions, the subheads of broad subjects are frequently to be found as main heads in their own right.

Most writers are given undivided entries, but in the case of the major writers, and in particular Voltaire, subdivision was necessary. Where this is so, general biographical matters come first, followed by thematic treatments, in alphabetical order; individual works are dealt with last, also in alphabetical order.

Within heads or subheads the titles of contributions are arranged chronologically. The format for each contribution is as follows: the name of the author(s), or occasionally editor(s); after a colon, the title is given, followed by the volume number; then, in parentheses, the year of publication; finally, for articles, the pagination within the volume.

A list of contributions arranged alphabetically by author (or editor) is also provided. Here too the arrangement under each head is chronological, but it should be noted that edited texts are collected together after individual works, and that collaborative works follow at the end.

Alphabetical list of subject headings

Abélard, Pierre
aborigines
absolutism
absurdity
academies: France: Châlons-sur-Marne
— — Dijon
— — Paris: Académie des inscriptions et
  belles lettres
— — — Académie française
— — — Académie royale des sciences
— Germany
— Italy
— Spain
Adam, Antoine
Addison, Joseph
Adhémar, Antoine-Honneste de Monteil
  de Brunier, marquis d'
Aeschylus
aesthetics
— antiquity
— art
— decadence
— music
Africa
agriculture
alchemy
Alembert, Jean Le Rond d'
Alexander the Great
Alfieri, Vittorio
Algarotti, Francesco
alien
alienation
Allart, Johannes
allegory
almanachs
America
— booktrade
— education
— law
— literature
— philosophy
— politics

America, *continued*
— religion
— revolution
— slavery
— Spanish and Portuguese
— views of
anarchism
anatomy
Anglomania
animals
Année littéraire
anthropology
antiquaries
antiquity
antisemitism
Antraigues, Emmanuel-Henri-Louis-
  Alexandre de Launay, comte d'
Arbuthnot, John
archaeology
architecture
Argens, Jean-Baptiste de Boyer,
  marquis d'
Argenson, René-Louis de Voyer,
  marquis d'
Argental, Charles-Augustin de Ferriol,
  comte d'
aristocracy
Aristophanes
Arnauld, Antoine
Arnold, Matthew
art
— criticism
— Gothic
— Italy
— monuments
— neo-classicism
— portraiture
— religious
— rococo
— Spain
— technique
— theory

art, *continued*
artisan
Assemblée des notables
astronomy
Astruc, Jean
atheism
Aucassin et Nicolette
Aufklärung
Augustine, saint
Austen, Jane
Australia
Austria
authority
autobiography
Bach, Johann Sebastian
Bachaumont, Louis Petit de
Bacon, Francis
Baculard d'Arnaud, François-Thomas-
  Marie Baculard, *called*
Bailly, Jean-Sylvain
Balkans
ballet
Bandini, Sallustio
Barbeyrac, Jean
Baretti, Giuseppe
Barnave, Antoine-Pierre-Joseph-Marie
baroque
Barthes, Roland
Bayle, Pierre
Beauharnais, Fanny de
Beaumarchais, Pierre-Augustin Caron de
Beauzée, Nicolas
Beccaria, Cesare
Beckford, William
Belgium
Bentham, Jeremy
Bentinck, Charlotte Sophia of Aldenburg,
  countess
Bentinck, John Albert
Bernardin de Saint-Pierre, Jacques-
  Henri
Bernini, Giovanni Lorenzo
Berthier, Guillaume-François
Besterman, Theodore
Beverland, Adriaan
Bible
bibliography
— Britain

bibliography, *continued*
— critical editions
— France
— Geneva
— Germany
— Greece
— Holland
— Italy
— New World
— Portugal
— Romania
— Scandinavia
— Spain
— travel
Bibliothèque universelle des romans
Bigex, Simon
Bignan, Anne
Bignon, Jean-Paul
biography
biology
blacks
Blackwell, Thomas
Blake, William
blasphemy
Boerhaave, Hermann
Bohemia
Boissel, François
Bolingbroke, Henry St John, Viscount
Bonald, Louis de
Boncerf, Pierre-François
Bonnet, Charles
booktrade
— almanachs
— Balkans
— Belgium
— Britain
— censorship
— clandestine
— colportage
— England
— France
— Geneva
— Germany
— Holland
— Italy
— printing
— privilege
— Russia

booktrade, *continued*
— Spain
— travel
Borde, Charles
Bordelon, Laurent
Bordeu, Théophile de
Bossuet, Jacques-Bénigne
Boswell, James
botany
Boudier de Villemert, Pierre-Joseph
Boufflers, Stanislas-Jean, chevalier de
Bougainville, Louis-Antoine de
Bouillon, Société typographique de
Boulainvilliers, Henri, comte de
Boulanger, Nicolas-Antoine
Boullée, Etienne-Louis
Boureau-Deslandes, André-François
bourgeoisie
Bourget, Paul
Boyer, Abel
Brazil
Brecht, Bertolt
Bret, Antoine
Breteuil, Louis-Auguste Le Tonnelier,
    baron de
Brissot de Warville, Jean-Pierre
Bristol journal
Brosses, Charles de
Brown, John
Brucker, Jakob
Bruhier, Jean-Jacques
Brumoy, Pierre
Brunetière, Ferdinand
Buffier, Claude
Buffon, Georges-Louis Leclerc, comte
    de
Bulkeley, comte de
Buñuel, Luis
bureaucracy
Bürger, Gottfried August
Burke, Edmund
burlesque
Burns, Robert
Bute, John Stuart, 3rd Earl of
Byron, George Noël Gordon, Lord
Cabanis, Pierre-Jean-Georges
Calas affair
Calmet, Augustin

Calvin, Jean
Camus, Albert
Canada
Canova, Antonio
Cantemir, Dimitrie
Carleton, Mary
Carlyle, Thomas
Carradori, Francesco
Casanova di Seingalt, Giacomo Girolamo
Castel, Louis-Bertrand
Cataneo, Jean de
Catargi, Dimitraki
Catherine II, Empress of Russia
Cato
Caumont, Joseph de Seytres, marquis de
Caylus, Anne-Claude-Philippe de
    Tubières, comte de
Cazotte, Jacques
censorship
Cerou, Pierre
Cervantes, Miguel de
Challe, Robert
Chambers, Ephraim
Chamfort, Sébastien-Roch-Nicolas
charity
Charles Edward Stuart
Charlevoix, Pierre-François-Xavier de
Charrière, Isabelle de [Belle de Zuylen]
Chastellux, François-Jean, marquis de
Chateaubriand, François-René, vicomte
    de
Chaudon, Louis-Mayeul
chemistry
Chénier, André-Marie de
Chénier, Marie-Joseph-Blaise de
children
Chile
China
Choiseul, Etienne-François, duc de
Choiseul, Louise-Honorine Crozat Du
    Châtel, duchesse de
Christ
Church
Cicero
cinema
circumcision
city
civilisation

5

civil rights
Clairon, Claire-Josèphe Lerys, *called* Mlle
clandestine writings
Clarke, Samuel
classicism
Clavijero, Francisco Xavier
Cléreaux, Marie
climate
Coger, François-Marie
Coleridge, Samuel Taylor
collectors
Collini, Cosimo Alessandro
colonialism
Combes, Louis
Comédie-Française
comedy
commerce
Condillac, Etienne Bonnot de
Condorcet, Jean-Antoine-Nicolas de
    Caritat, marquis de
Condorcet, Sophie de Grouchy, marquise
    de
Connaissance des beautés
conservatism
Constant, Benjamin
Constant d'Hermenches, David-Louis
    Constant de Rebecque, *called*
contes
continuity
Corneille, Marie
Corneille, Pierre
Corneille, Thomas
Correspondance littéraire
correspondence, political
Corsica
cosmology
costume
Coyer, Gabriel-François
Coypel, Charles-Antoine
Cramer family
Crashaw, Richard
Crébillon, Claude-Prosper Jolyot de
Crébillon, Prosper Jolyot de
crime
crisis
Croatia
culture
Cuppé, Pierre

Custine, Adam-Philippe de
Dacier, Anne
dance
Dancourt, Florent Carton, sieur
    d'Ancourt, *called*
Darwin, Erasmus
death
decadence
Defoe, Daniel
deism
Deleyre, Alexandre
Delille, Jacques
Delisle, Guillaume
Delisle de Sales, Jean-Baptiste-Claude
    Izouard, *called*
demagogy
democracy
demography
Denis, Marie-Louise
Denmark
Dennis, John
Denon, Dominique Vivant, baron
Desca, Anthony
Descartes, René
Deschamps, Léger-Marie
Desfontaines, Pierre-François Guyot,
    abbé
Deslandes, André-François
Desmahis, Joseph-François-Edouard
    Corsembleu de
despotism
destiny
Destutt de Tracy, Antoine-Louis-Claude
determinism
devils
Les Devises de la Cour
dictionaries
Dictionnaire de l'Académie française
Diderot, Denis
— bibliography
— correspondence
— criticism by
— criticism of
— philosophy
— politics
— works
— — *Les Bijoux indiscrets*
— — *Ceci n'est pas un conte*

England, *continued*
— influence
— literature
— medicine
— philosophy
— politics
— press
— religion
— theatre
— travellers
— views of
— visitors
— Voltaire
— women
epic
Epictetus
epicureanism
epistemology
equality
Erasmus
eroticism
Eskimoes
ethics
ethnology
Etudes sur le XVIIIe siècle
Europe, central
Europe, eastern
evil
evolution
Examen de la religion
exoticism
fables
fairy tales
Falconet, Etienne-Maurice
family
Farley, Felix
Farquhar, George
fascism
Fawkener, Everard
Fekete de Galánta, Janos
Feller, François-Xavier de
feminism
Fénelon, François de Salignac de La
　　Mothe
Ferdinand, prince
Féret, Jacques-Tranquillain
Ferguson, Adam
feudalism

Fiard, Jean-Baptiste
Fichte, Johann Gottlieb
Fielding, Henry
Filangieri, Gaetano
Finland
Fiske, John
Flanders
Flaubert, Gustave
Foigny, Gabriel de
folklore
Fontenelle, Bernard Le Bovier, sieur de
food
Forbes, Alexander
Formey, Jean-Henri-Samuel
Forner, Juan Pablo
Fourmont, Etienne
Franklin, Benjamin
Frederick II, King of Prussia
— works: *L'Anti-Machiavel*
— — *Art de la guerre*
Frederick II of Hesse-Kassel
freemasonry
Fréret, Nicolas
Fréron, Elie-Catherine
Freud, Sigmund
Friedel, Johann
friendship
Frisi, Paolo
Furetière, Antoine
Fuseli, Henry
Gaceta de Madrid
Galanti, Giuseppe Maria
Galeries des Etats-Généraux
Galiani, Ferdinando
Galileo
gambling
Garcilaso de la Vega
gardens
Garrick, David
Gauthey, Emiland-Marie
Gazette de Parme
Gazette d'Utrecht
Gazette littéraire
Gazette littéraire de l'Europe
Gédoyn, Nicolas
Geneva
Genlis, Caroline-Stéphanie-Félicité
　　Ducrest de Mézières, comtesse de

Genovesi, Antonio
genre
Gentleman's magazine
geography
geology
Germany
— booktrade
— education
— influence
— law
— literature
— philosophy
— politics
— press
— religion
— theatre
Gibbon, Edward
Girardin, René-Louis, marquis de
Gladstone, William Ewart
Gluck, Christoph Willibald
Godoy, Manuel
Godwin, William
Goethe, Johann Wolfgang von
Goezman, Louis-Valentin
Goldoni, Carlo
Goldsmith, Oliver
Golitsyn, Alexandre
Golitsyn, Dimitri
Gordon, Thomas
Gothic
Goya, Francisco de
Gozzi, Carlo
Gozzi, Gasparo
Graffigny, Françoise-Paule d'Issembourg
    d'Happoncourt Huguet de
Grafton, Augustus Henry Fitz Roy, 3rd
    Duke of
Graham, James
grammar
Grasset, François
Greece
Grimm, Friedrich Melchior
Guilleragues, Gabriel-Joseph de
    Lavergne, comte de
Guillotin, Ignace
Gustav III, King of Sweden
Habsburgs
Haller, Albrecht von

Hamann, Johann Georg
happiness
Harris, James
Harris, John
Hawkesworth, John
Haydn, Joseph
hedonism
Hegel, Georg Wilhelm Friedrich
Heinse, Wilhelm
Héloïse
Helvétius, Claude-Adrien
Hénault, Charles-Jean-François
Henríquez, Camilo
Herder, Johann Gottfried
Herodotus
heroic
Hervàs, José Gerardo de
Hervey, John, Baron Hervey of Ickworth
Highmore, Joseph
Hill, Aaron
Hirschel, Abraham
historiography
history
— ancient
— culture
Hobbes, Thomas
Hoffmann, Friedrich
Holbach, Paul Thiry, baron d'
Holland
Homer
Hommel, Karl Ferdinand
honour
Hooker, Richard
Horace
Houdon, Jean-Antoine
Huber, Jean
Hugo, Victor
Huguenots
humanism
humanitarianism
L'Humanité
Hume, David
Hungary
Hutcheson, Francis
idealism
ideas
— atheism
— bureaucracy

9

ideas, *continued*
— Cartesianism
— causality
— civilisation
— climate
— conscience
— continuity
— dialectics
— dogmatism
— élite
— encyclopedism
— equality
— essentialism
— evolution
— freemasonry
— Germany
— happiness
— hedonism
— hierarchy
— history
— honour
— humanism
— Ideologues
— innocence
— Jansenism
— language
— law
— legitimacy
— liberalism
— libertarianism
— literary history
— luxury
— mankind
— materialism
— modernisation
— nationalism
— natural law
— nature
— Newtonianism
— optimism
— pacifism
— perfectibility
— *philosophe*
— physiognomy
— pluralism
— prediction
— progress
— reason

ideas, *continued*
— reason of state
— reform
— relativism
— science
— scientism
— sovereignty
— supernatural
— teleology
— time
— toleration
— utopianism
— virtue
— war
ideologues
ideology
incest
India
Indians
industrial revolution
inequality
initiation
innocence
inoculation
Institut et musée Voltaire
institutions
international relations
Ireland
irony
irrationalism
Islam
Italy
— archaeology
— architecture
— art
— bibliography
— booktrade
— commerce
— cosmopolitanism
— diplomacy
— economics
— education
— history
— influence
— literature
— music
— philosophy
— politics

Italy, *continued*
— press
— religion
— social history
— theatre
— travel
— visitors
— Voltaire
Jacobi, Friedrich Heinrich
Jacobinism
Jansenism
Japan
Jaucourt, Louis, chevalier de
Jean-Paul
Jenyns, Soame
Jesuits
Jews
Joan of Arc
Jodin, Marie-Madeleine
Johnson, Samuel
Joseph II, Emperor of Austria-Hungary
Journal des dames
Journal des savants
Journal de Trévoux
Journal encyclopédique
Journal étranger
journalism
Jugoslavia
Julian
Jullien de La Drôme, Marc Antoine
Jung, Carl Gustav
Kant, Immanuel
Kantemir, Antioch
Karamzin, Nicholas
Kästner, Abraham Gotthelf
Keats, John
Klinger, Friedrich Maximilian
Knigge, Adolph Freiherr
Kotzwara, Franz
La Barre, François Poulain de
labour
Laclos, Pierre-Antoine-François
   Choderlos de
La Condamine, Charles-Marie de
La Fautrière, Louis Davy de
Lafayette, Marie-Joseph-Paul-Yves-Roch
   Gilbert Du Motier, marquis de

Lafayette, Marie-Madeleine Pioche de
   La Vergne, comtesse de
Lafitau, Joseph-François
La Harpe, Jean-François de
— correspondence
La Hontan, baron de
Lalande, Joseph-Jérôme François de
Lamarck, Jean-Baptiste-Pierre-Antoine
   de Monet, chevalier de
Lambert, Anne-Thérèse de Marguenat
   de Courcelles, marquise de
Lambert, Jean-Henri
La Mettrie, Julien Offray de
landscape
language
— origin
— semantics
— semiotics
La Noue, Jean-Baptiste Sauvé de, *called*
Larcher, Pierre-Henry
La Roche, Michel de
La Roche, Sophie
Lavater, Johann Caspar
Lavoisier, Antoine-Laurent
law
Le Bret, Alexis-Jean
Lebrun-Pindare, Ponce-Denis
   Ecouchard Lebrun, *called*
Le Clerc, Jean
Ledoux, Claude-Nicolas
Leibniz, Gottfried Wilhelm von
Le Mascrier, Jean-Baptiste
Lemercier, Louis-Jean-Népomucène
Le Mierre, Antoine-Marin
Lenclos, Ninon de
Lenglet Du Fresnoy, Nicolas
Lenz, Siegfried
Leopold I, Grand Duke of Tuscany
Le Prince de Beaumont, Jeanne-Marie
Leroux, Pierre
Lesage, Alain-René
Lessing, Gotthold Ephraim
lexicology
liberalism
libertarianism
libertinism
liberty
libraries

Liège
Ligne, Charles-Joseph, prince de
Lillo, George
Linguet, Simon-Nicolas-Henri
Linnaeus, Carl
Liotard, Jean-Etienne
Liston, Sir Robert
literary criticism
literary history
literary technique
literary theory
Loaisel de Tréogate, Joseph-Marie
Locke, John
Loen, Johann Michael von
logic
Louis, Antoine
Louis XIV
Louis XV
Louise-Dorothée, duchesse de Gotha
Louvet de Couvray, Jean-Baptiste
love
Low Countries
Lucian
Lucotte, J. R.
Lucretius
Luneau de Boisjermain, Pierre-Joseph-François
Luther, Martin
luxury
Mably, Gabriel Bonnot de
Machiavelli, Niccolò
Maillet, Benoît de
Maine de Biran, Marie-François-Pierre Gonthier de Biran, *called*
Maistre, Joseph de
Malebranche, Nicolas de
Malesherbes, Chrétien-Guillaume de Lamoignan de
Mandeville, Bernard
Manichean dualism
Marchand, Prosper
Maréchal, Sylvain
Marivaux, Pierre Carlet de Chamblain de
Marmontel, Jean-François
marriage
Marx, Karl
materialism
mathematics

Maupertuis, Pierre-Louis Moreau de
medicine
Meister, Johann Heinrich
melancholy
melodrama
Melon, Jean-François
Mémoires secrets
Mendelssohn, Moses
mentalities
Menuret de Chambaud, Jean-Jacques
Mercier, Louis-Sébastien
Mercier de La Rivière, Paul-Pierre
Mercure de France
Mercure galant
Mercure suisse
Mérimée, Prosper
Meslier, Jean
Mesmer, Anton
Messerschmidt, Franz Xaver
metaphysics
Metastasio, Pietro
methodology
Mexico
Mey, Mathieu
Middle ages
militarism
Milton, John
mimesis
Minet, Jean-Baptiste
minor writers
Mirabeau, Honoré-Gabriel Riqueti, comte de
missionaries
Missy, César de
modernisation
Molière
monarchy
Monbron, Fougeret de
monsters
Montaigne, Michel
Montesquieu
— politics
— works: *Considérations*
— — *L'Esprit des lois*
— — *Lettres persanes*
— — *Le Temple de Gnide*
morality

philosophy, *continued*
— idealism
— immoralism
— language
— materialism
— metaphysics
— natural law
— of history
— of medicine
— ontology
— optimism
— pessimism
— political
— propaganda
— rationalism
— realism
— rhetoric
— scepticism
— sensationalism
— sensualism
— society
— teleology
— utilitarianism
physics
physiocrats
physiognomy
physiology
picaresque
pietism
Pigalle, Jean-Baptiste
Pilati, Carlo Antonio
Pinto, Isaac de
Pirandello, Luigi
Piron, Alexis
Pivati, Gianfrancesco
Plato
Pluche, Noël-Antoine
pluralism
Plutarch
poetics
poetry
Poland
polemics
police
Polier de Bottens, Georges
politics
— absolutism
— anarchism

politics, *continued*
— aristocracy
— authoritarianism
— democracy
— despotism
— England
— France
— Germany
— institutions
— international relations
— Ireland
— Italy
— Jacobinism
— liberalism
— Low Countries
— monarchy
— morality
— nationalism
— pacifism
— patriotism
— Poland
— power
— realism
— religion
— republicanism
— Romania
— Scandinavia
— Scotland
— socialism
— sovereignty
— theory
— utopianism
Pombal, Sebastião José de Carvalho e
    Melo, Marquis of
Pompignan, Jean-Jacques Le Franc,
    marquis de
Pope, Alexander
population
Porée, Charles
pornography, *see also* Restif de La
    Bretonne, Sade
Porphyry
portrait
Port-Royal
Portugal
Potier, Pierre
Potocki, Jean
poverty

Prades, Jean-Martin de
prediction
prejudice
preromanticism
press
— Canada
— England
— France
— Germany
— Holland
— Hungary
— Italy
Prévost, Antoine-François
— works: *Cleveland*
— — *Le Doyen de Killerine*
— — *Histoire d'une Grecque moderne*
— — *Manon Lescaut*
— — *Mémoires d'un honnête homme*
— — *Le Pour et contre*
Price, Richard
Priestley, Joseph
printing
Prior, Matthew
privilege (publishing)
prize contests
progress
propaganda
prostitution
Protestantism
Providence
psychology
public opinion
Puisieux, Madeleine d'Arsant, Mme de
Quakers
Querelle des anciens et des modernes
Quesnay, François
Racine, Jean
Racine, Louis
Radichtchev, Alexandre
Rameau, Jean-Philippe
rationalism
Raudot, Antoine
Raynal, Guillaume-Thomas-François
reading
realism
Réaumur, René-Antoine Ferchault de
Recueil philosophique et littéraire
reform

Regency
Regnard, Jean-François
Reid, Thomas
relativism
religion
— apologetics
— atheism
— deism
— dissent
— dualism
— France
— Jansenism
— Judaism
— mysticism
— natural
— Protestantism
— providence
— Quakerism
— Scotland
— Socinianism
— Taoism
— toleration
Rémond de Saint-Mard, Toussaint
Renan, Ernest
Renout, Jean-Julien-Constantin
republicanism
Restif de La Bretonne, Nicolas-Edme
Restoration
revolution
— America
— counter-revolution
— Germany
— Italy
— Portugal
Rey, Marc-Michel
rhetoric
Ricardo, David
Riccoboni, Marie-Jeanne Laboras de
   Mézières, Mme
Richardson, Samuel
Richelieu, Louis-François-Armand Du
   Plessis, duc de
Rieu, Henri
Rivarol, Antoine
Robert, Hubert
Robertson, William
Robespierre, Maximilien-Marie-Isidore
   de

18

Voltaire, *continued*
— — *Micromégas*
— — *Le Monde comme il va*
— — *La Mort de César*
— — notebooks
— — *Œdipe*
— — *Olympie*
— — *Oreste*
— — *L'Orphelin de la Chine*
— — *La Philosophie de l'histoire*
— — *Poème sur le désastre de Lisbonne*
— — *La Princesse de Babylone*
— — *La Prude*
— — *La Pucelle*
— — *Questions sur l'Encyclopédie*
— — *Relation de Berthier*
— — *Rome sauvée*
— — *Le Siècle de Louis XIV*
— — *Les Singularités de la nature*
— — *Le Songe de Platon*
— — *Tancrède*
— — *Le Taureau blanc*
— — *Le Temple du Goût*
— — *Tout en dieu*
— — *Le Triumvirat*
— — *La Voix du sage et du peuple*
— — *Zadig*
— — *Zaïre*
Voyage à Paphos

Wales
Walpole, Horace
war
Warburton, William
Warens, Françoise-Louise-Eléonore de
    La Tour, baronne de
Warton, Thomas
Webb, Daniel
Wegelin, Jacob
Weise, Christian
Wendel, François-Ignace de
Whiston, William
widow
Wieland, Christoph Martin
Wilhelmine de Bayreuth
witchcraft
Wollstonecraft, Mary
women
— education
— religion
Wordsworth, William
Ximenès, Augustin-Marie, marquis de
Zanović, Stjepan
Zasulich, Vera Ivanovna
Zedler, Johann Heinrich
Zeno, Apostolo
Zola, Emile
Zuylen, Belle de, *see* Charrière

List of contents, volumes 1-249

Haac, L'amour dans les collèges jésuites: une satire anonyme du dix-huitième siècle; A. J. Bingham, The *Recueil philosophique et littéraire*; A. C. Keys, The vicissitudes of the *Mémoires* of Ninon de Lenclos; C. Duckworth, Flaubert and Voltaire's *Dictionnaire*; J. Vercruysse, La marquise Du Châtelet, prévote d'une confrérie bruxelloise; J. D. Candaux, La publication de *Candide* à Paris; M. Fields, La première édition française de *La Princesse de Babylone*; J. Th. de Booy, L'abbé Coger, dit Cogé Pecus, lecteur de Voltaire et d'Holbach; J. D. Candaux, Les débuts de François Grasset; Sir G. de Beer and A. M. Rousseau, Voltaire's British visitors: supplement; Th. Besterman, A provisional bibliography of Italian editions and translations of Voltaire.
ISBN 0 7294 0141 3   1961, 310 pages

19. L'Abbé Desfontaines et son rôle dans la littérature de son temps
Thelma Morris.
ISBN 0 7294 0072 7   1961, 390 pages

20. Collectaneous. M. Rezler, The Voltaire-d'Alembert correspondence; M. L. Perkins, Voltaire on the source of national power; M. Fields, Voltaire et le *Mercure de France*; H. T. Mason, Voltaire and Le Bret's digest of Bayle; J. Montagu, Inventaire des tableaux, sculptures, estampes, etc. de l'Institut et musée Voltaire; J. Vercruysse, Notes sur les imprimés et les manuscrits du collection Launoit; J. D. Candaux, Des documents nouveaux sur la mort de Voltaire?
ISBN 0 7294 0142 1   1962, 263 pages

21. The French image of China before and after Voltaire
Basil Guy.
ISBN 0 7294 0073 5   1963, 468 pages, 4 plates

22. Denis Diderot: *La Religieuse*
Edition critique par J. Parrish.
ISBN 0 7294 0074 3   1963, 345 pages

23. Collectaneous. P. Kra, The invisible chain of the *Lettres persanes*; J. Vercruysse, C'est la faute à Rousseau, c'est la faute à Voltaire; J. A. Perkins, Diderot's concept of virtue; S. J. Gendzier, Diderot's impact on the generation of 1830; J. Th. de Booy, Une anecdote de Diderot sur *Le Système de la nature*; J. Lough, Luneau de Boisjermain v. the publishers of the *Encyclopédie*; J. H. Broome, 'L'homme au cœur velu': the turbulent career of Fougeret de Monbron; J. Th. de Booy, Henri Meister et la première édition de la *Correspondance littéraire*; L. G. Crocker, L'analyse des rêves au XVIIIe siècle.
ISBN 0 7294 0143 X   1963, 315 pages

24-27. Transactions of the First international congress on the Enlightenment: Coppet 1963
ISBN 0 7294 0079 4   1963, 1918 pages

28. Voltaire: *La Philosophie de l'histoire*. Critical edition by J. H. Brumfitt. This edition has been superseded by the *Complete works of Voltaire*, volume 59.

29. Pierre Rousseau and the philosophes of Bouillon
Raymond F. Birn.
ISBN 0 7294 0080 8   1964, 212 pages

30. Collectaneous. *L'Akakia* de Voltaire, éd. C. Fleischauer; M. Rezler, Voltaire and the *Encyclopédie*; R. A. Brooks, Voltaire and Garcilo de la Vega; A. Ages, Voltaire's Biblical

criticism; J. Vercruysse, Bernard Nieuwentydt et les notes marginales de Voltaire; R. A. Leigh, Rousseau's letter to Voltaire on optimism; L. Gossman, Time and history in Rousseau; H. D. Rothschild, Benoît de Maillets's Leghorn letters; G. Barber, The Cramers of Geneva.
ISBN 0 7294 0144 8   1964, 414 pages

31. General index to volumes 1-30
ISBN 0 7294 0126 X   1967, 242 pages

32. Collectaneous. Th. Besterman, Voltaire, absolute monarchy, and the enlightened monarch; J. Rigal, L'iconographie de la *Henriade* au XVIIIe siècle; P. D. Jimack, Rousseau and the primacy of self; R. Mortier, Un adversaire vénitien des 'lumières', le comte de Cataneo; P. Laubriet, Les guides de voyages au début du XVIIIe siècle et la propagande philosophique; J. Lough, The problem of the unsigned articles in the *Encyclopédie*.
ISBN 0 7294 0145 6   1965, 390 pages

33. *Jacques le fataliste* et *La Religieuse* devant la critique révolutionnaire
Textes éd. J. Th. de Booy et A. J. Freer.
ISBN 0 7294 0127 8   1965, 340 pages

34-35. Le *Pour et contre* et son temps
Marie-Rose de Labriolle.
ISBN 0 7294 0128 6   1965, 584 pages

36. Voltaire's concept of international order
Merle L. Perkins.
ISBN 0 7294 0129 4   1965, 344 pages

37. Collectaneous. Articles inédits de Voltaire pour le *Dictionnaire* de l'Académie française, éd. J. Vercruysse; D. L. Gobert, Comic in *Micromégas* as expressive of theme; J. A. Perkins, Voltaire and the natural sciences; P. D. Jimack, Rousseau misquoting Voltaire?; J. Van Eerde, Aspects of social criticism in eighteenth-century French comedy; H. D. Rothschild, Benoît de Maillet's Marseilles letters; R. L. Meyers, Fréron's critique of Rémond de Saint Mard; R. M. Conlon, Additions to the bibliography of Bossuet.
ISBN 0 7294 0146 4   1965, 176 pages

38-40. Voltaire: *La Henriade*. Edition critique par O. R. Taylor. This edition has been superseded by the *Complete works of Voltaire*, volume 2.

41. Collectaneous. T. J. Barling, The literary art of the *Lettres philosophiques*; J. R. Monty, Notes sur le vocabulaire du *Dictionnaire philosophique*; A. Ages, Voltaire, Calmet and the Old testament; C. Thacker, The misplaced garden? Voltaire, Julian, and *Candide*; D. D. R. Owen, *Aucassin et Nicolette* and the genesis of *Candide*; N. Kotta, Voltaire's *Histoire du parlement de Paris*; Th. Braun, A forgotten letter from Voltaire to Le Franc de Pompignan; L. Gossman, The worlds of *La Nouvelle Héloïse*; P. van Bever, La religion du docteur A. N. R. Sanches; G. Périer de Féral, La descendance collatérale de Voltaire; P. M. Conlon, Dancourt assailed.
ISBN 0 7294 0147 2   1965, 364 pages

42-43. Marquis d'Argenson: *Notices sur les œuvres de théâtre*
Publié par H. Lagrave.
ISBN 0 7294 0130 8   1966, 851 pages

55-58. Transactions of the Second international congress on the Enlightenment: St Andrews 1967
ISBN 0 7294 0153 7   1967, 1992 pages

59A. The Enlightenment and science in 18th century France
Colm Kiernan.
ISBN 0 7294 0060 3   1973, 249 pages

60. Collectaneous. J. Vercruysse, Bibliographie des écrits français relatifs à Voltaire, 1719-1830; A. G. Bourassa, Polémique et propagande dans *Rome sauvée* et *Les Triumvirs*; O. R. Taylor, *La Henriade*: a complementary note; R. J. Howells, The metaphysic of nature in Rousseau; R. G. Saisselin, Rousseau and portraiture; N. Perry, A forged letter from Frederick to Voltaire; C. Kiernan, Helvétius and a science of ethics; J. A. Perkins, Irony and candour in certain *libertin* novels; R. L. Myers, Rémond dialogues; N. Perry, John Vansommer of Spitalfields; H. D. Rothschild, Benoît de Maillet's letters to the marquis de Caumont.
ISBN 0 7294 0154 5   1968, 338 pages

61. Voltaire's *Tancrède*
John S. Henderson.
ISBN 0 7294 0155 3   1968, 275 pages, 103 plates

62. Collectaneous. J. B. Shipley, Two Voltaire letters; T. J. Barling, Voltaire's correspondence with Lord Hervey; M. S. Staum, Newton and Voltaire; D. Williams, Voltaire and the language of the gods; A. Ages, Stendhal and Voltaire: the *philosophe* as target; E. Rostworowski, Voltaire et la Pologne; E. Bachmann, An unknown portrait of Voltaire by Jean Etienne Liotard?; N. Perry, Voltaire and Felix Farley's *Bristol journal*; C. Todd, Two lost plays by La Harpe; S. Chevalley, Le 'sieur Minet'; R. Grimsley, Maupertuis, Turgot and Maine de Biran on the origin of language; C. Thacker, M. A. D.: an editor of Voltaire's letters identified.
ISBN 0 7294 0156 1   1968, 310 pages, 1 colour plate

63. Beaumarchais: *Le Mariage de Figaro*
Publié par J. B. Ratermanis.
ISBN 0 7294 0157 X   1968, 604 pages

64. Collectaneous. Th. Besterman, Some eighteenth century Voltaire editions unknown to Bengesco; T. J. Barling, The problem of the poem in the 20th *Lettre philosophique*; T. E. Hall, The development of Enlightenment interest in eighteenth-century Corsica; L. Sozzi, Interprétations de Rousseau pendant la révolution; S. Pitou, The Comédie française and the Palais royal interlude of 1716-1723.
ISBN 0 7294 0271 1   1968, 264 pages, 80 illustrations

65. Petit de Bachaumont: his circle and the *Mémoires secrets*
R. S. Tate.
ISBN 0 7294 0158 8   1968, 211 pages on microfiche

66. A study of the works of Claude Buffier
K. S. Wilkins.
ISBN 0 7294 0159 6   1969, 233 pages

67. Collectaneous. Voltaire's dedication of *Oreste*, ed. Th. Besterman; E. Straub, A propos d'une lettre inconnue de Voltaire; S. Werner, Voltaire and Seneca; D. Schier, Aaron

26

Hill's translation of *Alzire*; E. T. Helmick, Voltaire and *Humphrey Clinker*, J. Vercruysse, Turgot et Vergennes contre la lettre de Voltaire à Boncerf; J. Vercruysse, Mme Denis et Ximenès; R. F. O'Reilly, The structure and meaning of the *Lettres persanes*; M. L. Perkins, Destiny, sentiment and time in Rousseau; R. A. Leigh, Rousseau and Mme de Warens; E. B. Hill, Virtue on trial: a defense of Prévost's *Théophé*; A. Jovicevich, Thirteen letters of La Harpe; P. Chevallier, Les idées religieuses de Davy de La Fautrière.
ISBN 0 7294 0160 X   1969, 241 pages

68. Collectaneous. J. Leduc, Les sources de l'athéisme et de l'immoralisme du marquis de Sade; G. B. Watts, C. J. Panckoucke, 'l'Atlas de la librairie française'.
ISBN 0 7294 0161 8   1969, 205 pages

69. Voltaire's *Candide*: the protean gardener, 1755-1762
Geoffrey Murray.
ISBN 0 7294 0162 6   1970, 386 pages on microfiche

70. Collectaneous. Gladstone on *Candide*; J. D. Hubert, Note malicieuse sur le jardin de Candide; R. S. Tate, *Manon Lescaut* and the Enlightenment; F. Plotkin, Mime as pander: Diderot's *Neveu de Rameau*; M. Molinier, Les relations de Deleyre et de Rousseau; M. J. Southworth, La notion de l'île chez Rousseau; R. G. Saisselin, The transformation of art into culture; D. G. Levy, Simon Linguet's sociological system.
ISBN 0 7294 0163 4   1970, 293 pages

71. General index to volumes 32-70
ISBN 0 7294 0164 2   1973, 352 pages

72. Religion in Montesquieu's *Lettres persanes*
P. Kra.
ISBN 0 7294 0165 0   1970, 224 pages on microfiche

73. Collectaneous. S. Pitou, The players' return to Versailles, 1723-1757; C. Hogsett, Jean Baptiste Dubos on art as illusion; C. Cherpack, *Jacques le fataliste* and *Le Compère Matthieu*; W. H. Trapnell, The 'philosophical' implications of Marivaux's *Dispute*; B. Ivker, Towards a definition of libertinism in 18th-century French fiction; M. Poster, The concepts of sexual identity and the life cycle in Restif's utopian thought.
ISBN 0 7294 0166 9   1970, 293 pages

74. Rémond de Saint-Mard: a study of his major works, followed by a modernized edition of *Lucilie*
R. L. Myers.
ISBN 0 7294 0167 7   1970, 198 pages

75. Voltaire's theatre: the cycle from *Œdipe* to *Mérope*
J. R. Vrooman.
ISBN 0 7294 0168 5   1970, 220 pages

76. Collectaneous. D. A. Bonneville, *Candide* as symbolic experience; Th. Besterman, A preliminary bibliography of Portuguese translations of Voltaire; C. Duckworth, Madame Denis's unpublished *Pamela*; M. B. May, Comte d'Argental; T. E. D. Braun, Le Franc de Pompignan et la moralité du théâtre; J. Renwick, Marmontel ... 1753-1765; E. Katz, Marmontel and the voice of experience.
ISBN 0 7294 0169 3   1970, 259 pages

77. Collectaneous. A. Brown, Calendar of Voltaire manuscripts other than correspon-

dence; W. H. Trapnell, Survey and analysis of Voltaire's collective editions, 1728-1789.
ISBN 0 7294 0170 7   1970, 199 pages, £20 (also on microfiche, £10)

78. Les Romans de l'abbé Prévost
J. R. Monty.
ISBN 0 7294 0171 5   1971, 272 pages

79. Collectaneous. Th. Besterman, Additions and corrections to the definitive edition of Voltaire's correspondence, I ; R. Kusch, Voltaire as symbol of the eighteenth century in Carlyle's *Frederick*; M. Gaulin, Montesquieu et l'attribution de la lettre XXXIV des *Lettres persanes*; S. Werner, Diderot's *Encyclopédie* article 'Agnus Scythius'; I. L. Greenberg, Narrative technique and literary intent in Diderot; R. C. Carroll, Rousseau's bookish ontology; D. W. Smith, Helvétius's library; L. J. Forno, Challe and the eighteenth century; L. Levin, Masque et identité dans *Le Paysan parvenu*; J. Vercruysse, La Harpe et la *Gazette d'Utrecht*; B. Ivker, On the darker side of the enlightenment; F. R. Frautschi, Some eighteenth-century stances of silence.
ISBN 0 7294 0172 3   1971, 234 pages

80,83,85,91-93. Inventory of Diderot's *Encyclopédie*
R. N. Schwab and W. E. Rex.
See also below, volume 223
ISBN 0 7294 0179 0   1971-1972, 1538 pages

81. Collectaneous. A. Ages, The private Voltaire; M. Alcover, La casuistique du père Tout à tous et *Les Provinciales*; B. N. Morton, Beaumarchais et le prospectus de l'édition de Kehl; L. J. Forno, The fictional letter in the memoir novel; R. C. Rosbottom, Parody and truth in Mme Riccoboni's *Vie de Marianne*; H. Häusser, The Thomasius article in the *Encyclopédie*; R. A. Leigh, The first edition of the *Lettre à Christophe de Beaumont*.
ISBN 0 7294 0173 1   1971, 216 pages, 2 plates

82. The Fortunes of Pope's *Essay on man* in 18th-century France
R. G. Knapp.
ISBN 0 7294 0174 X   1971, 156 pages

84. Collectaneous. D. L. Anderson, Abélard and Héloïse: eighteenth century motif; H. B. Applewhite and D. G. Levy, The concept of modernization and the French Enlightenment; J. Marx, Autour des *Pensées philosophiques*: une lettre inédite de Georges Polier de Bottens; R. L. Caldwell, Structure de la *Lettre sur les sourds et muets*; R. I. Boss, Rousseau's civil religion and the meaning of belief: an answer to Bayle's paradox; R. M. E. De Rycke, Des Grieux's confession; R. S. Tate, Bachaumont revisited: some unpublished papers and correspondence.
ISBN 0 7294 0175 8   1971, 273 pages

86. Collectaneous. N. Hampson and B. Behrens, Cultural history as infrastructure; N. Suckling, The unfulfilled Renaissance; C. G. Stricklen, The philosophe's political mission; S. Werner, Diderot's *Supplément* and late Enlightenment thought.
ISBN 0 7294 0176 6   1972, 228 pages

87-90. Transactions of the Third international congress on the Enlightenment: Nancy 1971
ISBN 0 7294 0177 4   1972, 1798 pages, 26 plates

94. Collectaneous. J. F. Hamilton, Parallel interpretations, religious and political, of

Rousseau's *Discours sur l'inégalité*; R. A. Leigh, Rousseau, Voltaire and Péravy; D. L. Anderson, Aspects of motif in *La Nouvelle Héloïse*; J. F. Hamilton, A theory of art in Rousseau's first discourse; R. A. Leigh, New light on the genesis of the *Lettres de la montagne*; S. P. Malueg, Diderot's descriptions of nature; J. Falvey, Psychological analysis ... Chasles, Prévost and Marivaux; C. Todd, The present state of La Harpe's correspondence; A. J. Bingham, Chénier, ideologue and critic; W. Moser, De la signification d'une poésie insignifiante; A. Magnan, Un épisode oublié de la lutte ... contre Th. Tronchin.
ISBN 0 7294 0180 4   1972, 429 pages

95. The Eagle and the dove: Corneille and Racine in eighteenth-century France
E. P. Kostoroski.
ISBN 0 7294 0181 2   1972, 343 pages

96. Collectaneous. C. Wilberger, Peter the great: an 18th-century hero of our times; W. R. Womack, Eighteenth century themes in ... Raynal.
ISBN 0 7294 0182 0   1972, 265 pages

97. Collectaneous. M. Vamos, Pascal's *Pensées* and the Enlightenment; E. B. Hill, The role of *le monstre* in Diderot's thought.
ISBN 0 7294 0183 9   1972, 261 pages

98. Collectaneous. A. O. Aldridge, The state of nature; D. Williams, Voltaire's guardianship of Marie Corneille; P. B. Daprini, Le *Discours aux welches*; S. Pitou, Voltaire, Linguet, and China; L. A. Segal, Lenglet du Fresnoy; J. F. Hamilton, Virtue in Rousseau's first discourse; K. M. Lambert, Some thoughts on Diderot and Sophie Volland; E. Lizé, *La Religieuse*, un roman épistolaire; D. A. Bonneville, Glanures du *Mercure* ... Diderot et Marivaux; J. Donohoe, Marivaux: the comedy of enlightenment; R. Galliani, Quelques lettres inédites de Mably; B. Ivker, Andréa de Nerciat; V. Lee, The Sade machine; A. C. Keys, Antoine Bret.
ISBN 0 7294 0272 X   1972, 230 pages

99. Crébillon fils: techniques of the novel
P. V. Conroy.
ISBN 0 7294 0184 7   1972, 238 pages

100. Diderot et l'amitié
Blandine L. McLaughlin.
ISBN 0 7294 0185 5   1973, 282 pages

101. The Influence of Hobbes and Locke in the shaping of the concept of sovereignty in eighteenth-century France
Ian M. Wilson.
ISBN 0 7294 0186 3   1973, 290 pages

102. Collectaneous. Th. Besterman, Additions and corrections to the definitive edition of Voltaire's correspondence, II; D. R. Thelander, The oak and the thinking reed; B. E. Schwarzbach, Etienne Fourmont; M. N. Crumpacker, The secret chain of the *Lettres persanes*; F. R. O'Reilly, Montesquieu: anti-feminist; E. M. Hine, Madame de Lambert; M. W. Beal, Condillac as precursor of Kant; R. H. McDonald, A forgotten Voltairean poem; N. Perry, Voltaire's London agents.
ISBN 0 7294 0187 1   1973, 299 pages

briand juge de Voltaire; S. Werner, Diderot, Sade and the gothic novel; R. L. Emerson, The social composition of enlightened Scotland; J. M. Blanchard, Style pastoral, style des Lumières.

ISBN 0 7294 0198 7   1973, 346 pages

115. Voltaire and Crébillon père: history of an enmity
Paul O. Le Clerc.

ISBN 0 7294 0021 2   1973, 157 pages

116. Collectaneous. A. Hunwick, Le patriotisme de Voltaire; J. Vercruysse, Bibliographie provisoire des traductions néerlandaises et flamandes de Voltaire; E. M. Hine, The woman question in early eighteenth-century French literature; M. P. Masterson, Montesquieu's stadtholder; J. McFadden, *Les Bijoux indiscrets*; R. P. Whitmore, Two essays on *Le Père de famille*; B. G. Mittman, Some sources of the André scene in Diderot's *Fils naturel*; A. R. Larsen, Ethical mutability in four of Diderot's tales; M. J. Silverthorne, Rousseau's Plato; L. A. Segal, Lenglet Du Fresnoy: the treason of a cleric; S. Pitou, Rameau's *Dardanus* at Fontainebleau in 1763.

ISBN 0 7294 0199 5   1973, 314 pages

117. Collectaneous. Th. Besterman, Additions and corrections to the definitive edition of Voltaire's correspondence, III; A. Lacombe, La lettre sur l'insertion de la petite vérole et les *Lettres philosophiques*; M. H. Gertner, Five comic devices in *Zadig*; P. Ilie, Voltaire and Spain: the meaning of *Don Pèdre*; R. Wokler, Rameau, Rousseau, and the *Essai sur l'origine des langues*; R. P. Thomas, *Jacques le fataliste*, the *Liaisons dangereuses*, and the autonomy of the novel; J. H. Batley, Amour et métaphore: analyse de la lettre 23 des *Liaisons dangereuses*; David Levy, Qui est l'auteur de l'*Oracle des anciens fidèles*?

ISBN 0 7294 0200 2   1974, 270 pages

118. Collectaneous. J. L. Curtis, La providence: vicissitudes du dieu voltairien; D. Berry, The technique of literary digression in the fiction of Diderot.

ISBN 0 7294 0014 X   1974, 272 pages

119. Denis Diderot: Ecrits inconnus de jeunesse 1737-1744
Publié par J. Th. de Booy.

ISBN 0 7294 0015 8   1974, 543 pages

120. Collectaneous. M. L. Perkins, Voltaire's alphabetical works; J. R. Monty, Voltaire's rhetoric; Th. Besterman, Voltaire bibliography; Young Hai Park, La carrière scénique de *L'Orphelin de la Chine*; D. S. Hawley, L'Inde de Voltaire; B. W. Maggs, Answers from eighteenth-century China ... on Voltaire's sinology; A. Ages, Voltaire and Horace; I. L. Greenberg, Destination in *Jacques le fataliste*; A. Attridge, The reception of *La Nouvelle Héloïse*; I. Wohlfarth, The irony of criticism; J. F. Jones, Visual communication in *Les Egarements du cœur*; E. Anderson, La collaboration de Sonnini de Manoncourt à l'*Histoire naturelle*.

ISBN 0 7294 0201 0   1974, 358 pages

121. Marmontel, Voltaire and the *Bélisaire* affair
John Renwick.

ISBN 0 7294 0027 1   1974, 401 pages

122. Voltaire and the Socinians
R. E. Florida.

ISBN 0 7294 0017 4   1974, 275 pages

123. Coyer and the Enlightenment
Leonard Adams.
ISBN 0 7294 0012 3   1974, 196 pages

124. Collectaneous. S. S. B. Taylor, The definitive text of Voltaire's works; H. N. Bakalar, An unpublished Voltaire letter; J. C. Guédon, Le retour d'Angleterre de Voltaire; D. Williams, Observations on an English translation of Voltaire's commentary on Corneille; A. Gunny, Voltaire and the novel: Sterne; A. O. Aldridge, The American revolution and a spurious letter from Voltaire; M. Waddicor, An unpublished satire of the regency: *Les Devises de la cour*; H. J. Batlay, L'art du portrait dans *Gil Blas*; A. Nabarra, L'influence de don Quichotte sur ... Marivaux; O. A. Haac, Rousseau and Marivaux; D. J. Adams, Style and social ideas in *Jacques le fataliste*; C. J. Block, The 'unnatural' versus the 'natural' in *La Religieuse*; J. Marx, L'abbé Fiard et ses sorciers; A. Morellet, *Le Préjugé vaincu*, ed. C. Vahlkamp; A. P. L. Kempton, Education and the child in eighteenth-century French fiction.
ISBN 0 7294 0202 9   1974, 362 pages, 4 plates

125. Voltaire et l'Islam
G. Badir.
ISBN 0 7294 0013 1   1974, 226 pages

126. A study of Voltaire's lighter verse
R. A. Nablow.
ISBN 0 7294 0025 5   1974, 321 pages

127. Collectaneous. R. E. A. Waller, Voltaire and the regent; D. I. Dalnekoff, The meaning of Eldorado; D. Eccheverria, Some unknown 18th-century editions of Voltaire's political pamphlets; M. F. Harris, Le séjour de Montesquieu en Italie; J. M. Rogister, Missing pages from the marquis d'Argenson's journal; V. R. Rossman, L'Onomancie ... dans l'*Encyclopédie*; J. F. Jones, Du Bos and Rousseau; A. D. Hytier, Les philosophes et ... la guerre.
ISBN 0 7294 0203 7   1974, 258 pages, 1 map

128. Diderot's great scroll: narrative art in *Jacques le fataliste*
S. Werner.
ISBN 0 7294 0030 1   1975, 153 pages

129. Collectaneous. K. Cameron, Aspects of Voltaire's style in *Mahomet*; E. Lizé, Une affaire de pommes à Ferney; S. Pitou, The opéra-ballet and *Scanderberg* in Fontainebleau; A. Miller, Vera Zasulich's *Jean-Jacques Rousseau*; A. Lacombe, Du théâtre au roman: Sade; G. Gullace, Brunetière on the eighteenth century.
ISBN 0 7294 0204 5   1975, 195 pages

130. Voltaire et son exégèse du Pentateuque
David Lévy.
ISBN 0 7294 0022 0   1975, 346 pages

131. Diderot's *Essai sur Sénèque*
W. T. Conroy.
ISBN 0 7294 0205 3   1975, 167 pages

132. Collectaneous. J. H. Batley, Analyse d'un chapitre de *Zadig*; R. Galliani, Voltaire cité par les brochures de 1789; R. Wokler, The influence of Diderot on the political

32

theory of Rousseau; H. N. Bakalar, Language and logic: Diderot; G. Mercken-Spaas, The social anthropology of Rousseau's *Emile*; B. W. Palmer, Crébillon fils and his reader; V. Link, The reception of Crébillon's *Le Sopha* in England; A. P. L. Kempton, The theme of childhood in French eighteenth-century memoir novels.
ISBN 0 7294 0206 1   1975, 225 pages

133. Sir Everard Fawkener, friend and correspondent of Voltaire
Norma Perry.
ISBN 0 7294 0026 3   1975, 160 pages

134. La Mettrie: *Discours sur le bonheur*
Critical edition by John Falvey.
ISBN 0 7294 0020 4   1975, 236 pages

135. Collectaneous. Th. Besterman, Additions and corrections to the definitive edition of Voltaire's correspondence, IV; D. Williams, Voltaire on the sentimental novel; N. Senior, The structure of *Zadig*; P. Henry, A different view of Voltaire's controversial *Tout en dieu*; S. S. B. Taylor, The duke and duchess of Grafton with Voltaire; S. S. B. Taylor, Voltaire's marginalia; E. Showalter, Sensibility at Cirey; J. Vercruysse, Lettre de Henri Rieu sur les derniers jours de Voltaire; R. P. Thomas, *Les Bijoux indiscrets* as a laboratory; J. Renwick, Encore des précisions nouvelles sur les débuts de Beaumarchais.
ISBN 0 7294 0207 X   1975, 227 pages, 5 plates

136. Voltaire's comic theatre: composition and critics
Lilian Willens.
ISBN 0 7294 0031 X   1975, 191 pages

137. Collectaneous. B. W. Maggs, Eighteenth-century Russian reflections on the Lisbon earthquake, Voltaire and optimism; P. C. Mitchell, An underlying theme in *La Princesse de Babylone*; D. W. Smith, The first edition of the *Relation de Berthier*; R. Setbon, Voltaire jugé par Charles Nodier; D. J. Fletcher, Aaron Hill; R. C. Carroll, Muse and Narcissus: Rousseau's *Lettres à Sara*; E. Thompsett, Love and libertinism in the novels of Duclos; P. Stewart, L'armature historique du *Cleveland* de Prévost; M. Waters, Unpublished letters from mlle Clairon to Jean de Vaines.
ISBN 0 7294 0208 8   1975, 189 pages

138. Voltaire and Camus: the limits of reason and the awareness of absurdity
Patrick Henry.
ISBN 0 7294 0018 2   1975, 261 pages

139. Voltaire et ses amis d'après la correspondance de Mme de Graffigny
English Showalter.
ISBN 0 7294 0028 X   1975, 233 pages

140. Collectaneous. A. Gunny, Voltaire's thoughts on prose fiction; S. Gearhart, Rationality and ... Voltaire's historiography; E. J. Weinraub, Plays as pedagogical laboratories: *Mahomet* and *Don Pèdre*; T. E. D. Braun, Voltaire, *Olympie*, and Alexander the great; A. Gunny, A propos de la date de ... *Micromégas*; M. L. Perkins, Motivation ... in the *Neveu de Rameau*; K. S. Wilkins, Some aspects of the irrational in 18th-century France; T. C. Newland, Holbach and religion versus morality.
ISBN 0 7294 0209 6   1975, 218 pages

141-142. Baculard d'Arnaud: life and prose fiction
R. L. Dawson.
ISBN 0 7294 0016 6   1975, 761 pages

143. Collectaneous. T. M. Carr, Dramatic structure and philosophy in *Brutus, Alzire* and *Mahomet*; G. A. Perla, Zadig, hero of the absurd; D. E. Highnam, *L'Ingénu*: flawed masterpiece or masterful innovation; P. E. Abanime, Voltaire as an anthropologist; Th. Besterman, Some eighteenth-century Voltaire editions unknown to Bengesco: supplement; L. J. Forno, The cosmic mysticism of Diderot; M. Kusch, *Manon Lescaut* ... dans la basse Romancie; L. A. Oliver, Bachaumont the chronicler; D. T. Siebert, Soames Jenyns's debt to Johnson.
ISBN 0 7294 0210 X   1975, 195 pages

144. Voltaire on war and peace
Henry Meyer.
ISBN 0 7294 0023 9   1975, 202 pages

145-147. L'Angleterre et Voltaire
André-Michel Rousseau.
ISBN 0 7294 0034 4   1976, 1085 pages, 1 plate

148. Collectaneous. Voltaire's notebooks, thirteen new fragments, ed. Th. Besterman; P. Ilie, The voices in Candide's garden; M. F. O'Meara, *Le Taureau blanc* and the activity of language; L. R. Free, Laclos and the myth of courtly love; M. R. Bruno, Fréron, police spy; L. Kerslake, J. G. Sulzer and the *Encyclopédie*.
ISBN 0 7294 0211 8   1976, 247 pages, 2 illustrations

149. Mme Riccoboni's letters to David Hume, David Garrick and Sir Robert Liston, 1764-1783
Edited by J. C. Nicholls.
ISBN 0 7294 0043 3   1976, 471 pages

150. Collectaneous. S. Vance, History as dramatic reinforcement; Diderot, *Réflexions sur le courage des femmes*, éd. J. Th. de Booy; H. Mydlarski, Vauvenargues; T. Murphy, J. B. R. Robinet.
ISBN 0 7294 0212 6   1976, 250 pages

151-155. Transactions of the Fourth international congress on the Enlightenment: Yale 1975
ISBN 0 7294 0038 7   1976, 2319 pages

156-157. Charles Bonnet contre les Lumières
Jacques Marx.
ISBN 0 7294 0044 1   1976, 782 pages, 2 plates

158. Voltaire and the form of the novel
D. A. Bonneville.
ISBN 0 7294 0035 2   1976, 149 pages

159. The Language theory, epistemology, and aesthetics of Jean Lerond d'Alembert
D. F. Essar.
ISBN 0 7294 0045 X   1976, 160 pages

160. Collectaneous. Steve Larkin, Voltaire and Prévost: a reappraisal; T. E. D. Braun

and G. R. Culley, Aeschylus, Voltaire, and Le Franc de Pompignan's *Prométhee*: a critical edition.
ISBN 0 7294 0046 8   1976, 226 pages

161. Collectaneous. Les notes marginales de Voltaire au *Dictionnaire philosophique*, ed. R. Galliani; J. Scull, Voltaire's reading of Pascal: his quotations compared to early texts; C. Todd, A provisional bibliography of published Spanish translations of Voltaire; D. J. Fletcher, *Candide* and the theme of the happy husbandman; J. Knowlson, Voltaire, Lucian and *Candide*; R. A. Dawson, ed. Une lettre inédite de Fanny de Beauharnais à Voltaire; S. Helein-Koss, Albert Camus et le *Contrat social*; R. Galliani, Le débat en France sur le luxe: Voltaire ou Rousseau; L. A. Olivier, The other Bachaumont: connoisseur and citizen; A. Ages, Merimée and the philosophes.
ISBN 0 7294 0213 4   1976, 252 pages

162. La Figure dialogique dans *Jacques le fataliste*
Huguette Cohen.
ISBN 0 7294 0047 6   1976, 243 pages

163. Collectaneous. R. Galliani, Quelques notes inédites de Voltaire à *L'Esprit des lois*; J. Vercruysse, La première d'*Olympie*: trois lettres de Mme Denis aux Constant d'Hermenches; J. Yashinsky, Voltaire's *Enfant prodigue*; Th. Besterman, William Beckford's marginal notes on a life of Voltaire; J. Patrick Lee, Voltaire and César de Missy; M. Cardy, Discussion of the theory of climate in the 'querelle des anciens et des modernes'; L. R. Free, Vivant Denon's *Point de lendemain*; P. L. Smith, The launching of the *Journal étranger* (1752-1754); S. Pitou, Renout's *La Mort d'Hercule*; A. A. Sokalski, Autour du *Vert galant*; J. P. Guicciardi, Tocqueville et les Lumières; Th. Besterman, The new Diderot edition.
ISBN 0 7294 0214 2   1976, 221 pages

164. Voltaire's Russia: window on the East
Carolyn H. Wilberger.
ISBN 0 7294 0051 4   1976, 287 pages

165. Concordance to the correspondence of Voltaire
Edited by Th. Besterman and A. Brown.
ISBN 0 7294 0055 7   1977, 154 pages

166. Diderot's 'femme savante'
Laurence L. Bongie.
ISBN 0 7294 0054 9   1977, 235 pages, 1 plate

167. Facets of education in the eighteenth century
Edited by James A. Leith.
ISBN 0 7294 0056 5   1977, 585 pages, 1 plate

168. Les Editions encadrées des œuvres de Voltaire de 1775
Jeroom Vercruysse.
ISBN 0 7294 0058 1   1977, 198 pages, 12 illustrations

169. Collectaneous. K. M. Baker, Condorcet's notes for a revised edition of his reception speech to the Académie française; R. Galliani, La présence de Voltaire dans les brochures de 1790; H. D. Rothschild, Benoît de Maillet's Cairo letters; M. Stern, Lettres inédites de madame de Genlis à Bernardin de Saint-Pierre.
ISBN 0 7294 0215 0   1977, 275 pages

170. Collectaneous. J. Vercruysse, Vauvenargues trahi: pour une édition authentique de ses œuvres; Restif de La Bretonne, *Le Généographe*, ed. D. Fletcher.
ISBN 0 7294 0216 9   1977, 234 pages

171. Collectaneous. L. L. Bongie, Voltaire's English, high treason and a manifesto for bonnie prince Charles; G. M. Russo, Sexual roles and religious images in Voltaire's *La Pucelle*; N. H. Severin, Voltaire's campaign againts saints' days; H. Watzlawick, Casanova and Voltaire's *Discours aux welches*; D. Medlin, Voltaire, Morellet, and Le Franc de Pompignan: a bibliographical error corrected; J. Whatley, Coherent worlds: Fénelon's *Télémaque* and Marivaux's *Télémaque travesti*; R. J. Howells, Marivaux and the heroic; D. J. Langdon, Interpolations in the *Encyclopédie* article 'Liberté'; G. A. Perla, The unsigned articles and Jaucourt's bibliographical sketches in the *Encyclopédie*; A. Martin, The origins of the *Contes moraux*: Marmontel and other authors of short fiction in the *Mercure de France* (1750-1761); M. G. Carroll, Sénac de Meilhan's *Les Deux cousins*: a monarchist paradox at the end of the ancien régime; E. Kennedy, Destutt de Tracy and the unity of the sciences.
ISBN 0 7294 0217 7   1977, 238 pages

172. Louis XIV and the age of the Enlightenment: the myth of the sun king from 1715 to 1789
N. R. Johnson.
ISBN 0 7294 0117 0   1978, 350 pages

173. *Le Mariage de Figaro*: essai d'interprétation
F. Levy.
ISBN 0 7294 0112 X   1978, 306 pages

174. Collectaneous. G. Gargett, Voltaire, Gilbert de Voisin's *Mémoires* and the problem of Huguenot civil rights (1767-1768); J. Vercruysse, Une épigramme de Voltaire à Frédéric II; C. Duckworth, Voltaire at Ferney: an unpublished description; R. Galliani, Voltaire et les autres philosophes dans la Révolution: les brochures de 1791, 1792, 1793; E. Lizé, Une lettre oubliée de Lebrun-Pindare à Voltaire; W. D. Howarth, Tragedy into melodrama: the fortunes of the Calas affair on the stage; A. Gunny, Montesquieu's view of Islam in the *Lettres persanes*; M. L. Perkins, The crisis of sensationalism in Diderot's *Lettre sur les aveugles*; D. Medlin, André Morellet, translator of liberal thought; M. Fletcher, N. Labbé, A. de Laforcade et D. Desplat, Le rétablissement des anciens parlements (1774-1775) vu de la correspondance inédite de Théophile de Bordeu.
ISBN 0 7294 0218 5   1978, 267 pages

175. Madame de Graffigny and Rousseau: between the two *Discours*
English Showalter.
ISBN 0 7294 0113 8   1978, 191 pages

176. Collectaneous. J. Hellegouarc'h, Genèse d'un conte de Voltaire; J. Hellegouarc'h, Encore la duchesse Du Maine: note sur les rubans jaunes de *Zadig*; P. Teissier, Une lettre de madame Denis au comte d'Argental sur *Rome sauvée*; J. Vercruysse, L'œuvre de 'poéshie' corrigée: notes marginales de Voltaire sur les poésies de Frédéric II; R. A. Nablow, Voltaire's indebtedness to Addison in the alphabetical works; A. Jovicevich, Voltaire and La Harpe – l'affaire des manuscrits: a reappraisal; G. Gargett, Voltaire, Richelieu and the problem of Huguenot emancipation in the reign of Louis XV; P. Henry, Sacred and profane gardens in *Candide*; C. M. Gillis, Private room and public space: the

paradox of form in *Clarissa*; J. P. Gilroy, Peace and the pursuit of happiness in the French utopian novel: Fénelon's *Télémaque* and Prévost's *Cleveland*; A. J. Singerman, L'abbé Prévost et la triple concupiscence: lecture augustinienne de *Manon Lescaut*; H. Mydlarski, Vauvenargues, critique de Corneille; W. T. Conroy, jr, Three neglected sources of Diderot's *Essai sur Sénèque*: Ponçol, Peyrilhe, L'Estoile; J. Renwick, Essai sur la première jeunesse de Jean-François Marmontel (1723-1745) ou Antimémoires; D. A. Coward, Restif de La Bretonne and the reform of prostitution; B. Guy, Toward a history of eighteenth-century French literature in the nineteenth century: 1810-1894; C. Duckworth, Louis XIV and English history: a French reaction to Walpole, Hume and Gibbon on Richard III; K. S. Wilkins, Children's literature in eighteenth-century France.

ISBN 0 7294 0219 3   1979, 444 pages

177. Voltaire and English literature: a study of English literary influences on Voltaire
Ahmad Gunny.
ISBN 0 7294 0119 7   1979, 309 pages

178. Denis Diderot: Ecrits inconnus de jeunesse 1745
Identifiés et présentés par J. Th. de Booy.
ISBN 0 7294 0061 1   1979, 284 pages

179. Voltaire and the English
R. Pomeau, Les *Lettres philosophiques*: le projet de Voltaire; A.-M. Rousseau, Naissance d'un livre et d'un texte: les *Letters concerning the English nation*; W. H. Barber, Voltaire and Samuel Clarke; P. Casini, Briarée en miniature: Voltaire et Newton; D. Williams, Voltaire's war with England: the appeal to Europe 1760-1764; S. S. B. Taylor, Voltaire's humour; J. Scherer, 'L'univers en raccourci': quelques ambitions du roman voltairien; J. Vercruysse, Voltaire, Sisyphe en 'Jermanie': vers la meilleure des éditions possibles; G. Barber, Voltaire and the English: catalogue of an exhibition; N. Perry, Voltaire's London haunts; W. H. Barber, Voltaire et Newton; W. H. Barber, Theodore Besterman.
ISBN 0 7294 0120 0   1979, 225 pages, 14 plates

180. Voltaire, Grimm et la *Correspondance littéraire*
Emile Lizé.
ISBN 0 7294 0121 9   1979, 253 pages

181. Bibliographie des œuvres de Jean-François de La Harpe
Christopher Todd.
ISBN 0 7294 0122 7   1979, 360 pages

182. Collectaneous. Ch. Porset, Discours d'un anonyme sur l'inégalité 1754; C. Lanau, 'Je tiens Jean-Jacques Rousseau': un point de l'affaire Rousseau-Hume; A. M. Laborde, Rousseau: sémiotique d'une phystie; R. J. P. Jordan, A new look at Rousseau as educator; D. Scott, Rousseau and flowers: the poetry of botany; P. France, Jean-Jacques Rousseau en Union Soviétique; J.-P. Le Bouler et C. Lafarge, Les emprunts de Mme Dupin à la Bibliothèque du roi dans les années 1748-1750; J.-P. Le Bouler et C. Lafarge, L'infortune littéraire des Dupin: essai de bibliographie critique; J. Vercruysse, Quinze lettres de Voltaire; J. L. Epstein, Voltaire's ventriloquism: voices in the first *Lettre philosophique*; E. Abanime, Voltaire anti-esclavagiste; J. Yashinsky, Voltaire's *L'Ecossaise*: background, structure, originality; P. Kra, The role of the harem in imitations of Montesquieu's *Lettres persanes*: P. Winnack, Some English influences on the abbé Prévost; D. Adams,

Experiment and experience in *Les Bijoux indiscrets*; M. Mat-Hasquin, L'image de Voltaire dans les *Mémoires secrets*; D. Johnson-Cousin, Quelques précisions à propos du voyage des Necker en Angleterre en 1776; A. M. Wilson, The McMaster series of essays on the eighteenth century.
ISBN 0 7294 0235 5   1979, 357 pages

183. Collectaneous. C. Mervaud, Voltaire, Baculard d'Arnaud et le prince Ferdinand; M. G. Carroll, Some implications of 'vraisemblance' in Voltaire's *L'Ingénu*; Z. Levy, *L'Ingénu* ou l'Anti-*Candide*; R. S. Wolper, The toppling of Jeannot; R. R. McGregor, Heraldic quarterings and Voltaire's *Candide*; E. Lizé, Quand Malesherbes entrait à l'Académie; R. Galliani, Voltaire en 1878; H. Gaston Hall, Piron's *La Métromanie* and Pierre Cerou's *L'Amant auteur et valet*; M. Benítez, Benoît de Maillet et la littérature clandestine; D. Johnson-Cousin, Les 'leçons' de déclamation de Germaine Necker; J. Renwick, Chamfort, patriote en coulisses; J. Bourgeac, A partir de la lettre XLVIII des *Liaisons dangereuses*; G. E. Rodmell, Laclos, Brissot, and the petition of the Champ de Mars; S. F. Davies, Louvet as social critic; J. Wagner, Anthropologie et histoire dans le *Journal encyclopédique*; B. W. Head, The origin of 'idéologue' and 'idéologie'; W. Hanley, Censorship in eighteenth-century France.
ISBN 0 7294 0236 3   1980, 295 pages

184. Jérôme Lalande: *Journal d'un voyage en Angleterre, 1763*
Publié avec une introduction par Hélène Monod-Cassidy.
ISBN 0 7294 0237 1   1980, 116 pages, 4 plates

185. Collectaneous. F. J. McLynn, Voltaire and the Jacobite rising of 1745; J. L. Schorr, A Voltaire letter in the *Journal historique*; H. A. Stavan, Voltaire et la duchesse de Gotha; J. Renwick, Voltaire et les antécédents de la *Guerre civile de Genève*; L. Willens, Voltaire's *Irène* and his illusion of theatrical success; M. Delon, Candide et Justine dans les tranchées; R. C. Knight, Anne Dacier and gardens; J. King and B. Lynn, The *Metamorphoses* in English eighteenth-century mythological handbooks; A. J. Singerman, Le sérail dans les *Lettres persanes*; N. Boothroyd, Les *Lettres de la Marquise de M. au Comte de R.*; J. Lough, The *Encyclopédie* and Chamber's *Cyclopaedia*; J. Chouillet, 'Etre Voltaire ou rien': réflexions sur le voltairianisme de Diderot; A. P. Kouidis, The *Praise of folly*: Diderot's model for *Le Neuveu de Rameau*; C. J. Betts, The function of analogy in Diderot's *Rêve de d'Alembert*; S. Baudiffier, La parole et l'écriture dans *Jacques le fataliste*; I. Kisliuk, Le symbolisme du jardin et l'imagination créatrice chez Rousseau, Bernardin de Saint-Pierre et Chateaubriand.
ISBN 0 7294 0241 X   1980, 418 pages

186. A preliminary bibliography of Isabelle de Charrière (Belle de Zuylen)
C. P. Courtney.
ISBN 0 7294 0240 1   1980, 157 pages, 1 plate, 21 illustrations

187. Etienne Bonnot de Condillac: *Les Monades*
Edited with an introduction and notes by Laurence L. Bongie.
ISBN 0 7294 0242 8   1980, 216 pages

188. Voltaire and Protestantism
Graham Gargett.
ISBN 0 7294 0243 6   1980, 532 pages

189. Collectaneous. R. Galliani, A propos de Voltaire, de Leibniz et de la *Théodicée*;

A. M. Redshaw, Voltaire and Lucretius; P. Haffter, Voltaire et les italiques; B. W. Maggs, Voltaire and the Balkans; R. S. Ridgway, Voltaire's operas; G. Klosko, Montesquieu's science of politics; L. L. Bongie, Diderot and the rue Taranne; J. A. Fleming, Texual autogenesis in Marivaux's *Paysan parvenu*; R. Galliani, Trois lettres inédites de Buffon; F. Barbier, Quelques documents inédits sur l'abbé Delille; R. F. O'Reilly, The spurious attribution of the *Voyage à Paphos*; D. Medlin, André Morellet and the idea of progress; M. Gutwirth, Laclos and *le sexe*; B. Brookes, The feminism of Condorcet and Sophie de Grouchy; D. A. Coward, Eighteenth-century attitudes to prostitution; R. Niklaus, *Etudes sur le XVIIIe siècle*.

199. Collectaneous. P. Robinson, Marivaux's poetic theatre of love: some considerations of genre; P. Koch, L'*Histoire de l'Ancien Théâtre-Italien*: la part des frères Parfaict; N. Jonard, La comédie des apparences dans le théâtre de Goldoni; W. D. Howarth, Voltaire, Ninon de L'Enclos and the evolution of a dramatic genre; V. Nachtergaele, *Micromégas*, ou le disfonctionnement des procédés de la narration; R. Démoris, Genèse et symbolique de l'*Histoire de Jenni*; R. Galliani, Voltaire, Porphyre et les animaux; F. Lafarga, Sur la fortune de la *Henriade* en Espagne; R. Price, Boulainviller and the myth of the Frankish conquest of Gaul; A. J. Hanou, Dutch periodicals from 1697 to 1721: in imitation of the English?; J. K. McLelland, Metaphor in Montesquieu's theoretical writings; J.-P. Le Bouler, Sur les écrits féministes de Rousseau; P. Hoffmann, La controverse entre Leibniz et Stahl sur la nature de l'âme; J. A. Perkins, Censorship and the Académie des sciences: a case study of Bonnet's *Considérations sur les corps organisés*; M. Sandoz, La peinture de l'histoire comme trait marquant du siècle des Lumières finissant; M. Coulaud, Les *Mémoires sur la matière étymologique* de Charles de Brosses; E. Kennedy, The French revolutionary catechisms: ruptures and continuities with Classical, Christian, and Enlightenment moralities; R. S. Ridgway, Camus's favourite moralist; A. Brown, Voltaire at the Bibliothèque nationale.

literary portrait of Garrick; L. Honoré, The philosophical satire of La Mettrie; D. Raynor, Hume's critique of Helvétius's *De l'esprit*; A. Ridehalgh, Preromantic attitudes and the birth of a legend: French pilgrimages to Ermenonville, 1778-1789; J.-C. David, Un théiste chez le baron d'Holbach: l'abbé Morellet; D. Wood, Isabelle de Charrière et Benjamin Constant: à propos d'une découverte récente; H. A. Stavan, Are Voltaire's tales narrative fantasies? a reply to Wolper.
ISBN 0 7294 0297 5   1982, 293 pages, 4 plates

216. Transactions of the Sixth international congress on the Enlightenment: Brussels 1983
ISBN 0 7294 0298 3   1983, 494 pages

217. Collectaneous. J. Chouillet, Images continentales du *Marchand de Londres*; J. Feather, The merchants of culture: bookselling in early industrial England; G. Festa, Images et réalités de la vie commerciale italienne à travers le *Voyage d'Italie* de Sade; J. Hoock, Structures de l'échange et mentalités marchandes: les marchands de Rouen, 1650-1750; G. Lamoine, Le personnage du *merchant* à Bristol, dans la réalité et dans la littérature au dix-huitième siècle; Edna Hindie Lemay, Une minorité au sein d'une minorité: un banquier et quelques négociants à l'Assemblée constituante 1789-1791; J. McVeagh, George Farquhar and commercial England; A. Strugnell, Diderot on luxury, commerce and the merchant; Janet Todd, Marketing the self: Mary Carleton, Miss F and Susannah Gunning; Françoise Weil, Le marchand-libraire en France pendant le second quart du dix-huitième siècle; J. K. Welcher, Gulliver in the market-place: R. Galliani, La date de composition du *Crocheteur borgne* par Voltaire; J. Yashinsky, Voltaire's *La Prude*: influences, philosophy, dramaturgy; R. Galliani, Quelques faits inédits sur la mort de Voltaire; P. Aubery, Voltaire and antisemitism: a reply to Hertzberg; R. A. Nablow, Addison's indebtedness to Pascal in *Spectator* no.420; P. V. Conroy, Jr, Image claire, image trouble dans l'*Histoire d'une Grecque moderne* de Prévost; C. H. Kullman, James Boswell, compassionate lawyer and harsh criminologist: a divided self; G. Dulac, Grimm et la *Correspondance littéraire* envoyée à Catherine II (d'après les lettres de Dimitri Golitsyn et de F. M. Grimm au vice-chancelier Alexandre Golitsyn); R. F. O'Reilly, Desire in Sade's *Les 120 Journées de Sodome*; R. G. Saisselin, Painting, writing and primitive purity: from expression to sign in eighteenth-century French painting and architecture; D. J. Adams, *Le Neveu de Rameau* since 1950.
ISBN 0 7294 0302 5   1983, 394 pages

218. Montesquieu and the history of French laws
Iris Cox
ISBN 0 7294 0303 3   1983, 210 pages

219. Collectaneous. L. G. Crocker, Voltaire and the political philosophers; R. Galliani, Voltaire, Astruc, et la maladie vénérienne; R. Galliani, La date de composition du *Songe de Platon* par Voltaire; R. Waller, Voltaire's 'pension from the Regent': Foulet was right; D. W. Smith, The publication of *Micromégas*; Maureen F. O'Meara, Linguistic powerplay: Voltaire's considerations on the evolution, use, and abuse of language; J. Lavička, Voltaire et la Bohême; F. Lafarga, Essai de bibliographie critique de 'Voltaire et l'Espagne'; S. O'Cathasaigh, Bayle and the authorship of the *Avis aux Réfugiez*; Geneviève Menant-Artigas, Boulainvilliers et madame de Lambert; B. L. H. Lewis, The influence of Chasles's *Illustres Françoises* on Prévost's *Cleveland*; P. Saint-Amand, Rousseau contre la science: l'exemple de la botanique dans les textes autobiographiques; Colette Piau-

Gillot, La misogynie de J. J. Rousseau; Suzanne Guerlac, The tableau and authority in Diderot's aesthetics; J. -C. David, Documents inédits concernant l'*Histoire d'Hérodote* de Pierre Henry Larcher (1786); Sylvette Milliot, L'évolution du violon et du violoncelle au dix-huitième siècle; A. G. Cross, The eighteenth-century Russian theatre through British eyes; A. H. Huussen Jr. et H. J. Wedman, L'émancipation des Juifs aux Pays-Bas: aspects politiques et socio-culturels; Mireille Gille, La 'Lettre d'Italie' au dix-huitième siècle: forme et signification; P. Swiggers, Studies on the French eighteenth-century grammatical tradition; C. P. Courtney, *The Portrait of Zélide*: Geoffrey Scott and Belle de Zuylen; D. Coward, Laclos studies, 1968-1982.

ISBN 0 7294 0304 1 1983, 336 pages

220. L'Exégèse du Nouveau Testament dans la philosophie française du dix-huitième siècle
Marie-Hélène Cotoni
ISBN 0 7294 0306 8 1984, 454 pages

221. Thémiseul de Saint-Hyacinthe, 1684-1746
Elisabeth Carayol
ISBN 0 7294 0308 4 1984, 216 pages

222. Correspondance entre Prosper Marchand et le marquis d'Argens
Steve Larkin
ISBN 0 7294 0309 2 1984, 278 pages

223. Inventory of Diderot's *Encyclopédie*: vii. Inventory of the plates
Richard N. Schwab with the collaboration of Walter E. Rex; with a study of the contributors to the *Encyclopédie* by John Lough.
See also above, volumes 80, 83, 85, 91-93
ISBN 0 7294 0310 6 1984, 576 pages, 3 plates

224. Russia and 'le rêve chinois': China in eighteenth-century Russian literature
Barbara Widenor Maggs
ISBN 0 7294 0311 4 1984, 190 pages

225-227. Inventaire de la *Correspondance littéraire* de Grimm et Meister
Ulla Kölving et Jeanne Carriat
ISBN 0 7294 0316 5 1984, 1340 pages

228. Collectaneous. R. Porter, Sex and the singular man: the seminal ideas of James Graham; P. -G. Boucé, Sex, amours and love in *Tom Jones*; Margarette Smith, Smollett and matrimonial bawdy; R. J. Wolfe, The hang-up of Franz Kotwara and its relationship to sexual quackery in late 18th-century London; E. James, Voltaire and the 'Ethics' of Spinoza; Christiane Mervaud, Voltaire, saint Augustin et le duc Du Maine aux sources de *Cosi-Sancta*; Anne Sanderson, Voltaire and the problem of dramatic structure: the evolution of the form of *Eriphyle*; Anne Sanderson, In the playwright's workshop: Voltaire's corrections to *Irène*; A. Niderst, Fontenelle et la science de son temps; C. Lloyd, Illusion and seduction: Diderot's rejection of traditional authority in works prior to *Le Neveu de Rameau*; A. J. Singerman, L'abbé Prévost et la quête du bonheur: lecture morale et philosophique de l'*Histoire de M. Cleveland*; J. P. Gilroy, Prévost's *Le Doyen de Killerine*: the career of an imperfect mentor; R. Waller, Louis-Mayeul Chaudon against the *philosophes*; G. Stenger, Diderot lecteur de *L'Homme*: une nouvelle approche de la *Réfutation d'Helvétius*; Olga Cragg, Les maximes dans *Le Paysan parvenu*; M. Cook,

Laclos and the *Galeries des Etats-Généraux*; P. Testud, Du conte moral au conte total: *L'Année des dames nationales* de Rétif de La Bretonne.
ISBN 0 7294 0318 1   1984, 342 pages

229. Marmontel et *Polymnie*
James M. Kaplan
ISBN 0 7294 0319 X   1984, 190 pages

230. Collectaneous. W. Doyle, Dupaty (1746-1788): a career in the late Enlightenment; Carol Kleiner Willen, From protégé to persona: the evolution of the Voltaire-Desmahis relationship; R. Granderoute, Quatre lettres inédites de Collini à Voltaire; J.-C. David, Quelques actes notariés inédits concernant Voltaire; Susan C. Strong, Why a *secret* chain?: oriental *topoi* and the essential mystery of the *Lettres persanes*; C. J. Betts, Some doubtful passages in the text of Montesquieu's *Lettres persanes*; D. Beeson, ed. Maupertuis, *Lettre d'un horloger anglois à un astronome de Pékin*; R. J. Howells, Désir et distance dans *La Nouvelle Héloïse*; G. A. Wells, Condillac, Rousseau and Herder on the origin of language; Claudine Hunting, Les mille et une sources du *Diable amoureux* de Cazotte; J. V. Harari, D'une raison à l'autre: le dispositif Sade; N. Waszek, Bibliography of the Scottish Enlightenment in Germany; J. Mitchell, The spread and fluctuation of eighteenth-century printing; J. Vercruysse, Joseph Marie Durey de Morsan chroniqueur de Ferney (1769-1772) et l'édition neuchâteloise des *Questions sur l'Encyclopédie*; Helen Rosenau-Carmi, Ledoux's *L'Architecture*; Anne Boës and R. L. Dawson, The legitimation of *contrefaçons* and the police stamp of 1777.
ISBN 0 7294 0320 3   1985, 394 pages

231. La *Bibliothèque universelle des romans*, 1775-1789: présentation, table analytique et index
Angus Martin
ISBN 0 7294 0321 1   1985, 480 pages

232. Tacite et Montesquieu
Catherine Volpilhac-Auger
ISBN 0 7294 0322 X   1985, 210 pages

233. Rhétorique et roman au dix-huitième siècle: l'exemple de Prévost et de Marivaux (1728-1742)
Jean-Paul Sermain
ISBN 0 7294 0323 8   1985, 170 pages

234. Voltaire et Frédéric II: une dramaturgie des Lumières, 1736-1778
Christiane Mervaud
ISBN 0 7294 0324 6   1985, 631 pages

235. Gambling: a social and moral problem in France, 1685-1792
John Dunkley
ISBN 0 7294 0326 2   1985, 251 pages

236. Additions to the bibliographies of French prose fiction, 1618-1806
Robert L. Dawson
ISBN 0 7294 0327 0   1985, 428 pages

237. Diderot et Galiani: étude d'une amitié philosophique
Rosena Davison
ISBN 0 7294 0328 9   1985, 143 pages

P. Bonolas, Fénelon et le luxe dans le *Télémaque*; B. E. Schwarzbach and A. W. Fairbairn, The *Examen de la religion*: a bibliographical note; A. Rivara, L'exotisme barbaresque dans *La Provençale*: fonction culturelle, pratiques éditoriales et de lecture; F. Sturzer, Narration and the creative process in *Pharsamon ou les nouvelles folies romanesques*; C. Mervaud, La narration interrompue dans *Le Sopha* de Crébillon; S. Larkin, The abbé Prévost, a convert to the Church of England?; F. Weil, Les libraires parisiens propriétaires d'éditions sans véritable privilège: l'exemple de Voltaire; D. Beeson, Maupertuis at the crossroads: dating the *Réflexions philosophiques*; J. Hope Mason, Reading Rousseau's first Discourse; R. J. Howells, Deux histoires, un discours: *La Nouvelle Héloïse* et le récit des amours d'Emile et Sophie dans l'*Emile*; S. L. Arico, The arrangement of St Preux's first letter to Julie in *La Nouvelle Héloïse*; R. A. Leigh, Wegelin's visit to Rousseau in 1763; M.-H. Chabut, Diderot's *Jacques le fataliste*: a reflection on historiography and 'truth'; T. M. Pratt, Glittering prizes: Marmontel's theory and practice of epic; J. M. Kaplan, The Stockholm manuscript of Marmontel's *Les Incas*; J. M. Kaplan, Some unpublished letters to Marmontel found in Swedish collections; X. Coyer, L'élection de l'abbé Coyer à la Royal Society of London: deux lettres inédites de Voltaire et de d'Alembert; R. Benhamou, The sincerest form of flattery: the professional life of J. R. Lucotte; R. F. O'Reilly, Language and the transcendent subject in three works of the marquis de Sade: *Les 120 journées de Sodome, La Philosophie dans le boudoir*, and *Justine*; M. Tilby, Ducray-Duminil's *Victor, ou l'enfant de la forêt* in the context of the Revolution; G. Festa, Le voyage en Sardaigne au siècle des Lumières; M. G. Badir, Législation et définition de la prostitution au dix-huitième siècle.

ISBN 0 7294 0345 9   1987, 466 pages

Subject index

Abélard, Pierre

aborigines

absolutism

absurdity

academies: France: Châlons-sur-Marne

— — Dijon

— — Paris: Académie des inscriptions et belles lettres

Renée Simon: *Nicolas Fréret, académicien* 17 (1961)

— — — Académie française

P. M. Conlon: *Voltaire's literary career from 1728 to 1750* 14 (1961)

Articles inédits de Voltaire pour le dictionnaire de l'Académie française, éd. J. Vercruysse 37 (1965) 7-51

Karlis Racevskis: Le règne des philosophes à l'Académie française, vu par les historiens du dix-neuvième siècle 154 (1976) 1801-12

Keith Michael Baker: Condorcet's notes for a revised edition of his reception speech to the Académie française 169 (1977) 7-68

Emile Lizé: Quand Malesherbes entrait à l'Académie ... 183 (1980) 89-90

Karlis Racevskis: Le discours philosophique à l'Académie française: une sémiotique de la démagogie et de l'arrivisme 190 (1980) 343-50

— — — Académie royale des sciences

Maria Teresa Marcialis: Pirronismo e perfettibilità della scienza nell'*Histoire de l'Académie royale des sciences* (1676-1776) 190 (1980) 472-80

Jean A. Perkins: Censorship and the Académie des sciences: a case study of Bonnet's *Considérations sur les corps organisés* 199 (1981) 251-62

— Germany

Harcourt Brown: Maupertuis *philosophe*: Enlightenment and the Berlin academy 24 (1963) 255-69

— Italy

P. M. Conlon: Voltaire's election to the Accademia della Crusca 6 (1958) 133-39

— Spain

Alberto Gil Novales: Il concetto di accademia delle scienze in Spagna, secolo XVIII 190 (1980) 470-71

Adam, Antoine

Emile Lizé: Une affaire de pommes à Ferney: Simon Bigex contre Antoine Adam 129 (1975) 19-26

Addison, Joseph

Calhoun Winton: Addison and Steele in the English Enlightenment 27 (1963) 1901-18

Ralph Arthur Nablow: Voltaire's indebtedness to Addison in the alphabetical works 176 (1979) 63-75

Ralph Arthur Nablow: Addison's indebtedness to Pascal in *Spectator* no.420 217 (1983) 183-85

Adhémar, Antoine-Honneste de Monteil de Brunier, marquis d'

Edgar Mass: *Le Marquis d'Adhémar: la correspondance inédite d'un ami des philosophes à la cour de Bayreuth* 109 (1973)

Aeschylus

Theodore E. D. Braun and Gerald R. Culley: Aeschylus, Voltaire, and Le Franc de Pompignan's *Prométhée*: a critical edition 160 (1976) 137-226

aesthetics

Charles Jacques Beyer: Montesquieu et le relativisme esthétique 24 (1963) 171-82

R. G. Saisselin: The rococo muddle 47 (1966) 233-55

Patrick Brady: The *Lettres persanes*: rococo or neo-classical? 53 (1967) 47-77

Patrick Brady: *Manon Lescaut*: classical, romantic, or rococo? 53 (1967) 339-60

Herbert Dieckmann: Diderot's *Promenade du sceptique*: a study in the relationship of thought and form 55 (1967) 417-38

John Falvey: The aesthetics of La Mettrie 87 (1972) 397-479

Norman Suckling: The aesthetic light that failed 90 (1972) 1489-504

Lenore R. Kreitman: Diderot's aesthetic paradox and created reality 102 (1973) 157-72

Jenny H. Batlay: L'art du portrait dans *Gil Blas*: effet d'esthétique à travers le mouvement 124 (1974) 181-89

Michael Cartwright: Luxe, goût et l'ivresse de l'objet: un problème moral et esthétique chez Diderot 151 (1976) 405-15

David Irwin: The industrial revolution and the dissemination of neoclassical taste 153 (1976) 1087-98

Dennis F. Essar: *The Language theory, epistemology, and aesthetics of Jean Lerond d'Alembert* 159 (1976)

Judith Sloman: Dryden's preface to the *Fables*: translation as aesthetic experience 193 (1980) 1587-95

Garry Retzleff: *Ut pictura poesis* once again: picturesque aesthetics and imagism 193 (1980) 1614-21

Andrzej Siemek: *La Recherche morale et esthétique dans le roman de Crébillon fils* 200 (1981)

Michael Cardy: *The Literary doctrines of Jean-François Marmontel* 210 (1982)

Merle L. Perkins: *Diderot and the time-space continuum: his philosophy, aesthetics and politics* 211 (1982)

Calvin Seerveld: The moment of truth and evidence of sterility within neoclassical art and aesthetic theory of the later Enlightenment 216 (1983) 149-51

Teresa Kostkiewiczowa: Les doctrines littéraires dans la Pologne des 'Lumières' et leurs relations avec l'esthétique française 216 (1983) 457-58

agriculture

Anand C. Chitnis: Agricultural improvement, political management and civic virtue in enlightened Scotland: an historiographical critique 245 (1986) 475-88

alchemy

Kay S. Wilkins: Some aspects of the irrational in 18th-century France 140 (1975) 107-201

Alembert, Jean Le Rond d'

Marta Rezler: The Voltaire-d'Alembert correspondence: an historical and bibliographical re-appraisal 20 (1962) 9-139

Paul M. Spurlin: Diderot, Alembert and the *Encyclopédie* in the United States, 1760-1800 57 (1967) 1417-33

John Pappas: L'esprit de finesse contre l'esprit de 'géométrie: un débat entre Diderot et Alembert 89 (1972) 1229-53

Edgar Mass: *Le Marquis d'Adhémar: la correspondance inédite d'un ami des philosophes à la cour de Bayreuth* 109 (1973)

Ralph S. Pomeroy: Locke, Alembert, and the anti-rhetoric of the Enlightenment 154 (1976) 1657-75

Dennis F. Essar: *The Language theory, epistemology, and aesthetics of Jean Lerond d'Alembert* 159 (1976)

Orest Ranum: D'Alembert, Tacitus and the political sociology of despotism 191 (1980) 547-58

John Pappas: Inventaire de la correspondance de d'Alembert 245 (1986) 131-276

Xavier Coyer: L'élection de l'abbé Coyer à la Royal Society of London: deux lettres inédites de Voltaire et de d'Alembert 249 (1986) 379-80

Alexander the Great

Theodore E. D. Braun: Voltaire, *Olympie*, and Alexander the Great 140 (19) 63-72

Alfieri, Vittorio

Rita Falke: Alfieri and his autobiography: the question of 'veracity' 56 (1967) 501-508

Algarotti, Francesco

Anna Vittoria Migliorini: Spunti di cosmopolitismo in Francesco Algarotti 190 (1980) 395-402

alien

Roger Mercier: Image de l'autre et image de soi-même dans le discours ethnologique au XVIIIe siècle 154 (1976) 1417-35

Raymonde Robert: Le comte de Caylus et l'orient: la littérature aux prises avec le même et l'autre 154 (1976) 1825-53

alienation

Roger Clark: Aliénation et utopie: fonctions du héros dans la littérature utopique française du XVIIIe siècle 191 (1980) 661-62

Allart, Johannes

Ton Broos: Johannes Allart (1754-1816): Dutch printer, publisher and bookseller 193 (1980) 1822-30

allegory

Georges May: Diderot et l'allégorie 89 (1972) 1049-76

almanachs

Neal R. Johnson: Almanachs français et les mentalités collectives au dix-huitième siècle 191 (1980) 1023-30

America

David Fate Norton: Francis Hutcheson in America 154 (1976) 1547-68

Grzegorz L. Seidler and Maria Smolka: Poland as seen by Americans 1785-1795 191 (1980) 965-70

Philip Stewart: Du sauvage au colon anglais: l'Américain au dix-huitième siècle 216 (1983) 120-21

— booktrade

Giles Barber: Books from the old world and for the new: the British international trade in books in the eighteenth century 151 (1976) 185-224

— education

Jurgen Herbst: The eighteenth-century American colonial college: responses to religious pluralism 167 (1977) 85-104

Peter N. Moogk: Manual education and economic life in New France 167 (1977) 125-68

Jeanne Chenu: Littérature scientifique en Nouvelle Grenade à la veille de l'indépendance: du discours à la pratique 167 (1977) 313-36

José Augusto Dos Santos: Education in Portuguese America in the eighteenth century 167 (1977) 395-425

Gregorio Weinberg: The Enlightenment and some aspects of culture and higher education in Spanish America 167 (1977) 491-522

— law

— literature

— philosophy

— politics

— religion

— revolution

— slavery

— Spanish and Portuguese

— views of

Edouard Guitton: L'architecture d'un nouveau monde dans *Les Mois* de Roucher 153 (1976) 937-49

Edna Lemay: Histoire de l'antiquité et découverte du nouveau monde chez deux auteurs du XVIIIe siècle 153 (1976) 1313-28

Sara Ellen Malueg: America in the *Encyclopédie* 153 (1976) 1381-94

Pierre Peyronnet: L'exotisme américain sur la scène française du XVIIIe siècle 154 (1976) 1617-27

Maurice Roelens: L'expérience de l'espace américain dans les récits de voyage entre La Hontan et Charlevoix 155 (1976) 1861-95

Claudia-Anne Lopez: L'utopie americaine du dr Guillotin 191 (1980) 694-98

Mathé Allain: The coloniser's viewpoint: Louisiana Indians as seen by the French 216 (1983) 87-88

Julie Andresen: L'image des langues américaines au dix-huitième siècle 216 (1983) 88-89

Townsend W. Bowling: European man encounters the New World native in the French novel 1751-1800 216 (1983) 95-97

Howard Brofsky: Rameau and the Indians: the popularity of *Les Sauvages* 216 (1983) 99-100

Marie-Thérèse Isaac: L'Européen à la rencontre du noir-esclave des Etats-Unis d'Amérique d'après les *Voyages* du marquis de Chastellux 216 (1983) 111-12

Jeffrey Smitten: Robertson's *History of America*: the Enlightenment's exploration of the Other 216 (1983) 118-19

anarchism

Alberto Andreatta: Alle origini dell'anarchismo moderno: Dom Deschamps: la metafisica al servizio dell'utopia 191 (1980) 637-43

Maria Ludassy: Tendances autoritaires et tendances anarchiques dans les utopies du XVIIIe siècle 191 (1980) 699-701

anatomy

Robert Wokler: Tyson and Buffon on the orang-utan 155 (1976) 2301-19

Miguel Benítez: Anatomie de la matière: matière et mouvement dans le naturalisme clandestin du XVIIIe siècle en France 205 (1982) 7-30

Anglomania

Josephine Grieder: Supercheries plus que littéraires: ouvrages et observateurs dits 'anglais' en France, 1740-1789 216 (1983) 453-54

animals

Robert Wokler: Tyson and Buffon on the orang-utan 155 (1976) 2301-19

Robert Wokler: The ape debates in Enlightenment anthropology 192 (1980) 1164-75

R. Galliani: Voltaire, Porphyre et les animaux 199 (1981) 125-38

Camiel Hamans: The ape in Dutch linguistics of the 18th century 216 (1983) 108-109

Année littéraire

George B. Watts: Charles Joseph Panckoucke, 'l'Atlas de la librairie française' 68 (1969) 67-205

anthropology

Godelieve Mercken-Spaas: The social anthropology of Rousseau's *Emile* 132 (1975) 137-81

P. Emeka Abanime: Voltaire as an anthropologist: the case of the albino 143 (1975) 85-104

Jacques Wagner: 'Comme l'eau le sucre' ou anthropologie et histoire dans le *Journal encyclopédique* (1756-1778) 183 (1980) 239-56

Sergio Moravia: The Enlightenment and the sciences of man 192 (1980) 1153-57

Giulio Barsanti: L'homme et les classifications: aspects du débat anthropologique dans les sciences naturelles de Buffon à Lamarck 192 (1980) 1158-64

Robert Wokler: The ape debates in Enlightenment anthropology 192 (1980) 1164-75

Irina Badescu: Une hypostase roumaine de la problématique des origines 192 (1980) 1199

Antonio Verri: Antropologia e linguistica in Rousseau 192 (1980) 1205-18

Daniel Droixhe: Le cercle et le gland: linguistique et anthropologie chez Hamann 192 (1980) 1246-56

Ann Thomson: From 'l'histoire naturelle de l'homme' to the natural history of mankind 216 (1983) 121-22

antiquaries

R. D. Thornton: The influence of the Enlightenment upon eighteenth-century British antiquaries 1750-1800 27 (1963) 1593-618

Seymour Howard: The antiquarian market in Rome and the use of neo-classicism: a basis for Canova's new classics 153 (1976) 1057-68

antiquity

Günter Gawlick: Cicero and the Enlightenment 25 (1963) 657-82

Joseph Gallanar: Argenson's 'Platonic republics' 56 (1967) 557-75

Raymond Trousson: Grandeur et décadence de Socrate chez Jean Jacques Rousseau 58 (1967) 1659-69

Stephen Werner: Voltaire and Seneca 67 (1969) 29-44

antisemitism

Antraigues, Emmanuel-Henri-Louis-Alexandre de Launay, comte d'

Colin Duckworth: D'Antraigues and the quest for happiness: nostalgia and commitment 152 (1976) 625-45

Colin Duckworth: Voltaire at Ferney: an unpublished description 174 (1978) 61-67

Arbuthnot, John

Alain Bony: *The History of John Bull* et les comédies d'Aristophane: le modèle grec dans la propagande torie 241 (1986) 41-64

archaeology

Françoise Waquet: Les souscriptions au *Museum etruscum* et la diffusion de l'étruscologie au dix-huitième siècle 208 (1982) 305-13

architecture

Claire McGlinchee: 'The smile of reason': its metamorphosis in late 18th-century architecture and literature 89 (1972) 993-1001

David Irwin: The industrial revolution and the dissemination of neoclassical taste 153 (1976) 1087-98

Rémy G. Saisselin: Architecture in the age of Louis XVI: from private luxury to public power 155 (1976) 1957-70

Monique Mosser et Jean-Pierre Mouilleseaux: Architecture, politique et utopie: vers une *Foederapolis europeana*: les monuments à la paix de Louis Combes 191 (1980) 712-16

James A. Leith: Symbolising a new era: some architectural projects under the Constituent and Legislative assemblies 216 (1983) 134-35

Monique Nemer: Ledoux et Boullée: une écriture monumentale 216 (1983) 137-38

Giuliana Ricci: L'architettura del neoclassicismo e i sui rapporti con le preesistenze gotiche a Milano nella seconda metà del '700 216 (1983) 141-43

Maria Grazia Sandri: Lo scienziato Paolo Frisi e la polemica sulla guglia del duomo di Milano: origine di un contrasto 216 (1983) 147-49

Philippe Stiennon: Les églises néo-classiques de Wallonie 216 (1983) 151-55

Guy Walton: The Chapelle royale of Versailles, an early neo-gothic building 216 (1983) 158-59

Rémy G. Saisselin: Painting, writing and primitive purity: from expression to sign in eighteenth-century French painting and architecture 217 (1983) 257-369

Helen Rosenau-Carmi: Ledoux's *L'Architecture* 230 (1985) 393-459

Argens, Jean-Baptiste de Boyer, marquis d'

Steve Larkin: *Correspondance entre Prosper Marchand et le marquis d'Argens* 222 (1984)

Argenson, René-Louis de Voyer, marquis d'

Marquis d'Argenson: *Notices sur les œuvres de théâtre*, éd. H. Lagrave 42-43 (1966)

Joseph Gallanar: Argenson's 'Platonic republics' 56 (1967) 557-75

J. M. J. Rogister: Missing pages from the marquis d'Argenson's journal 127 (1974) 199-221

N. Johnson: L'idéologie politique du marquis d'Argenson, d'après ses œuvres inédites 216 (1983) 185

Argental, Charles-Augustin de Ferriol, comte d'

M. B. May: Comte d'Argental: a magistrate in the literary world 76 (1970) 55-114

Philippe Teissier: Une lettre de madame Denis au comte d'Argental sur *Rome sauvée* 176 (1979) 41-50

aristocracy

Adrienne Koch: The contest of democracy and aristocracy in the American Enlightenment 26 (1963) 999-1018

Paul Janssens: L'influence sur le continent du modèle aristocratique britannique au dix-huitième siecle 216 (1983) 183-84

Joachim Schmitt-Sasse: J. M. v. Loen and A. Freiherr Knigge: bourgeois ideals in the writings of German aristocrats 216 (1983) 187-88

Aristophanes

Alain Bony: *The History of John Bull* et les comédies d'Aristophane: le modèle grec dans la propagande torie 241 (1986) 41-64

Arnauld, Antoine

Theodore Besterman: Review: W. H. Barber, *Leibniz in France from Arnauld to Voltaire* 2 (1956) 317-18

Arnold, Matthew

J. W. Frierson: Matthew Arnold, *philosophe* 25 (1963) 645-56

art

Rémy Gilbert Saisselin: Le passé, le goût, et l'histoire 27 (1963) 1445-55

James A. Leith: Nationalism and the fine arts in France, 1750-1789 89 (1972) 919-37

Emita B. Hill: The role of 'le monstre' in Diderot's thought 97 (1972) 147-261

Marianne Roland Michel: Représentations de l'exotisme dans la peinture en France dans la première moitié du XVIIIe siècle 154 (1976) 1437-57

Jean Seznec: L'invention de l'antiquité 155 (1976) 2033-47

N. R. Johnson: *Louis XIV and the age of the Enlightenment: the myth of the Sun King from 1715 to 1789* 172 (1978)

Calvin Seerveld: The influence of periodisation upon art historiography of the Enlightenment 190 (1980) 183-89

Seymour Howard: The revival of ancient archaic art in the late eighteenth century and the use of archaising postures and modes in drama and living sculpture 192 (1980) 1453-60

Jack Richtman: Seven *canevas* for the Théâtre-Italien: early theatrical ventures by Charles-Antoine Coypel, court painter under Louis XV 192 (1980) 1469-77

Giuseppe Galigani: Some homologies between *The Rape of the lock* and the visual arts 193 (1980) 1577-86

Marc Sandoz: La 'peinture d'histoire' comme trait marquant du siècle des Lumières finissant 193 (1980) 1663-64

Judith Colton: Pigalle's *Voltaire*: realist manifesto or tribute *all'antica?* 193 (1980) 1680-87

Roberta Roani Villani: Lo scultore pistoiese Francesco Carradori 193 (1980) 1707-10

Marc Sandoz: La peinture de l'histoire comme trait marquant du siècle des Lumières finissant 199 (1981) 263-85

Thomas R. Cleary: Illusion in late baroque painting and complex perspective in Enlightenment satire 216 (1983) 131

Marc Sandoz: Les encyclopédistes et la peinture d'histoire 216 (1983) 145-46

Paul H. Meyer: The breakdown of hierarchial concepts in 18th-century French society, literature, and art 216 (1983) 210-11

Rémy G. Saisselin: Painting, writing and primitive purity: from expression to sign in eighteenth-century French painting and architecture 217 (1983) 257-369

Rosena Davison: *Diderot et Galiani: étude d'une amitié philosophique* 237 (1985)

Paula Rea Radisich: Hubert Robert's Paris: truth, artifice, and spectacle 245 (1986) 501-18

— criticism

Virgil W. Topazio: Art criticism in the Enlightenment 27 (1963) 1639-56

Michael T. Cartwright: Diderot et l'expression: un problème de style dans la formation d'une critique d'art 55 (1967) 345-59

Leslie Carr: Painting and the paradox of the spectator in Diderot's art criticism 193 (1980) 1690-98

Suzanne Guerlac: The tableau and authority in Diderot's aesthetics 219 (1983) 183-94

— Gothic

Gustavo Costa: German antiquities and Gothic art in the early Italian Enlightenment 191 (1980) 559-61

Michel Baridon: Le réveil du gothique et l'imaginaire politique: naissance d'un mythe créateur au siècle des Lumières 193 (1980) 1667-69

François Pupil: Aux sources du néo-gothique français: la représentation du moyen âge au dix-huitième siècle 216 (1983) 139-41

— Italy

Seymour Howard: The antiquarian market in Rome and the use of neo-classicism: a basis for Canova's new classics 153 (1976) 1057-68

David Irwin: The Italian Renaissance viewed by an 18th-century sculptor 193 (1980) 1664-67

Edward J. Olszewski: A repudiation of baroque extravagance: cardinal Pietro Ottoboni's project for the tomb of Alexander VIII in St Peter's 216 (1983) 138-39

G. Festa: Images du Bernin au dix-huitième siècle: l'œuvre du sculpteur jugée par les voyageurs français en Italie 241 (1986) 87-94

— monuments

June Hargrove: The public monument as an image of authority in the age of the Enlightenment 193 (1980) 1752

James A. Leith: Space and revolution: public monuments and urban planning at the peak of the Terror 193 (1980) 1752-53

David Irwin: Death in the landscape: the neo-classic tomb 216 (1983) 132-33

Monique Nemer: Ledoux et Boullée: une écriture monumentale 216 (1983) 137-38

Edward J. Olszewski: A repudiation of baroque extravagance: cardinal Pietro Ottoboni's project for the tomb of Alexander VIII in St Peter's 216 (1983) 138-39

— neo-classicism

David Irwin: The industrial revolution and the dissemination of neoclassical taste 153 (1976) 1087-98

József Pál: Le motif de la mort dans l'art et la littérature néoclassiques 193 (1980) 1743-51

Pierre Van Bever: Néo-classicisme et Lumières: Parini 216 (1983) 157-58

— portraiture

Rémy G. Saisselin: Rousseau and portraiture: from representation to fiction 60 (1968) 201-24

— religious

William L. Barcham: Giambattista Tiepolo's *Translation of the holy house*: a sacred image in the Enlightenment 193 (1980) 1688-89

— rococo

Rémy G. Saisselin: The rococo muddle 47 (1966) 233-55

— Spain

Edward J. Sullivan: The revival of classical themes in painting and the academic style at the Court of Madrid in the 18th century 216 (1983) 155-57

— technique

Lucia Tongiorgi Tomasi: Un problème artistique dans l'*Encyclopédie*: le débat sur les techniques en France à la moitié du XVIIIe siècle 193 (1980) 1701-1706

Silvia Bordini: Art et imitation à l'époque néo-classique: les techniques de reproduction du 'Panorama' 216 (1983) 129-31

— theory

Rémy G. Saisselin: The transformation of art into culture: from Pascal to Diderot 70 (1970) 193-218

Charlotte Hogsett: Jean Baptiste Dubos on art as illusion 73 (1970) 147-64

Theodore Besterman: Art in the age of reason 87 (1972) 17-36

Norman Suckling: The aesthetic light that failed 90 (1972) 1489-504

James F. Hamilton: A theory of art in Rousseau's first discourse 94 (1972) 73-87

Michael Fried: Absorption and theatricality: painting and beholder in the age of Diderot 152 (1976) 753-77

François Jost: *Ut sculptura poesis*: littérature et arts plastiques 193 (1980) 1722-29

Rémy G. Saisselin: Langage et peinture: la dialectique du regard 193 (1980) 1735-36

Maurice Colgan: The language of landscape: truth or pleasing delusion? 193 (1980) 1736-41

Jean Renaud: De la théorie à la fiction: les *Salons* de Diderot 201 (1982) 143-62

Calvin Seerveld: The moment of truth and evidence of sterility within neoclassical art and aesthetic theory of the later Enlightenment 216 (1983) 149-51

artisan

F. G. Healey: The Enlightenment view of 'homo faber' 25 (1963) 837-59

Robert Shackleton: The Enlightenment and the artisan 190 (1980) 53-62

Assemblée des notables

Vivian R. Gruder: Paths to political consciousness: the Assembly of notables, 1787 191 (1980) 886-91

astronomy

Hélène Monod-Cassidy: Un astronome-philosophe, Jérôme de Lalande 56 (1967) 907-30

David Beeson (ed.): Maupertuis, *Lettre d'un horloger anglois à un astronome de Pékin* 230 (1985) 189-222

Astruc, Jean

R. Galliani: Voltaire, Astruc, et la maladie vénérienne 219 (1983) 19-36

atheism

Jean Wahl: *Cours sur l'athéisme éclairé de dom Deschamps* 52 (1967)

Jean Leduc: Les sources de l'athéisme et de l'immoralisme du marquis de Sade 68 (1969) 7-66

Marie Souviron: Les *Pensées philosophiques* de Diderot ou les 'Provinciales' de l'athéisme 238 (1985) 197-267

Aucassin et Nicolette

D. D. R. Owen: *Aucassin et Nicolette* and the genesis of *Candide* 41 (1966) 203-17

Aufklärung

Janine Buenzod: De l'*Aufklärung* au *Sturm und Drang*: continuité ou rupture? 24 (1963) 289-313

Peter Horwath: Literature in the service of enlightened absolutism: the age of Joseph II (1780-1790) 56 (1967) 707-34

Dominique Bourel: Aufklärung contra siècle des Lumières 190 (1980) 160

Walter Moser: L'*Aufklärung* et sa renaissance au vingtième siècle 190 (1980) 249-52

Walter Moser: L'*Aufklärung* et sa renaissance au vingtième siècle 205 (1982) 191-209

Hans Erich Bödeker: La conscience politique de l'*Aufklärung*: les philosophes allemands au service de l'état 216 (1983) 381-83

Augustine, saint

Christiane Mervaud: Voltaire, saint Augustin et le duc Du Maine aux sources de *Cosi-Sancta* 228 (1984) 89-96

Austen, Jane

Mildred Greene: 'A chimera of her own creating': love and fantasy in novels from madame de Lafayette to Jane Austen 193 (1980) 1940-42

Australia

C. P. Hanlon: Some observations on French contacts with aboriginal society (1801-1803) 216 (1983) 109-10

Austria

authority

autobiography

Bach, Johann Sebastian

Bachaumont, Louis Petit de

Bacon, Francis

Baculard d'Arnaud, François-Thomas-Marie Baculard, *called*

Bailly, Jean-Sylvain

Jeroom Vercruysse: Les vraies lettres de Voltaire à J. S. Bailly 201 (1982) 81-84

Balkans

Barbara W. Maggs: Voltaire and the Balkans: aspects of the Enlightenment in 18th-century Croatia and Serbia 189 (1980) 81-118

Gabrijela Vidan: Quelques aspects de la diffusion de la culture dans les terres slaves balkaniques 193 (1980) 1782-90

ballet

Spire Pitou: The *opéra-ballet* and *Scanderberg* at Fontainebleau in 1763 129 (1975) 27-66

Bandini, Sallustio

Jean Claude Waquet: La composition du *Discorso sopra la Maremma di Siena* de Sallustio Bandini: pensée française et politique locale dans la Toscane des Médicis 242 (1986) 233-42

Barbeyrac, Jean

Ian M. Wilson: *The Influence of Hobbes and Locke in the shaping of the concept of sovereignty in eighteenth-century France* 101 (1973)

Baretti, Giuseppe

Alan T. McKenzie: Giuseppe Baretti and the 'republic of letters' in the eighteenth century 193 (1980) 1813-22

Barnave, Antoine-Pierre-Joseph-Marie

Rosanna Albertini: Storiografia e arte della politica nel testo originale dei *Cahiers* di Barnave 191 (1980) 540-47

baroque

Thomas R. Cleary: Illusion in late baroque painting and complex perspective in Enlightenment satire 216 (1983) 131

Edward J. Olszewski: A repudiation of baroque extravagance: cardinal Pietro Ottoboni's project for the tomb of Alexander VIII in St Peter's 216 (1983) 138-39

Barthes, Roland

Patrick Henry: Contre Barthes 249 (1986) 19-36

Bayle, Pierre

H. T. Mason: Voltaire and Le Bret's digest of Bayle 20 (1962) 217-21

Elisabeth Labrousse: Obscurantisme et Lumières chez Pierre Bayle 26 (1963) 1037-48

Ronald Ian Boss: Rousseau's civil religion and the meaning of belief: an answer to Bayle's paradox 84 (1971) 123-93

Henri Mydlarski: Vauvenargues, juge littéraire de son siècle 150 (1976) 149-81

Paul Burrell: Pierre Bayle's *Dictionnaire historique et critique* 194 (1981) 83-103

Sean O'Cathasaigh: Bayle and the authorship of the *Avis aux Réfugiez* 219 (1983) 133-45

Marie-Hélène Cotoni: *L'Exégèse du Nouveau Testament dans la philosophie française du dix-huitième siècle* 220 (1984)

Margaret D. Thomas: Michel de La Roche: a Huguenot critic of Calvin 238 (1985) 97-195

Beauharnais, Fanny de

Robert L. Dawson (ed.): Une lettre inédite de Fanny de Beauharnais à Voltaire 161 (1976) 161-63

Beaumarchais, Pierre-Augustin Caron de

Theodore Besterman: The terra-cotta statue of Voltaire made by Houdon for Beaumarchais 12 (1960) 21-27

John Hampton: The literary technique of the first two *Mémoires* of Beaumarchais against Goezman 47 (1966) 177-205

Robert Niklaus: La genèse du *Barbier de Séville* 57 (1967) 1081-95

Pierre Augustin Caron de Beaumarchais: *La Folle journée ou le mariage de Figaro*, publiée par J. B. Ratermanis 63 (1968)

Brian N. Morton: Beaumarchais et le prospectus de l'édition de Kehl 81 (1971) 133-47

J. P. de Beaumarchais: Les *Mémoires contre Goezman* et la morale rousseauiste de l'intention 87 (1972) 101-13

Samuel S. B. Taylor: Le développement du genre comique en France de Molière à Beaumarchais 90 (1972) 1545-66

Monique Wagner: *Molière and the age of Enlightenment* 112 (1973)

John Renwick: Encore des précisions nouvelles sur les débuts de Beaumarchais 135 (1975) 213-27

J. P. de Beaumarchais: Beaumarchais, propagandiste de l'Amérique 151 (1976) 249-60

Francine Levy: *Le Mariage de Figaro*, essai d'interprétation 173 (1978)

Janette Gatty: Les *Six époques* de Beaumarchais: chronique de l'histoire vue et vécue 191 (1980) 574-81

Donald C. Spinelli: Beaumarchais's opera *Tarare* 193 (1980) 1721

Robert Niklaus: L'idée de vertu chez Beaumarchais et la morale implicite dans ses pièces de théâtre 216 (1983) 358-59

Beauzée, Nicolas

Sylvain Auroux: Le concept de détermination: Port-Royal et Beauzée 192 (1980) 1236-45

Beccaria, Cesare

Paul M. Spurlin: Beccaria's *Essay on crimes and punishments* in eighteenth-century America 27 (1963) 1489-504

Mario A. Cattaneo: La discussione su Beccaria in Germania: K. F. Hommel e J. E. F. Schall 191 (1980) 935-43

Seizo Hotta: Quesnay or Hume: Beccaria between France and Britain 216 (1983) 281-83

Seizo Hotta: Quesnay or Hume: Beccaria between France and Britain 245 (1986) 457-65

Beckford, William

B. Didier: L'exotisme et la mise en question du système familial et moral dans le roman à la fin du XVIIIe siècle: Beckford, Sade, Potocki 152 (1976) 571-86

Th. Besterman: William Beckford's notes on a life of Voltaire 163 (1976) 53-55

Belgium

J. Vercruysse: La marquise Du Châtelet, prévote d'une confrérie bruxelloise 18 (1961) 169-71

Bentham, Jeremy

Robert Shackleton: The greatest happiness of the greatest number: the history of Bentham's phrase 90 (1972) 1461-82

Bentinck, Charlotte Sophia of Aldenburg, countess

Margaret Chenais: The 'man of the triangle' in Voltaire's correspondence with countess Bentinck 10 (1959) 421-24

André Magnan: *Dossier Voltaire en Prusse (1750-1753)* 244 (1986)

Bentinck, John Albert

Theodore Besterman: Rousseau, conseiller familial: deux lettres de John Albert Bentinck à Jean Jacques Rousseau 1 (1955) 175-81

Bernardin de Saint-Pierre, Jacques-Henri

Monique Stern: Lettres inédites de madame de Genlis à Bernardin de Saint-Pierre 169 (1977) 187-275

Ingrid Kisliuk: Le symbolisme du jardin et l'imagination créatrice chez Rousseau, Bernardin de Saint-Pierre et Chateaubriand 185 (1980) 297-418

Jean-Michel Racault: Système de la toponymie et organisation de l'espace romanesque dans *Paul et Virginie* 242 (1986) 377-418

Jean-Michel Racault: *Paul et Virginie* et l'utopie: de la 'petite société' au mythe collectif 242 (1986) 419-71

Bernini, Giovanni Lorenzo

G. Festa: Images du Bernin au dix-huitième siècle: l'œuvre du sculpteur jugée par les voyageurs français en Italie 241 (1986) 87-94

Berthier, Guillaume-François

John N. Pappas: *Berthier's 'Journal de Trévoux' and the philosophes* 3 (1957)

John Pappas: Buffon vu par Berthier, Feller et les *Nouvelles ecclésiastiques* 216 (1983) 26-28

Besterman, Theodore

William H. Barber: Obituary: Theodore Besterman 179 (1979) 221-25

Beverland, Adriaan

Willem Elias: La 'vertu' dans l'œuvre de Adriaan Beverland 216 (1983) 347-48

Bible

Alfred J. Bingham: Voltaire and the New testament 24 (1963) 183-218

J. Deshayes: De l'abbé Pluche au citoyen Dupuis: à la recherche de la clef des fables 24 (1963) 457-86

Arnold Ages: Voltaire's Biblical criticism: a study in thematic repetitions 30 (1964) 205-21

Arnold Ages: Voltaire, Calmet and the Old testament 41 (1966) 87-187

Arnold Ages: Voltaire and the Old testament: the testimony of his correspondence 55 (1967) 43-63

Günter Gawlick: Abraham's sacrifice of Isaac viewed by the English deists 56 (1967) 577-600

Rebecca Price Parkin: Alexander Pope's use of Biblical and ecclesiastical allusions 57 (1967) 1183-216

Pauline Kra: *Religion in Montesquieu's 'Lettres persanes'* 72 (1970)

Arnold Ages: The private Voltaire: three studies in the correspondence 81 (1971) 7-125

Bertram Eugene Schwarzbach: Etienne Fourmont, *philosophe* in disguise? 102 (1973) 65-119

David Lévy: *Voltaire et son exégèse du Pentateuque: critique et polémique* 130 (1975)

Walter Moser: Pour et contre la Bible: croire et savoir au XVIIIe siècle 154 (1976) 1509-28

William H. Trapnell: *Voltaire and the eucharist* 198 (1981)

Bertram Eugene Schwarzbach: The sacred genealogy of a Voltairean polemic: the development of critical hypotheses regarding the composition of the canonical and apocryphal gospels 216 (1983) 72-73

Marie-Hélène Cotoni: *L'Exégèse du Nouveau Testament dans la philosophie française du dix-huitième siècle* 220 (1984)

Bertram Eugene Schwarzbach: The sacred genealogy of a Voltairean polemic: the development of critical hypotheses regarding the composition of the canonical and apocryphal gospels 245 (1986) 303-50

bibliography

J. Rustin: Les 'suites' de Candide au XVIIIe siècle 90 (1972) 1395-416

Raymond Birn: *Livre et société* after ten years: formation of a discipline 151 (1976) 287-312

Richard L. Frautschi: Quelques paramètres de la production romanesque de 1751 à 1800 152 (1976) 741-52

C. Berkvens-Stevelinck et A. Nieuweboer: Le livre annoté: un moyen de communication souvent négligé entre auteur, éditeur et lecteur 216 (1983) 231-32

— Britain

Norma Perry: Voltaire's London agents for the *Henriade*: Simond and Bénézet, Huguenot merchants 102 (1973) 265-99

Giles Barber: Books from the old world and for the new: the British international trade in books in the eighteenth century 151 (1976) 185-224

— critical editions

Jean Varloot: Terminologie et édition critique 193 (1980) 1759-62

— France

George B. Watts: Charles Joseph Panckoucke, 'l'Atlas de la librairie française' 68 (1969) 67-205

Richard L. Frautschi: La diffusion du roman francophone au dix-huitième siècle: relevé provisoire de quelques collections en Europe centrale 216 (1983) 243-44

Angus Martin: La *'Bibliothèque universelle des romans', 1775-1789: présentation, table analytique, et index* 231 (1985)

bibliography

Robert L. Dawson: *Additions to the bibliographies of French prose fiction 1618-1806* 236 (1985)

— Geneva

Giles Barber: The Cramers of Geneva and their trade in Europe between 1755 and 1766 30 (1964) 377-413

— Germany

Norbert Waszek: Bibliography of the Scottish Enlightenment in Germany 230 (1985) 283-303

— Greece

C. Th. Dimaras: Notes sur la présence de Voltaire en Grèce 55 (1967) 439-44

— Holland

Jeroom Vercruysse: Bibliographie provisoire des traductions néerlandaises et flamandes de Voltaire 116 (1973) 19-64

— Italy

Theodore Besterman: A provisional bibliography of Italian editions and translations of Voltaire 18 (1961) 263-310

— New World

Giles Barber: Books from the old world and for the new: the British international trade in books in the eighteenth century 151 (1976) 185-224

— Portugal

Theodore Besterman: Provisional bibliography of Portuguese editions of Voltaire 76 (1970) 15-35

— Romania

Iacob Mârza: Horizon livresque des Lumières dans les bibliothèques roumaines de Transylvanie depuis le milieu du 18e siècle jusqu'aux premières décennies du 19e 216 (1983) 251-52

— Scandinavia

Theodore Besterman: A provisional bibliography of Scandinavian and Finnish editions and translations of Voltaire 47 (1966) 53-92

— Spain

Daniel Henri Pageaux: La *Gaceta de Madrid* et les traductions espagnoles d'ouvrages français (1750- 1770) 57 (1967) 1147-68

Christopher Todd: A provisional bibliography of published Spanish translations of Voltaire 161 (1976) 43-136

José Miguel Caso Gonzales: Traduction de livres dans l'Espagne du dix-huitième siècle 216 (1983) 237-38

73

Francisco Lafarga: Essai de bibliographie critique de 'Voltaire et l'Espagne' 219 (1983) 117-31

— travel

Peter Boerner: The great travel collections of the eighteenth century: their scope and purpose 193 (1980) 1798-1805

Bibliothèque universelle des romans

Angus Martin: La *'Bibliothèque universelle des romans', 1775-1789: présentation, table analytique, et index* 231 (1985)

Bigex, Simon

D. Lévy: Qui est l'auteur de *L'Oracle des anciens fidèles?* 117 (1974) 259-70

Emile Lizé: Une affaire de pommes à Ferney: Simon Bigex contre Antoine Adam 129 (1975) 19-26

Bignan, Anne

Robert H. McDonald: A forgotten Voltairean poem: *Voltaire et le comte de Maistre* by Anne Bignan 102 (1973) 231-64

Bignon, Jean-Paul

Françoise Bléchet: Deux lettres inédites de l'abbé Bignon, bibliothécaire du roi, à Voltaire 208 (1982) 315-22

biography

O M Brack: The art of dying in eighteenth-century English biography and fiction 191 (1980) 985

William L. Lipnick: Criminal biographies in eighteenth-century French popular literature 193 (1980) 1857-64

R. Veasey: *La Vie de mon père*: biography, autobiography, ethnography? 212 (1982) 213-24

biology

Miguel Benítez: Entre le mythe et la science: Benoît de Maillet et l'origine des êtres dans la mer 216 (1983) 307-309

blacks

Carminella Biondi: L'image du noir dans la littérature française du dix-huitième siècle 192 (1980) 1175-81

Blackwell, Thomas

K. K. Simonsuuri: Thomas Blackwell and the study of classical mythology 216 (1983) 117-18

Blake, William

Jean H. Hagstrum: William Blake rejects the Enlightenment 25 (1963) 811-28

Harold Orel: *English Romantic poets and the Enlightenment: nine essays on a literary relationship* 103 (1973)

Seymour Howard: Blake, classicism, gothicism, and nationalism 216 (1983) 132

blasphemy

Walter Rex: 'Blasphemy' in the refuge in Holland and in the French Enlightenment 57 (1967) 1307-20

Boerhaave, Hermann

Maurice Crosland: The development of chemistry in the eighteenth century 24 (1963) 369-441

Bohemia

Jan Lavička: Voltaire et la Bohême 219 (1983) 105-15

Boissel, François

Makoto Takahashi: François Boissel et ses principes de l'égalité en 1789 216 (1983) 220-21

Bolingbroke, Henry St John, Viscount

Dennis J. Fletcher: The fortunes of Bolingbroke in France in the eighteenth century 47 (1966) 207-32

Dennis J. Fletcher: Bolingbroke and the diffusion of Newtonianism in France 53 (1967) 29-46

Bonald, Louis de

L. Barclay: Louis de Bonald, prophet of the past? 55 (1967) 167-204

David M. Klinck: An examination of the *notes de lecture* of Louis de Bonald: at the origins of the ideology of the radical right in France 216 (1983) 18-19

Boncerf, Pierre-François

Jeroom Vercruysse: Turgot et Vergennes contre la lettre de Voltaire à Boncerf 67 (1969) 65-71

75

Bonnet, Charles

Jacques Marx: *Charles Bonnet contre les Lumières* 156-157 (1976)

Jean A. Perkins: Censorship and the Académie des sciences: a case study of Bonnet's *Considérations sur les corps organisés* 199 (1981) 251-62

Renato G. Mazzolini and Shirley A. Roe: *Science against the unbelievers: the correspondence of Bonnet and Needham, 1760-1780* 243 (1986)

booktrade

Jean-Daniel Candaux: L'annonce des livres nouveaux au 18e siècle 216 (1983) 234-37

Richard L. Frautschi: La diffusion du roman francophone au dix-huitième siècle: relevé provisoire de quelques collections en Europe centrale 216 (1983) 243-44

— almanachs

Neal R. Johnson: Almanachs français et les mentalités collectives au dix-huitième siècle 191 (1980) 1023-30

— Balkans

Gabrijela Vidan: Quelques aspects de la diffusion de la culture dans les terres slaves balkaniques 193 (1980) 1782-90

— Belgium

Jeroom Vercruysse: Les livres clandestins de Bouillon 193 (1980) 1840-52

G. Biart: L'organisation de l'edition à la Société typographique de Bouillon 216 (1983) 232-33

C. Bruneel: La diffusion du livre dans la société bruxelloise (1750-1796) 216 (1983) 233-34

— Britain

Giles Barber: Books from the old world and for the new: the British international trade in books in the eighteenth century 151 (1976) 185-224

— censorship

William Hanley: The policing of thought: censorship in eighteenth-century France 183 (1980) 265-95

Jean A. Perkins: Censorship and the Académie des sciences: a case study of Bonnet's *Considérations sur les corps organisés* 199 (1981) 251-62

Anne Boës: *La Lanterne magique de l'histoire: essai sur le théâtre historique en France de 1750 à 1789* 213 (1982)

Anne Boës and Robert L. Dawson: The legitimation of *contrefaçons* and the police stamp of 1777 230 (1985) 461-84

Geraldine Sheridan: Censorship and the booktrade in France in the early eighteenth century: Lenglet Dufresnoy's *Méthode pour étudier l'histoire* 241 (1986) 95-107

— clandestine

Raymond Birn: Book smuggling and book seizures in Paris at the dawn of the Enlightenment 193 (1980) 1762-63

Jeroom Vercruysse: Les livres clandestins de Bouillon 193 (1980) 1840-52

B. E. Schwarzbach and A. W. Fairbairn: The *Examen de la religion*: a bibliographical note 249 (1986) 91-156

— colportage

Lise Andries: Le roman de colportage au 18e siècle: évolution et analyse de contenu 216 (1983) 229-31

— England

Bernhard Fabian: The importation of English books into Germany in the eighteenth-century 193 (1980) 1780-82

Gae Brack: English literary ladies and the booksellers 193 (1980) 1932-39

Betty Rizzo: 'Hail, printing!': the Commonwealthman's salute to the printed word in eighteenth-century England 216 (1983) 258-59

P. Hunter: Print culture and the developing audience in England: fiction 216 (1983) 266-67

Shirley Strum Kenny: Print culture and the developing audience in England: dramatic literature 216 (1983) 267-69

John Feather: The merchants of culture: bookselling in early industrial England 217 (1983) 11-21

— France

Jacques Rychner: A l'ombre des Lumières: coup d'œil sur la main d'œuvre de quelques imprimeurs du XVIIIe siècle 155 (1976) 1925-55

Neal R. Johnson: Almanachs français et les mentalités collectives au dix-huitième siècle 191 (1980) 1023-30

Raymond Birn: Book smuggling and book seizures in Paris at the dawn of the Enlightenment 193 (1980) 1762-63

J. D. Woodbridge: The Parisian book trade in the early Enlightenment: an update on the Prosper Marchand project 193 (1980) 1763-72

Eugenio di Rienzo: Diffusione del libro, classe intellettuale e problemi istituzionali dell'editoria nel Settecento francese 193 (1980) 1772-79

William L. Lipnick: Criminal biographies in eighteenth-century French popular literature 193 (1980) 1857-64

Richard L. Frautschi: La diffusion du roman francophone au dix-huitième siècle: relevé provisoire de quelques collections en Europe centrale 216 (1983) 243-44

Françoise Weil: Le marchand-libraire en France pendant le second quart du dix-huitième siècle 217 (1983) 107-23

Anne Boës and Robert L. Dawson: The legitimation of *contrefaçons* and the police stamp of 1777 230 (1985) 461-84

77

Geraldine Sheridan: Censorship and the booktrade in France in the early eighteenth century: Lenglet Dufresnoy's *Méthode pour étudier l'histoire* 241 (1986) 95-107

Françoise Weil: Les libraires parisiens propriétaires d'éditions sans véritable privilège: l'exemple de Voltaire 249 (1986) 227-39

— Geneva

Giles Barber: The Cramers of Geneva and their trade in Europe between 1755 and 1766 30 (1964) 377-413

— Germany

Bernhard Fabian: The importation of English books into Germany in the eighteenth-century 193 (1980) 1780-82

— Holland

Ton Broos: Johannes Allart (1754-1816): Dutch printer, publisher and bookseller 193 (1980) 1822-30

— Italy

Anne Machet: Librairie et commerce du livre en Italie dans la deuxième moitié du XVIIIe siècle 153 (1976) 1347-80

Franco Piva: Le livre français dans les bibliothèques vicentines du dix-huitième siècle 193 (1980) 1791-98

Anne Machet: Edition populaire et colporteurs italiens dans la deuxième moitié du XVIIIe siècle 193 (1980) 1852-57

— printing

Betty Rizzo: 'Hail, printing!': the Commonwealthman's salute to the printed word in eighteenth-century England 216 (1983) 258-59

Jim Mitchell: The spread and fluctuation of eighteenth-century printing 230 (1985) 305-21

— privilege

Anne Boës and Robert L. Dawson: The legitimation of *contrefaçons* and the police stamp of 1777 230 (1985) 461-84

— Russia

Kenneth Craven: Publish and languish: the fate of Nikolai Ivanovich Novikov (1743-1818), propagator of the Enlightenment under Catherine II 216 (1983) 238-39

— Spain

José Miguel Caso Gonzales: Traduction de livres dans l'Espagne du dix-huitième siècle 216 (1983) 237-38

— travel

Peter Boerner: The great travel collections of the eighteenth century: their scope and purpose 193 (1980) 1798-1805

Borde, Charles

Jean Daniel Candaux: Charles Borde et la première crise d'antimilitarisme de l'opinion publique européenne 24 (1963) 315-44

Bordelon, Laurent

George Levitine: Goya and l'abbé Bordelon 216 (1983) 135-36

Bordeu, Théophile de

Paul Hoffmann: L'idée de liberté dans la philosophie médicale de Théophile de Bordeu 88 (1972) 769-87

Martha Fletcher, Nadine Labbé, A. de Laforcade et Christian Desplat: Le rétablissement des anciens parlements (1774-1775) vu de la correspondance inédite de Théophile de Bordeu 174 (1978) 203-67

Bossuet, Jacques-Bénigne

Pierre M. Conlon: Additions to the bibliography of Bossuet 37 (1965) 165-75

Louis Trenard: L'historiographie française d'après les manuels scolaires, de Bossuet à Voltaire 155 (1976) 2083-111

Boswell, James

Robert Folkenflik: Genre and the Boswellian imagination 192 (1980) 1287-95

Colby H. Kullman: James Boswell, compassionate lawyer and harsh criminologist: a divided self 217 (1983) 199-205

Jean Viviès: Boswell, la Corse et l'*Encyclopédie* 245 (1986) 467-73

botany

David Scott: Rousseau and flowers: the poetry of botany 182 (1979) 73-86

Pierre Saint-Amand: Rousseau contre la science: l'exemple de la botanique dans les textes autobiographiques 219 (1983) 159-67

Boudier de Villemert, Pierre-Joseph

David Williams: Boudier de Villemert: 'philosopher of the fair sex' 193 (1980) 1899-1901

Boufflers, Stanislas-Jean, chevalier de

H. Stavan: *Ah! si...*: 'nouvelle allemande' du chevalier de Boufflers 90 (1972) 1483-97

Bougainville, Louis-Antoine de

Lionello Sozzi: Bougainville e i selvaggi 192 (1980) 1181-83

Bouillon, Société typographique de

Jeroom Vercruysse: Les livres clandestins de Bouillon 193 (1980) 1840-52

G. Biart: L'organisation de l'edition à la Société typographique de Bouillon 216 (1983) 232-33

Boulainvilliers, Henri, comte de

Norman L. Torrey: Boulainvilliers: the man and the mask 1 (1955) 159-73

Robin Price: Boulainviller and the myth of the Frankish conquest of Gaul 199 (1981) 155-85

G. Gerhardi: L'idéologie du sang chez Boulainvilliers et sa réception au dix-huitième siècle 216 (1983) 177-79

Geneviève Menant-Artigas: Boulainvilliers et madame de Lambert 219 (1983) 147-51

Boulanger, Nicolas-Antoine

Paul Sadrin: *Nicolas-Antoine Boulanger (1722-1759) ou avant nous le déluge* 240 (1986)

Boullée, Etienne-Louis

Monique Nemer: Ledoux et Boullée: une écriture monumentale 216 (1983) 137-38

Boureau-Deslandes, André-François

Gregorio Piaia: Dal libertinismo erudito all'illuminismo: l'*Histoire critique de la philosophie* di A.-F. Boureau-Deslandes 191 (1980) 595-601

bourgeoisie

Katharine Whitman Carson: *Aspects of contemporary society in 'Gil Blas'* 110 (1973)

P. J. Buijnsters: The tutor/governess between nobility and bourgeoisie: some considerations with reference to an essay of 1734 by Justus van Effen 216 (1983) 164-66

Joachim Schmitt-Sasse: J. M. v. Loen and A. Freiherr Knigge: bourgeois ideals in the writings of German aristocrats 216 (1983) 187-88

Eric Golay: Egalité populaire et égalité bourgeoise a Genève au temps de la Révolution 216 (1983) 203-204

Bourget, Paul

Rémy G. Saisselin: Le dix-huitième siècle de Paul Bourget 216 (1983) 436-37

Boyer, Abel

James Flagg: Abel Boyer: a Huguenot intermediary 242 (1986) 1-73

Brazil

José Augusto Dos Santos: Education in Portuguese America in the eighteenth century 167 (1977) 395-425

Leopoldo Jobim: A la découverte du Mato Grosso au siècle des Lumières 216 (1983) 112

Brecht, Bertolt

Retta M. Taney: The effect of Brecht's techniques in the Berliner Ensemble's *Trumpets and drums* on the staging of *The Recruiting officer* by the National Theatre of Great Britain 192 (1980) 1440-46

Bret, Antoine

A. C. Keys: Bret, Douxménil and the *Mémoires* of Ninon de Lanclos 12 (1960) 43-54

A. C. Keys: An eighteenth-century editor of Molière: Antoine Bret 98 (1972) 219-30

Breteuil, Louis-Auguste Le Tonnelier, baron de

Louis Auguste Le Tonnelier, baron de Breteuil: *Réflexions sur la manière de rendre utiles les gens de lettres et d'arrêter la licence des écrits*, ed. P. M. Conlon 1 (1955) 125-31

Brissot de Warville, Jean-Pierre

Graham E. Rodmell: Laclos, Brissot, and the petition of the Champ de Mars 183 (1980) 189-222

Bristol journal

Norma Perry: Voltaire and Felix Farley's *Bristol journal* 62 (1968) 137-50

Brosses, Charles de

Micheline Coulaud: Les *Mémoires sur la matière étymologique* de Charles de Brosses 199 (1981) 287-352

Brown, John

James E. Crimmins: 'The study of true politics': John Brown on manners and liberty 241 (1986) 65-86

Brucker, Jakob

Mario Longo: Illuminismo e storiografia filosofica: Brucker e l'*Encyclopédie* 191 (1980) 581-87

Bruhier, Jean-Jacques

Paola Vecchi: Mort apparente et procédés de 'ressuscitation' dans la littérature médicale du 18e siècle (Bruhier, Louis, Réaumur, Menuret de Chambaud) 216 (1983) 330-32

Brumoy, Pierre

Lucette Perol: Diderot, les tragiques grecs et le père Brumoy 154 (1976) 1593-1616

Brunetière, Ferdinand

Giovanni Gullace: Brunetière on the eighteenth century 129 (1975) 145-95

Buffier, Claude

Kathleen Sonia Wilkins: *A study of the works of Claude Buffier* 66 (1969)

Buffon, Georges-Louis Leclerc, comte de

Otis Fellows: Buffon's place in the Enlightenment 25 (1963) 603-29

Elizabeth Anderson: La collaboration de Sonnini de Manoncourt à l'*Histoire naturelle* de Buffon 120 (1974) 329-58

Robert Wokler: Tyson and Buffon on the orang-utan 155 (1976) 2301-19

R. Galliani: Trois lettres inédites de Buffon 189 (1980) 205-10

Giulio Barsanti: L'homme et les classifications: aspects du débat anthropologique dans les sciences naturelles de Buffon à Lamarck 192 (1980) 1158-64

Geoffrey Bremner: Buffon and the casting out of fear 205 (1982) 75-88

John Pappas: Buffon vu par Berthier, Feller et les *Nouvelles ecclésiastiques* 216 (1983) 26-28

Giulio Barsanti: Linné et Buffon: deux images différentes de la nature et de l'histoire naturelle 216 (1983) 306-307

Bulkeley, comte de

Gunnar von Proschwitz: Lettres inédites de madame Du Deffand, du président Hénault et du comte de Bulkeley au baron Carl Fredrik Scheffer 1751-1756 10 (1959) 267-412

Buñuel, Luis

Jacqueline Marchand: De Voltaire à Buñuel 89 (1972) 1003-16

bureaucracy

G. L. Seidler: The concept of bureaucracy in the Enlightenment 216 (1983) 70-72

Calvin

Bürger, Gottfried August

Peter Boerner: 'Les morts vont vite' or the European success of Bürger's ballad *Lenore* 216 (1983) 448-49

Burke, Edmund

Michel Fuchs: Edmund Burke vu par Joseph de Maistre 216 (1983) 14-15

burlesque

Virgil W. Topazio: Voltaire's *Pucelle*: a study in burlesque 2 (1956) 207-23

Burns, Robert

Robert D. Thornton: Robert Burns and the Scottish Enlightenment 58 (1967) 1533-49

William James Murray: Robert Burns: the poet as liberationist 193 (1980) 1969-80

Bute, John Stuart, 3rd Earl of

John B. Shipley: Two Voltaire letters: to the third earl of Bute and to the duc de Richelieu 62 (1968) 7-11

Byron, George Noël Gordon, Lord

Harold Orel: Lord Byron's debt to the Enlightenment 26 (1963) 1275-90

Harold Orel: *English Romantic poets and the Enlightenment: nine essays on a literary relationship* 103 (1973)

Cabanis, Pierre-Jean-Georges

Aram Vartanian: Cabanis and La Mettrie 155 (1976) 2149-66

Calas affair

W. D. Howarth: Tragedy into melodrama: the fortunes of the Calas affair on the stage 174 (1978) 121-50

Calmet, Augustin

Arnold Ages: Voltaire, Calmet and the Old testament 41 (1966) 87-187

Calvin, Jean

Graham Gargett: *Voltaire and Protestantism* 188 (1980)

Elizabeth I. Nybakken: The Enlightenment and Calvinism: mutual support systems for the eighteenth-century American wilderness 192 (1980) 1126-35

83

Margaret D. Thomas: Michel de La Roche: a Huguenot critic of Calvin 238 (1985) 97-195

Camus, Albert

Patrick Henry: *Voltaire and Camus: the limits of reason and the awareness of absurdity* 138 (1975)

George A. Perla: Zadig, hero of the absurd 143 (1975) 49-70

Suzanne Hélein-Koss: Albert Camus et le *Contrat social* 161 (1976) 165-204

R. S. Ridgway: Camus's favourite moralist 199 (1981) 363-73

Canada

Roger Ouellet: Une bataille, quatre récits: quelques mises en scène de l'histoire au XVIIIe siècle 191 (1980) 573-74

Alain Tichoux: Théorie et pratique du libéralisme réformateur: le paradoxe canadien (1760-1765) 191 (1980) 971-79

C. Rouben: Propagande anti-philosophique dans les gazettes de Montréal et de Québec après la fin du régime français 216 (1983) 30-32

Françoise Weil: La découverte des Indiens du Canada et des Esquimaux au début du dix-huitième siècle par Antoine Raudot 216 (1983) 124-25

Canova, Antonio

Seymour Howard: The antiquarian market in Rome and the use of neo-classicism: a basis for Canova's new classics 153 (1976) 1057-68

Cantemir, Dimitrie

Alexandru Dutu: Structures mentales et communication internationale: l'image de la civilisation européene chez Vico, Montesquieu, et Dimitrie Cantemir 191 (1980) 601

Carleton, Mary

Janet Todd: Marketing the self: Mary Carleton, Miss F and Susannah Gunning 217 (1983) 95-106

Carlyle, Thomas

Robert Kusch: Voltaire as symbol of the eighteenth century in Carlyle's *Frederick* 79 (1971) 61-72

John Boening: Carlyle versus the Enlightenment: the curious case of Lessing 216 (1983) 419-21

Carradori, Francesco

Roberta Roani Villani: Lo scultore pistoiese Francesco Carradori 193 (1980) 1707-10

Casanova di Seingalt, Giacomo Girolamo

H. Watzlawick: Casanova and Voltaire's *Discours aux Welches* 171 (1977) 71-75

Alberto Beretta Anguissola: Désir et utopie chez Foigny, Rétif et Casanova 191 (1980) 645-47

Elena Gascón-Vera: A feminist writer of the eighteenth century: Giacomo Casanova 193 (1980) 1995-96

Castel, Louis-Bertrand

Huguette Cohen: The intent of the digressions on father Castel and father Porée in Diderot's *Lettre sur les sourds et muets* 201 (1982) 163-83

Cataneo, Jean de

Roland Mortier: Un adversaire vénitien des 'Lumières', le comte de Cataneo 32 (1965) 91-268

Catargi, Dimitraki

C. Th. Dimaras: D. Catargi, 'philosophe' grec 25 (1963) 509-18

Catherine II, Empress of Russia

C. H. Wilberger: *Voltaire's Russia: window on the east* 164 (1976)

Valerie A. Tumins: Catherine II, Frederick II and Gustav III: three enlightened monarchs and their impact on literature 190 (1980) 350-56

Daniel L. Schlafly: Western Europe discovers Russia: foreign travellers in the reign of Catherine the Great 216 (1983) 115-17

Kenneth Craven: Publish and languish: the fate of Nikolai Ivanovich Novikov (1743-1818), propagator of the Enlightenment under Catherine II 216 (1983) 238-39

Georges Dulac: Grimm et la *Correspondance littéraire* envoyée à Catherine II (d'après les lettres de Dimitri Golitsyn et de F. M. Grimm au vice-chancelier Alexandre Golitsyn) 217 (1983) 207-48

Cato

Enrico Nuzzo: The theme of equality in Trenchard's and Gordon's *Cato's letters* 216 (1983) 211-13

Caumont, Joseph de Seytres, marquis de

Harriet Dorothy Rothschild: Benoît de Maillet's letters to the marquis de Caumont 60 (1968) 311-38

Caylus, Anne-Claude-Philippe de Tubières, comte de

René Godenne: Un inédit de Caylus: *Les Ages ou la fée du Loreau*, comédie en prose et en un acte (1739) 106 (1973) 175-224

Raymonde Robert: Le comte de Caylus et l'orient: la littérature aux prises avec le même et l'autre 154 (1976) 1825-53

Cazotte, Jacques

Nadia Minerva: Des Lumières à l'Illuminisme: Cazotte et son monde 191 (1980) 1015-22

Claudine Hunting: Les mille et une sources du *Diable amoureux* de Cazotte 230 (1985) 247-71

censorship

William Hanley: The policing of thought: censorship in eighteenth-century France 183 (1980) 265-95

Jean A. Perkins: Censorship and the Académie des sciences: a case study of Bonnet's *Considérations sur les corps organisés* 199 (1981) 251-62

Anne Boës: *La Lanterne magique de l'histoire: essai sur le théâtre historique en France de 1750 à 1789* 213 (1982)

Anne Boës and Robert L. Dawson: The legitimation of *contrefaçons* and the police stamp of 1777 230 (1985) 461-84

Geraldine Sheridan: Censorship and the booktrade in France in the early eighteenth century: Lenglet Dufresnoy's *Méthode pour étudier l'histoire* 241 (1986) 95-107

Cerou, Pierre

H. Gaston Hall: From extravagant poet to the writer as hero: Piron's *La Métromanie* and Pierre Cerou's *L'Amant auteur et valet* 183 (1980) 117-32

Cervantes, Miguel de

Alain Nabarra: L'influence de *Don Quichotte* sur les premiers romans de Marivaux 124 (1974) 191-219

Challe, Robert

Lawrence J. Forno: Robert Challe and the eighteenth century 79 (1971) 163-75

Lawrence J. Forno: The fictional letter in the memoir novel: Robert Challe's *Illustres Françoises* 81 (1971) 149-61

Eva Maria Knapp-Tepperberg: Deux cas d'adultère dans la littérature française de la première moitié du XVIIIe siècle 88 (1972) 859-70

Marie Laure Swiderski: L'image de la femme dans le roman au début du XVIIIe siècle: les *Illustres Françaises* de Robert Challe 90 (1972) 1505-18

John Falvey: Psychological analysis and moral ambiguity in the narrative processes of Chasles, Prévost and Marivaux 94 (1972) 141-58

Lois Ann Russell: A colonial utopia: the Acadia of Robert Challe 191 (1980) 729-31

F. Deloffre: Une crise de conscience exemplaire à l'orée du siècle des Lumières: le cas de Robert Challe 192 (1980) 1063-71

Melâhat Menemencioglu: Les adaptations dramatiques des *Illustres Françaises* 192 (1980) 1496-1506

Robert Challe: *Difficultés sur la religion proposées au père Malebranche*. Edition critique d'après un manuscrit inédit par Frédéric Deloffre et Melâhat Menemencioglu 209 (1982)

J. Chupeau: Le voyageur philosophe ou Robert Challe au miroir du *Journal d'un voyage aux Indes* 215 (1982) 45-61

B. L. H. Lewis: The influence of Chasles's *Illustres Françoises* on Prévost's *Cleveland* 219 (1983) 153-58

Michèle Weil: La 'peur' de Gallouïn: un scénario et deux interprétations de la sixième histoire des *Illustres Françaises* 242 (1986) 75-81

Chambers, Ephraim

J. Lough: The *Encyclopédie* and Chambers's *Cyclopaedia* 185 (1980) 221-24

Lael Ely Bradshaw: Ephraim Chambers's *Cyclopaedia* 194 (1981) 123-40

Chamfort, Sébastien-Roch-Nicolas

John Renwick: Chamfort, patriote en coulisses: réflexions sur une lettre inédite à Roland 183 (1980) 165-76

R. S. Ridgway: Camus's favourite moralist 199 (1981) 363-73

John Renwick: *Chamfort devant la postérité (1794-1984)* 247 (1986)

charity

Thomas M. Adams: Charitable reform and the diffusion of economic ideas in eighteenth-century France 191 (1980) 858-66

Luigi Cajani: L'assistenza ai poveri nell'Italia del Settecento 191 (1980) 914-20

Charles Edward Stuart

Laurence L. Bongie: Voltaire's English, high treason and a manifesto for bonnie prince Charles 171 (1977) 7-29

Charlevoix, Pierre-François-Xavier de

Maurice Roelens: L'expérience de l'espace américain dans les récits de voyage entre La Hontan et Charlevoix 155 (1976) 1861-95

Charrière, Isabelle de [Belle de Zuylen]

Les Années de formation de F. H. Jacobi, d'après ses lettres inédites à M. M. Rey (1763-1771) avec Le Noble, de madame de Charrière, textes présentées par J. Th. de Booy et Roland Mortier 45 (1966)

C. P. Courtney: *A preliminary bibliography of Isabelle de Charrière (Belle de Zuylen)* 186 (1980)

Béatrice Didier: La femme à la recherche de son image: Mme de Charrière et l'écriture féminine dans la seconde moitié du XVIIIe siècle 193 (1980) 1981-88

Dennis Wood: Isabelle de Charrière et Benjamin Constant: à propos d'une découverte récente 215 (1982) 273-79

C. P. Courtney: *The Portrait of Zélide*: Geoffrey Scott and Belle de Zuylen 219 (1983) 281-88

Chastellux, François-Jean, marquis de

Marie-Thérèse Isaac: L'Européen à la rencontre du noir-esclave des Etats-Unis d'Amérique d'après les *Voyages* du marquis de Chastellux 216 (1983) 111-12

Donald Schier: Prima le parole? Chastellux on the aesthetics of opera 245 (1986) 351-57

Chateaubriand, François-René, vicomte de

Robert J. Buyck: Chateaubriand juge de Voltaire 114 (1973) 141-272

Ingrid Kisliuk: Le symbolisme du jardin et l'imagination créatrice chez Rousseau, Bernardin de Saint-Pierre et Chateaubriand 185 (1980) 297-418

Chaudon, Louis-Mayeul

R. E. A. Waller: Louis-Mayeul Chaudon against the *philosophes* 216 (1983) 39-41

R. E. A. Waller: Louis-Mayeul Chaudon against the *philosophes* 228 (1984) 259-65

chemistry

Maurice Crosland: The development of chemistry in the eighteenth century 24 (1963) 369-441

Robert L. Walters: Chemistry at Cirey 58 (1967) 1807-27

Louis S. Greenbaum: The humanitarianism of Antoine Laurent Lavoisier 88 (1972) 651-75

Arthur Donovan: Chemistry in the Scottish Enlightenment 152 (1976) 587-605

David Beeson (ed.): Maupertuis, *Lettre d'un horloger anglois à un astronome de Pékin* 230 (1985) 189-222

Huguette Cohen: Diderot and the image of China in eighteenth-century France 242 (1986) 219-32

Gloria Bien: Chénier and China 242 (1986) 363-75

Choiseul, Etienne-François, duc de

Jeroom Vercruysse: La Harpe et la *Gazette d'Utrecht*: une lettre inédite à Choiseul 79 (1971) 193-98

Choiseul, Louise-Honorine Crozat Du Châtel, duchesse de

Benedetta Craveri: Mme Du Deffand e Mme de Choiseul: un'amicizia femminile 193 (1980) 1956-63

Christ

Marie-Hélène Cotoni: L'image du Christ dans les courants déiste et matérialiste français du XVIIIe siècle 192 (1980) 1093-1100

Church

Rebecca Price Parkin: Alexander Pope's use of Biblical and ecclesiastical allusions 57 (1967) 1183-216

William H. Williams: Voltaire and the utility of the lower clergy 58 (1967) 1869-91

James K. Cameron: The Church of Scotland in the age of reason 58 (1967) 1939-51

Katharine Whitman Carson: *Aspects of contemporary society in 'Gil Blas'* 110 (1973)

B. Robert Kreiser: Witchcraft and ecclesiastical politics in early eighteenth-century Provence: the Cadière-Girard affair 192 (1980) 1072

Marina Caffiero Trincia: Il problema della riforma della Chiesa e le istanze cattoliche de rinnovamento culturale in Italia nel XVIII secolo 192 (1980) 1135-41

Oscar A. Haac: A monstrous proposition: the Church stands in need of reform 216 (1983) 427-29

Cicero

Günter Gawlick: Cicero and the Enlightenment 25 (1963) 657-82

cinema

Jacqueline Marchand: De Voltaire à Buñuel 89 (1972) 1003-16

Jacqueline Marchand: Diderot et le cinéma 190 (1980) 244-49

circumcision

R. S. Wolper: 'Child of circumcision': the myths behind the image in eighteenth-century English literature and print 191 (1980) 1050-51

city

Silvia Bordini Porretta: Tendenze riformatrici e città nuove nella Sicilia del Settecento 191 (1980) 907-14

Vittorio E. Giuntella: La città dell'Illuminismo 191 (1980) 927-35

Edward A. Bloom: Eden betray'd: city motifs in satire 191 (1980) 956-62

Richard A. Etlin: From charnel house to Elysium: transformation in the image of the cemetery (1744-1804) 193 (1980) 1669-70

James A. Leith: Space and revolution: public monuments and urban planning at the peak of the Terror 193 (1980) 1752-53

Annette Bridgman: Heavenly cities on earth: urban planning and mass culture in 18th-century utopias 193 (1980) 1753-54

Siegfried Jüttner: La ville dans les débats entre encyclopédistes et économistes 216 (1983) 283-84

civilisation

Simon Davies: *Paris and the provinces in prose fiction* 214 (1982)

civil rights

G. Gargett: Voltaire, Gilbert de Voisins's *Mémoires* and the problem of Huguenot civil rights (1767-1768) 174 (1978) 7-57

Clairon, Claire-Josèphe Lerys, *called* Mlle

Michael Waters: Unpublished letters from Mlle Clairon to Jean de Vaines 137 (1975) 141-89

Jack Richtman: Mademoiselle Clairon: actress-philosopher 154 (1976) 1813-24

Danielle Johnson-Cousin: Les 'leçons de déclamation' de Germaine Necker: note sur le 'mystère Clairon' 183 (1980) 161-64

clandestine writings

Marie-Hélène Cotoni: Dénigrement de la providence et défense des valeurs humaines dans les manuscrits clandestins de la première moitié du dix-huitième siècle 152 (1976) 497-513

Miguel Benítez: Benoît de Maillet et la littérature clandestine: étude de sa correspondance avec l'abbé Le Mascrier 183 (1980) 133-59

Miguel Benítez: Naturalisme et atomisme: le refus des atomes et du vide dans la littérature clandestine 215 (1982) 121-38

B. E. Schwarzbach and A. W. Fairbairn: The *Examen de la religion*: a bibliographical note 249 (1986) 91-156

Clarke, Samuel

William H. Barber: Voltaire and Samuel Clarke 179 (1979) 47-61

Margaret D. Thomas: Michel de La Roche: a Huguenot critic of Calvin 238 (1985) 97-195

classicism

A. Kibédi Varga: La désagrégation de l'idéal classique dans le roman français de la première moitié du XVIIIe siècle 26 (1963) 965-98

Patrick Brady: *Manon Lescaut*: classical, romantic, or rococo? 53 (1967) 339-60

Clavijero, Francisco Xavier

Giovanni Marchetti: Cultura e nazione in Clavijero 190 (1980) 402-11

Cléreaux, Marie

Hans-Jürgen Lüsebrink: L'affaire Cléreaux (Rouen 1785-1790): affrontements idéo-logiques et tensions institutionnelles sur la scène judiciaire de la fin du XVIIIe siècle 191 (1980) 892-900

Hans-Jürgen Lüsebrink: *Mémoire pour la fille Cléreaux* (Rouen 1785) 208 (1982) 323-72

climate

Michael Cardy: Discussion of the theory of climate in the *querelle des anciens et des modernes* 163 (1976) 73-88

Coger, François-Marie

J. Th. de Booy: L'abbé Coger, dit Coge Pecus, lecteur de Voltaire et de d'Holbach 18 (1961) 183-96

Coleridge, Samuel Taylor

Harold Orel: *English Romantic poets and the Enlightenment: nine essays on a literary relationship* 103 (1973)

collectors

Krzysztof Pomian: Médailles/coquilles = érudition/philosophie 154 (1976) 1677-1703

Collini, Cosimo Alessandro

    Enrico Straub: A propos d'une lettre inconnue de Voltaire 67 (1969) 21-27

    Robert Granderoute: Quatre lettres inédites de Collini à Voltaire 230 (1985) 137-44

colonialism

    John Francis McDermott: The Enlightenment on the Mississippi frontier, 1763-1804 26 (1963) 1129-42

    Mathé Allain: The coloniser's viewpoint: Louisiana Indians as seen by the French 216 (1983) 87-88

    Philip Stewart: Du sauvage au colon anglais: l'Américain au dix-huitième siècle 216 (1983) 120-21

    Robert Toupin: Pierre Potier, jésuite belge chez les Hurons du Détroit (1744-1781): les chemins d'un espace *nouveau* à explorer 216 (1983) 122-24

Combes, Louis

    Monique Mosser et Jean-Pierre Mouilleseaux: Architecture, politique et utopie: vers une *Foederapolis europeana*: les monuments à la paix de Louis Combes 191 (1980) 712-16

Comédie-Française

    P. M. Conlon: *Voltaire's literary career from 1728 to 1750* 14 (1961)

    Christopher Todd: La Harpe quarrels with the actors: unpublished correspondence 53 (1967) 223-337

    Spire Pitou: The Comédie-Française and the Palais royal interlude of 1716-1723 64 (1968) 225-64

    Spire Pitou: The players' return to Versailles, 1723-1757 73 (1970) 7-145

    Alexander A. Sokalski: Le poète Mey et son double 212 (1982) 163-81

comedy

    David L. Gobert: Comic in *Micromégas* as expressive of theme 37 (1965) 53-60

    John Van Eerde: Aspects of social criticism in eighteenth-century French comedy 37 (1965) 81-107

    James S. Munro: Moral and social preoccupations in early eighteenth-century French comedy 57 (1967) 1031-54

    Samuel S. B. Taylor: Le développement du genre comique en France de Molière à Beaumarchais 90 (1972) 1545-66

    Joseph I. Donohoe: Marivaux: the comedy of Enlightenment 98 (1972) 169-81

    Jack Yashinsky: Les comédies de Voltaire: popularité et influence 114 (1973) 99-111

Michael H. Gertner: Five comic devices in *Zadig* 117 (1974) 133-52

Liliane Willens: *Voltaire's comic theatre: composition, conflict and critics* 136 (1975)

Oscar A. Haac: Comedy in utopia: the literary imagination of Marivaux and the abbé Prévost 191 (1980) 684-85

Lynn Salkin Sbiroli: L'emploi du comique dans *Jacques le fataliste* 192 (1980) 1409-16

Peter L. Smith: Natural order and social code in eighteenth-century French comedy 192 (1980) 1527

Theodore E. D. Braun: La conscience de la présence des spectateurs dans la comédie larmoyante et dans le drame 192 (1980) 1527-34

Roseann Runte: The widow in eighteenth-century French comedy 192 (1980) 1537-44

Norbert Jonard: La comédie des apparences dans le théâtre de Goldoni 192 (1980) 1544

Norbert Jonard: La comédie des apparences dans le théâtre de Goldoni 199 (1981) 47-61

David G. John: Women and men as equals in German comedy of the Enlightenment 216 (1983) 208-209

commerce

Nicholas Phillipson: Virtue, commerce, and the science of man in early eighteenth-century Scotland 191 (1980) 750-53

Georges Festa: Images et réalités de la vie commerciale italienne à travers le *Voyage d'Italie* de Sade 217 (1983) 23-26

Jochen Hoock: Structures de l'échange et mentalités marchandes: les marchands de Rouen, 1650-1750 217 (1983) 27-35

Georges Lamoine: Le personnage du *merchant* à Bristol, dans la réalité et dans la littérature au dix-huitième siècle 217 (1983) 37-47

Edna Hindie Lemay: Une minorité au sein d'une minorité: un banquier et quelques négociants à l'Assemblée constituante 1789-1791 217 (1983) 49-64

John McVeagh: George Farquhar and commercial England 217 (1983) 65-81

Anthony Strugnell: Diderot on luxury, commerce and the merchant 217 (1983) 83-93

J. K. Welcher: Gulliver in the market-place: 217 (1983) 125-39

Condillac, Etienne Bonnot de

M. W. Beal: Condillac as precursor of Kant 102 (1973) 193-229

Ellen McNiven Hine: Condillac and the problem of language 106 (1973) 21-62

John Frederick Logan: Condillac, Volney, and the lessons of the past 153 (1976) 1329-35

Etienne Bonnot de Condillac: *Les Monades*, edited with and introduction and notes by Laurence L. Bongie 187 (1980)

G. A. Wells: Condillac, Rousseau and Herder on the origin of language 230 (1985) 233-46

Condorcet, Jean-Antoine-Nicolas de Caritat, marquis de

L. A. Boiteux: Voltaire et le ménage Suard 1 (1955) 19-109

K. M. Baker: Scientism, elitism and liberalism: the case of Condorcet 55 (1967) 129-65

L. Barclay: Louis de Bonald, prophet of the past? 55 (1967) 167-204

Richard A. Brooks: Condorcet and Pascal 55 (1967) 297-307

Louis S. Greenbaum: Health-care and hospital-building in eighteenth-century France: reform proposals of Du Pont de Nemours and Condorcet 152 (1976) 895-930

Keith Michael Baker: Condorcet's notes for a revised edition of his reception speech to the Académie française 169 (1977) 7-68

Barbara Brookes: The feminism of Condorcet and Sophie de Grouchy 189 (1980) 297-361

Colette Verger Michael: Condorcet and the inherent contradiction in the American affirmation of natural rights and slaveholding 191 (1980) 768-74

Condorcet, Sophie de Grouchy, marquise de

Barbara Brookes: The feminism of Condorcet and Sophie de Grouchy 189 (1980) 297-361

Takaho Ando: Mme de Condorcet et la philosophie de la 'sympathie' 216 (1983) 335-36

Connaissance des beautés

Theodore Besterman: Note on the authorship of the *Connaissance des beautés* 4 (1957) 291-94

conservatism

David Nokes: The radical conservatism of Swift's Irish pamphlets 216 (1983) 25-26

Constant, Benjamin

Jean Ehrard: De Meilcour à Adolphe, ou la suite des *Egarements* 190 (1980) 101-17

Dennis Wood: Isabelle de Charrière et Benjamin Constant: à propos d'une découverte récente 215 (1982) 273-79

Emile Lizé: *Voltaire, Grimm et la 'Correspondance littéraire'* 180 (1979)

Georges Dulac: Grimm et la *Correspondance littéraire* envoyée à Catherine II (d'après les lettres de Dimitri Golitsyn et de F. M. Grimm au vice-chancelier Alexandre Golitsyn) 217 (1983) 207-48

Ulla Kölving et Jeanne Carriat: *Inventaire de la 'Correspondance littéraire' de Grimm et Meister* 225-227 (1984)

correspondence, political

Cécile Douxchamps-Lefèvre: La correspondance politique secrète sur la cour de France: 1er juillet 1774 – 22 décembre 1779 216 (1983) 241-42

Corsica

F. G. Healey: Rousseau, Voltaire and Corsica: some notes on an interesting enigma 10 (1959) 413-19

Thadd E. Hall: The development of Enlightenment interest in eighteenth-century Corsica 64 (1968) 165-85

Jean Viviès: Boswell, la Corse et l'*Encyclopédie* 245 (1986) 467-73

cosmology

Alain-Marc Rieu: Kant: critique du 'Cosmologisme' et fin des Lumières 216 (1983) 324

costume

Anne-Marie Jaton: Morale et vertu: histoire parallèle du costume et de la cosmétique 216 (1983) 351-52

Coyer, Gabriel-François

Leonard Adams: *Coyer and the Enlightenment* 123 (1974)

L. Adams: Anson in Frivola: an exercise in social criticism: Coyer's *Découverte de l'île Frivole* (1751) 191 (1980) 851-58

Xavier Coyer: L'élection de l'abbé Coyer à la Royal Society of London: deux lettres inédites de Voltaire et de d'Alembert 249 (1986) 379-80

Coypel, Charles-Antoine

Jack Richtman: Seven *canevas* for the Théâtre-Italien: early theatrical ventures by Charles-Antoine Coypel, court painter under Louis XV 192 (1980) 1469-77

Cramer family

Giles Barber: The Cramers of Geneva and their trade in Europe between 1755 and 1766 30 (1964) 377-413

Crashaw, Richard

Robert P. Kalmey: Pope's *Eloisa to Abelard* and some 'pretty conceptions' from Crashaw 241 (1986) 29-40

Crébillon, Claude-Prosper Jolyot de

Marguerite Marie D. Stevens: L'idéalisme et le réalisme dans *Les Egarements du cœur et de l'esprit* de Crébillon fils 47 (1966) 157-76

P. L. M. Fein: Crébillon fils, mirror of his society 88 (1972) 485-91

R. Niklaus: Crébillon fils et Richardson 89 (1972) 1169-85

Peter V. Conroy: *Crébillon fils: techniques of the novel* 99 (1972)

James F. Jones: Visual communication in *Les Egarements du cœur et de l'esprit* 120 (1974) 319-28

Benjamin W. Palmer: Crébillon *fils* and his reader 132 (1975) 183-97

Viktor Link: The reception of Crébillon's *Le Sopha* in England: an unnoticed edition and some imitations 132 (1975) 199-203

P. L. M. Fein: Crébillon fils and eroticism 152 (1976) 723-28

Ninette Boothroyd: *Les Lettres de la Marquise de M*** au Comte de R**** – le discours de la passion: structure et modulations 185 (1980) 199-220

Jean Ehrard: De Meilcour à Adolphe, ou la suite des *Egarements* 190 (1980) 101-17

Andrzej Siemek: Crébillon fils et le dilemme du narrateur 192 (1980) 1359-68

Andrzej Siemek: *La Recherche morale et esthétique dans le roman de Crébillon fils* 200 (1981)

Jeannette Geffriaud Rosso: Libertinage et 'surcompensation' dans les rapports entre les sexes au dix-huitième siècle', d'après Laclos, Diderot et Crébillon fils 216 (1983) 348-49

Christiane Mervaud: La narration interrompue dans *Le Sopha* de Crébillon 249 (1986) 183-95

Crébillon, Prosper Jolyot de

André G. Bourassa: Polémique et propagande dans *Rome sauvée* et *Les Triumvirs* de Voltaire 60 (1968) 73-103

Paul O. LeClerc: *Voltaire and Crébillon père: history of an enmity* 115 (1973)

crime

Paul M. Spurlin: Beccaria's *Essay on crimes and punishments* in eighteenth-century America 27 (1963) 1489-504

Diana Guiragossian: *Manon Lescaut* et la justice criminelle sous l'ancien régime 56 (1967) 679-91

William L. Lipnick: Criminal biographies in eighteenth-century French popular literature 193 (1980) 1857-64

Hans-Jürgen Lüsebrink: *Mémoire pour la fille Cléreaux* (Rouen 1785) 208 (1982) 323-72

Colby H. Kullman: James Boswell, compassionate lawyer and harsh criminologist: a divided self 217 (1983) 199-205

crisis

Franco Venturi: La prima crisi dell'antico regime: 1768-1776 190 (1980) 63-80

Croatia

Barbara W. Maggs: Voltaire and the Balkans: aspects of the Enlightenment in 18th-century Croatia and Serbia 189 (1980) 81-118

culture

Norman Hampson and Betty Behrens: Cultural history as infrastructure 86 (1971) 7-24

Jean Marie Goulemot: Démons, merveilles et philosophie à l'âge classique 191 (1980) 1009-15

Annette Bridgman: Heavenly cities on earth: urban planning and mass culture in 18th-century utopias 193 (1980) 1753-54

J. C. Stewart-Robertson: Reid's anatomy of culture: a Scottish response to the eloquent Jean-Jacques 205 (1982) 141-63

Cuppé, Pierre

E. R. Briggs: Pierre Cuppé's debts to England and Holland 6 (1958) 37-66

Custine, Adam-Philippe de

George Armstrong Kelly: War, revolution and terror: a public biography of Adam-Philippe de Custine 205 (1982) 211-95

Dacier, Anne

R. C. Knight: Anne Dacier and gardens ancient and modern 185 (1980) 119-29

dance

Jacques Chouillet: Figures chorégraphiques dans le théâtre de Diderot 193 (1980) 1721-22

Dancourt, Florent Carton, sieur d'Ancourt, *called*

P. M. Conlon: Dancourt assailed 41 (1966) 343-44

Alexander A. Sokalski: Autour du *Vert galant* 163 (1976) 155-202

Darwin, Erasmus

Donald M. Hassler: Erasmus Darwin and Enlightenment origins of science fiction 153 (1976) 1045-56

death

O M Brack: The art of dying in eighteenth-century English biography and fiction 191 (1980) 985

Paola Vecchi: La mort dans l'*Encyclopédie* 191 (1980) 986-94

Valentini Brady-Papadopoulou: Separation, death and sexuality: Diderot's *La Religieuse* and rites of initiation 192 (1980) 1199-1205

Giuseppe Scaraffia: La presenza della morte in *Jacques le fataliste* di Diderot 192 (1980) 1416-20

Richard A. Etlin: From charnel house to Elysium: transformation in the image of the cemetery (1744-1804) 193 (1980) 1669-70

József Pál: Le motif de la mort dans l'art et la littérature néoclassiques 193 (1980) 1743-51

David Irwin: Death in the landscape: the neo-classic tomb 216 (1983) 132-33

Paola Vecchi: Mort apparente et procédés de 'ressuscitation' dans la littérature médicale du 18e siècle (Bruhier, Louis, Réaumur, Menuret de Chambaud) 216 (1983) 330-32

decadence

Roland Mortier: L'idée de décadence littéraire au XVIIIe siècle 57 (1967) 1013-29

J. G. A. Pocock: Gibbon and the stages of society: progress, ambivalence and corruption in the *Decline and fall* 191 (1980) 537

Defoe, Daniel

Lucette Desvignes: Vues de la terre promise: les visages de l'Amérique dans *Moll Flanders* et dans l'*Histoire de Manon Lescaut* 152 (1976) 543-57

Marialuisa Bignami: Utopian elements in Daniel Defoe's novels 191 (1980) 647-53

Jean Ducrocq: Relations de voyages et récits symboliques: *Robinson* et *Gulliver* 215 (1982) 1-0008

Ton Broos: Robinson Crusoe and the Low Countries 216 (1983) 449

Anne Molet-Sauvaget: La *Relation de Robert Everard*, ébauche probable du *Journal de Robert Drury* de Daniel Defoe 241 (1986) 1-28

deism

Günter Gawlick: Abraham's sacrifice of Isaac viewed by the English deists 56 (1967) 577-600

David Lévy: *Voltaire et son exégèse du Pentateuque: critique et polémique* 130 (1975)

Günter Gawlick: The English deists' contribution to the theory of toleration 152 (1976) 823-35

Marie-Hélène Cotoni: L'image du Christ dans les courants déiste et matérialiste français du XVIIIe siècle 192 (1980) 1093-1100

Deleyre, Alexandre

M. Molinier: Les relations de Deleyre et de Rousseau, 1753-1778, suivi de la correspondance inédite de Deleyre et du marquis de Girardin, août-décembre 1778 70 (1970) 43-176

Delille, Jacques

Frédéric Barbier: Quelques documents inédits sur l'abbé Delille 189 (1980) 211-28

Delisle, Guillaume

Renée Simon: *Nicolas Fréret, académicien* 17 (1961)

Delisle de Sales, Jean-Baptiste-Claude Izouard, *called*

Pierre Malandain: *Delisle de Sales: philosophe de la nature 1741-1816* 203-204 (1982)

demagogy

Karlis Racevskis: Le discours philosophique à l'Académie française: une sémiotique de la démagogie et de l'arrivisme 190 (1980) 343-50

democracy

Adrienne Koch: The contest of democracy and aristocracy in the American Enlightenment 26 (1963) 999-1018

Maria Evelina Zoltowska: La démocratisation de l'idée de l'honneur dans le *Manuscrit trouvé à Saragosse* de Jean Potocki 216 (1983) 224-26

demography

Julian Huxley: A factor overlooked by the *philosophes*: the population explosion 25 (1963) 861-83

Agnes Raymond: Le problème de la population chez les encyclopédistes 26 (1963) 1379-88

Denis, Marie-Louise

Jeroom Vercruysse: Madame Denis et Ximenès ou la nièce aristarque 67 (1969) 73-90

Colin Duckworth: Madame Denis's unpublished *Pamela*: a link between Richardson, Goldoni and Voltaire 76 (1970) 37-53

Jeroom Vercruysse: La première d'*Olympie*: trois lettres de Mme Denis aux Constant d'Hermenches 163 (1976) 19-29

Philippe Teissier: Une lettre de madame Denis au comte d'Argental sur *Rome sauvée* 176 (1979) 41-50

André Magnan: *Dossier Voltaire en Prusse (1750-1753)* 244 (1986)

Denmark

Carol Gold: Educational reform in Denmark, 1784-1814 167 (1977) 49-64

Dennis, John

W. P. Albrecht: John Dennis and the sublime pleasures of tragedy 87 (1972) 65-85

Denon, Dominique Vivant, baron

Lloyd R. Free: Point of view and narrative space in Vivant Denon's *Point de lendemain* 163 (1976) 89-115

Giuliana Toso Rodinis: Vivant Denon e le sue note al *Voyage di H. Swinburne dans les deux Siciles* 193 (1980) 1669

Desca, Anthony

Christopher Thacker: M. A. D.: an editor of Voltaire's letters identified 62 (1968) 309-10

Descartes, René

Jean Deprun: Jean Meslier et l'héritage cartésien 24 (1963) 443-55

Mariafranca Spallanzani: Notes sur le cartésianisme dans l'*Encyclopédie* 216 (1983) 326-28

Jürgen von Stackelberg: Pope cartésien? L'*Essay on Man* traduit, faussé, et propagé à travers l'Europe par l'abbé Du Resnel 216 (1983) 467-68

Deschamps, Léger-Marie

Jean Wahl: *Cours sur l'athéisme éclairé de dom Deschamps* 52 (1967)

Alberto Andreatta: Alle origini dell'anarchismo moderno: Dom Deschamps: la metafisica al servizio dell'utopia 191 (1980) 637-43

G. Barthel: L'égalitarisme de dom Deschamps 216 (1983) 193-94

Desfontaines, Pierre-François Guyot, abbé

Thelma Morris: *L'Abbé Desfontaines et son rôle dans la littérature de son temps* 19 (1961)

Deslandes, André-François

J. Macary: L'esprit encyclopédique avant l'*Encyclopédie*: André François Deslandes 89 (1972) 975-92

Desmahis, Joseph-François-Edouard Corsembleu de

Carol Kleiner Willen: From protégé to persona: the evolution of the Voltaire-Desmahis relationship 230 (1985) 127-36

despotism

Orest Ranum: D'Alembert, Tacitus and the political sociology of despotism 191 (1980) 547-58

Darline Gay Levy: Despotism in Simon-Nicolas-Henri Linguet's science of society: theory and application 191 (1980) 761-68

destiny

Merle L. Perkins: Destiny, sentiment and time in the *Confessions* of Jean Jacques Rousseau 67 (1969) 133-64

Destutt de Tracy, Antoine-Louis-Claude

Emmet Kennedy: Destutt de Tracy and the unity of the sciences 171 (1977) 223-39

determinism

Judith McFadden: *Les Bijoux indiscrets*: a deterministic interpretation 116 (1973) 109-35

J. Peter Verdurmen: Varieties of determinism in Racine and Rowe: dramatic structure and the role of society 192 (1980) 1545-47

devils

Jean Marie Goulemot: Démons, merveilles et philosophie à l'âge classique 191 (1980) 1009-15

Nadia Minerva: Des Lumières à l'Illuminisme: Cazotte et son monde 191 (1980) 1015-22

Nadia Minerva: Démonologie tératologique et Lumières: un aspect de l'imaginaire fantastique et de l'anti-philosophie au dix-huitième siècle 216 (1983) 22-23

Les Devises de la Cour

Mark Waddicor: An unpublished satire of the regency: *Les Devises de la cour* 124 (1974) 167-79

dictionaries

Frank A. Kafker (ed.): *Notable encyclopedias of the seventeenth and eighteenth centuries: nine precursors of the 'Encyclopédie'* 194 (1981)

Arnold Miller: Louis Moréri's *Grand dictionnaire historique* 194 (1981) 13-52

Walter W. Ross: Antoine Furetière's *Dictionnaire universel* 194 (1981) 53-67

Walter W. Ross: Thomas Corneille's *Dictionnaire des arts et des sciences* 194 (1981) 69-81

Paul Burrell: Pierre Bayle's *Dictionnaire historique et critique* 194 (1981) 83-103

Lael Ely Bradshaw: John Harris's *Lexicon technicum* 194 (1981) 107-21

Lael Ely Bradshaw: Ephraim Chambers's *Cyclopaedia* 194 (1981) 123-40

Lael Ely Bradshaw: Thomas Dyche's *New general English dictionary* 194 (1981) 141-61

Peter E. Carels and Dan Flory: Johann Heinrich Zedler's *Universal Lexicon* 194 (1981) 165-96

Silvano Garofalo: Gianfrancesco Pivati's *Nuovo dizionario* 194 (1981) 197-219

Dictionnaire de l'Académie française

Articles inédits de Voltaire pour le dictionnaire de l'Académie française, éd. J. Vercruysse 37 (1965) 7-51

Diderot, Denis

Paul M. Spurlin: Diderot, Alembert and the *Encyclopédie* in the United States, 1760-1800 57 (1967) 1417-33

P. Vernière: Marie Madeleine Jodin, amie de Diderot et témoin des Lumières 58 (1967) 1765-75

Georges May: Diderot et l'allégorie 89 (1972) 1049-76

Kathleen Murphy Lambert: Some thoughts on Diderot and Sophie Volland 98 (1972) 131-41

Douglas A. Bonneville: Glanures du *Mercure* 1739-1748: Diderot et Marivaux 98 (1972) 165-68

Blandine L. McLaughlin: *Diderot et l'amitié* 100 (1973)

Gary Bruce Rogers: *Diderot and the eighteenth-century French press* 107 (1973)

Paulette Charbonnel: Remarques sur la futurologie politique du groupe Holbach-Diderot, 1773-1776 151 (1976) 449-66

Jacques Chouillet: 'Etre Voltaire ou rien': réflexions sur le voltairianisme de Diderot 185 (1980) 225-36

Laurence L. Bongie: Diderot and the rue Taranne 189 (1980) 179-90

Jacqueline Marchand: Diderot et le cinéma 190 (1980) 244-49

Aldo Maffey: Morelly-Diderot: un'amicizia nascosta 191 (1980) 701-706

Blake T. Hanna: Diderot et le frère Ange 216 (1983) 56-58

Rosena Davison: *Diderot et Galiani: étude d'une amitié philosophique* 237 (1985)

Emile Lizé: Notes bio-bibliographiques sur Diderot 241 (1986) 285-96

J. M. Moureaux: La place de Diderot dans la correspondance de Voltaire: une présence d'absence 242 (1986) 169-217

Huguette Cohen: Diderot and the image of China in eighteenth-century France 242 (1986) 219-32

— bibliography

Theodore Besterman: Review: The new Diderot edition 143 (1975) 189-95

Diana Guiragossian Carr: Les traductions anglaises des œuvres de Diderot au dix-huitième siècle 216 (1983) 455

Emile Lizé: Notes bio-bibliographiques sur Diderot 241 (1986) 285-96

— correspondence

Gabrijela Vidan: Style libertin et imagination ludique dans la correspondance de Diderot 90 (1972) 1731-45

Emile Lizé: Notes bio-bibliographiques sur Diderot 241 (1986) 285-96

— criticism by

G. Roth: Diderot 'renverse' *Le Siège de Calais* de Saurin 2 (1956) 233-40

Michael T. Cartwright: Diderot et l'expression: un problème de style dans la formation d'une critique d'art 55 (1967) 345-59

Rémy G. Saisselin: The transformation of art into culture: from Pascal to Diderot 70 (1970) 193-218

Lenore R. Kreitman: Diderot's aesthetic paradox and created reality 102 (1973) 157-72

Monique Wagner: *Molière and the age of Enlightenment* 112 (1973)

Michael Fried: Absorption and theatricality: painting and beholder in the age of Diderot 152 (1976) 753-77

Leslie Carr: Painting and the paradox of the spectator in Diderot's art criticism 193 (1980) 1690-98

— criticism of

Jean Seznec: Falconet, Voltaire et Diderot 2 (1956) 43-59

John N. Pappas: *Berthier's 'Journal de Trévoux' and the philosophes* 3 (1957)

Stephen J. Gendzier: Diderot's impact on the generation of 1830 23 (1963) 93-103

'Jacques le fataliste' et 'La Religieuse' devant la critique révolutionnaire, textes éd. J. Th. de Booy et A. J. Freer 33 (1965)

Anne-Marie Chouillet: Dossier du *Fils naturel* et du *Père de famille* 208 (1982) 73-166

— philosophy

Jean A. Perkins: Diderot and La Mettrie 10 (1959) 49-100

Jean A. Perkins: Diderot's concept of virtue 23 (1963) 77-91

J. Robert Loy: Nature, reason and enlightenment, Voltaire, Rousseau and Diderot 26 (1963) 1085-107

Dorothy B. Schlegel: Diderot as the transmitter of Shaftesbury's Romanticism 27 (1963) 1457-78

Otis Fellows: Metaphysics and the *Bijoux indiscrets*: Diderot's debt to Prior 56 (1967) 509-40

Ellen Marie Strenski: Diderot, for and against the physiocrats 57 (1967) 1435-55

Carol Blum: Diderot and the problem of virtue 87 (1972) 167-79

John Pappas: L'esprit de finesse contre l'esprit de géométrie: un débat entre Diderot et Alembert 89 (1972) 1229-53

Sara Procious Malueg: Diderot's descriptions of nature, 1759-1762 94 (1972) 121-39

Emita B. Hill: The role of 'le monstre' in Diderot's thought 97 (1972) 147-261

H. Nicholas Bakalar: Language and logic: Diderot and the *grammairiens-philosophes* 132 (1975) 113-35

Lawrence J. Forno: The cosmic mysticism of Diderot 143 (1975) 113-40

Michael Cartwright: Luxe, goût et l'ivresse de l'objet: un problème moral et esthétique chez Diderot 151 (1976) 405-15

Jean Macary: Le dialogue de Diderot et l'anti-rhétorique 153 (1976) 1337-46

Gabrijela Vidan: Diderot: la construction scientifique et son relais par l'imagination 155 (1976) 2207-22

Merle L. Perkins: The crisis of sensationalism in Diderot's *Lettre sur les aveugles* 174 (1978) 167-88

Paolo Casini: Tahiti, Diderot e l'utopia 191 (1980) 653-60

Jacques Proust: Le philosophe et la diseuse de bonne aventure 191 (1980) 1022-23

Franco Crispini: Mostri e mostruosità: un problema delle 'sciences de la vie' da Diderot a I. Geoffroy Saint-Hilaire 192 (1980) 1189-98

Johann Werner Schmidt: Diderot and Lucretius: the *De rerum natura* and Lucretius's legacy in Diderot's scientific, aesthetic, and ethical thought 208 (1982) 183-294

Merle L. Perkins: *Diderot and the time-space continuum: his philosophy, aesthetics and politics* 211 (1982)

Daniel Brewer: Diderot and the image of the other (woman) 216 (1983) 97-98

S. Baudiffier: La notion d'évidence: Le Mercier de La Rivière, Diderot, Mably 216 (1983) 278-80

Anthony Strugnell: Diderot on luxury, commerce and the merchant 217 (1983) 83-93

Suzanne Guerlac: The tableau and authority in Diderot's aesthetics 219 (1983) 183-94

Lynn Salkin Sbiroli: L'emploi du comique dans *Jacques le fataliste* 192 (1980) 1409-16

Giuseppe Scaraffia: La presenza della morte in *Jacques le fataliste* di Diderot 192 (1980) 1416-20

Marie-Hélène Chabut: Diderot's *Jacques le fataliste*: a reflexion on historiography and truth 249 (1986) 333-39

— — *Lettres sur les aveugles*

Merle L. Perkins: The crisis of sensationalism in Diderot's *Lettre sur les aveugles* 174 (1978) 167-88

— — *Lettre sur les sourds et muets*

Ruth L. Caldwell: Structure de la *Lettre sur les sourds et muets* 84 (1971) 109-22

Huguette Cohen: The intent of the digressions on father Castel and father Porée in Diderot's *Lettre sur les sourds et muets* 201 (1982) 163-83

— — *Le Neveu de Rameau*

Roland Desné: *Le Neveu de Rameau* dans l'ombre et la lumière du XVIIIe siècle 25 (1963) 493-507

Frederick Plotkin: Mime as pander: Diderot's *Neveu de Rameau* 70 (1970) 27-41

Raymond Joly: Entre *Le Père de famille* et *Le Neveu de Rameau*: conscience morale et réalisme romanesque dans *La Religieuse* 88 (1972) 845-57

Morris Wachs: The identity of the *renégat d'Avignon* in the *Neveu de Rameau* 90 (1972) 1747-56

Merle L. Perkins: Motivation and behaviour in the *Neveu de Rameau* 140 (1975) 85-106

Apostolos P. Kouidis: *The Praise of folly*: Diderot's model for *Le Neveu de Rameau* 185 (1980) 237-66

Jean Garagnon: La culture populaire dans *Le Neveu de Rameau* 190 (1980) 318-20

D. J. Adams: *Le Neveu de Rameau* since 1950 217 (1983) 371-87

— — *Paradoxe sur le comédien*

Virginia Edith Swain: Diderot's *Paradoxe sur le comédien*: the paradox of reading 208 (1982) 1-71

— — *Pensées philosophiques*

J. Marx: Autour des *Pensées philosophiques*: une lettre inédite de Georges Polier de Bottens 84 (1971) 99-108

Marie Souviron: Les *Pensées philosophiques* de Diderot ou les 'Provinciales' de l'athéisme 238 (1985) 197-267

— — *Le Père de famille*

Raymond Joly: Entre *Le Père de famille* et *Le Neveu de Rameau*: conscience morale et réalisme romanesque dans *La Religieuse* 88 (1972) 845-57

Diderot

— — *Supplément au voyage de Bougainville*

Stephen Werner: Diderot's *Supplément* and late Enlightenment thought 86 (1971) 229-92

C. Joel Block: The 'unnatural' versus the 'natural' in *La Religieuse* and *Le Supplément au Voyage de Bougainville* 124 (1974) 249-52

Alice M. Laborde: Madame de Puisieux et Diderot: de l'égalité entre les sexes 216 (1983) 209

diplomacy

Harriet Dorothy Rothschild: Benoît de Maillet's Leghorn letters 30 (1964) 351-75

Harriet Dorothy Rothschild: Benoît de Maillet's Marseilles letters 37 (1965) 109-45

J. L. Lecercle: Mably et la théorie de la diplomatie 88 (1972) 899-913

Harriet Dorothy Rothschild: Benoît de Maillet's Cairo letters 169 (1977) 115-85

dissent

Martin Fitzpatrick: Truth and tolerance in rational dissent in late eighteenth-century England 192 (1980) 1124-26

Dix-huitième siècle

Dennis Fletcher: Review: *Dix-huitième siècle* 205 (1982) 297-304

dogmatism

Louise Marcil-Lacoste: Le 'dogmatisme' des philosophes: l'origine d'une distortion 190 (1980) 209-14

Dolivier, Pierre

Hernâni A. Resende: Jean-Jacques Rousseau, l'abbé Dolivier, Hegel, sur la théorie des droits naturels 190 (1980) 381

domesticity

Charlotte C. Prather: Liberation and domesticity: two feminine ideals in the works of C. M. Wieland 193 (1980) 2002-2009

Elizabeth Fox-Genovese: Female identity: symbol and structure of bourgeois domesticity 193 (1980) 2016

Doublet, Marie-Anne

Robert S. Tate: *Petit de Bachaumont: his circle and the 'Mémoires secrets'* 65 (1968)

Douxménil

A. C. Keys: Bret, Douxménil and the *Mémoires* of Ninon de Lanclos 12 (1960) 43-54

Dryden, John

Judith Sloman: Dryden's preface to the *Fables*: translation as aesthetic experience 193 (1980) 1587-95

Theodore E. D. Braun: *Alzire* and *The Indian emperour*: Voltaire's debt to Dryden 205 (1982) 57-63

Dubos, Jean-Baptiste

Enzo Caramaschi: Du Bos et Voltaire 10 (1959) 113-236

Charlotte Hogsett: Jean Baptiste Dubos on art as illusion 73 (1970) 147-64

James F. Jones: Du Bos and Rousseau: a question of influence 127 (1974) 231-41

Du Châtelet, Gabrielle-Emilie Le Tonnelier de Breteuil, marquise

Ruth T. Murdoch: Voltaire, James Thomson, and a poem for the marquise Du Châtelet 6 (1958) 147-53

Jeroom Vercruysse: La marquise Du Châtelet, prévote d'une confrérie bruxelloise 18 (1961) 169-71

English Showalter: Sensibility at Cirey: Mme Du Châtelet, Mme de Graffigny, and the *Voltairomanie* 135 (1975) 181-92

Linda Gardiner Janik: Searching for the metaphysics of science: the structure and composition of Mme Du Châtelet's *Institutions de physique*, 1737-1740 201 (1982) 85-113

Duclos, Charles Pinot

René Duthil et Paul Dimoff: Une lettre inédite de Baculard d'Arnaud à Duclos sur l'affaire de Berlin 6 (1958) 141-46

E. Thompsett: Love and libertinism in the novels of Duclos 137 (1975) 109-19

Ducray-Duminil, François-Guillaume

Michael Tilby: Ducray-Duminil's *Victor, ou l'enfant de la forêt* in the context of the Revolution 249 (1986) 407-38

Du Deffand, Marie de Vichy de Chamrond, marquise

Gunnar von Proschwitz: Lettres inédites de madame Du Deffand, du président Hénault et du comte de Bulkeley au baron Carl Fredrik Scheffer 1751-1756 10 (1959) 267-412

Benedetta Craveri: Mme Du Deffand e Mme de Choiseul: un'amicizia femminile 193 (1980) 1956-63

Dufresny, Charles

François Moureau: Le *'Mercure galant' de Dufresny 1710-1714* 206 (1982)

Du Laurens, Henri-Joseph

Clifton Cherpack: *Jacques le fataliste* and *Le Compère Mathieu* 73 (1970) 165-91

Du Maine, Anne-Louise-Bénédicte de Bourbon-Condé, duchesse

Jacqueline Hellegouarc'h: Encore la duchesse Du Maine: note sur les rubans jaunes de *Zadig* 176 (1979) 37-40

Du Maine, Louis-Auguste de Bourbon, duc

Christiane Mervaud: Voltaire, saint Augustin et le duc Du Maine aux sources de *Cosi-Sancta* 228 (1984) 89-96

Du Marsais, César Chesneau

A. W. Fairbairn: Dumarsais and *Le Philosophe* 87 (1972) 375-95

Silvia Berti: César Chesneau Du Marsais entre gallicanisme et 'philosophie': l'*Exposition de la doctrine de l'Eglise gallicane par rapport aux prétentions de la cour de Rome* (1757) 216 (1983) 45-46

Silvia Berti: César Chesneau Du Marsais entre gallicanisme et 'philosophie': l'*Exposition de la doctrine de l'Eglise gallicane, par rapport aux prétentions de la Cour de Rome* (1757) 241 (1986) 237-51

Dupaty, Charles-Marguerite-Jean-Baptiste Mercier

William Doyle: Reforming the French criminal law at the end of the old regime: the example of president Dupaty 191 (1980) 866-72

William Doyle: Dupaty (1746-1788): a career in the late Enlightenment 230 (1985) 1-125

Dupin, Claude

Jean-Pierre Le Bouler, Catherine Lafarge: L'infortune littéraire des Dupin: essai de bibliographie critique 182 (1979) 187-201

Dupin, Louise-Marie-Madeleine

Jean-Pierre Le Bouler, Catherine Lafarge: Les emprunts de Mme Dupin à la Bibliothèque du roi dans les années 1748-1750 182 (1979) 107-85

Jean-Pierre Le Bouler, Catherine Lafarge: L'infortune littéraire des Dupin: essai de bibliographie critique 182 (1979) 187-201

Jean-Pierre Le Bouler et Robert Thiéry: Une partie retrouvée de l'*Ouvrage sur les femmes*, ou Mme Dupin dans la maison des 'Commères', avec un inventaire des papiers Dupin acquis à Monte Carlo le 8 octobre 1980 208 (1982) 373-403

Jean-Pierre Le Bouler: Un chapitre inédit de l'*Ouvrage sur les femmes* de Mme Dupin 241 (1986) 253-69

Du Pont de Nemours, Pierre-Samuel

Louis S. Greenbaum: Health-care and hospital-building in eighteenth-century France: reform proposals of Du Pont de Nemours and Condorcet 152 (1976) 895-930

Jochen Schlobach: Les physiocrates et une tentative de réalisation de leur doctrine en Allemagne (d'après les correspondances de Mirabeau et de Du Pont de Nemours avec le margrave de Bade) 216 (1983) 293-96

Dupuis, Charles-François

J. Deshayes: De l'abbé Pluche au citoyen Dupuis: à la recherche de la clef des fables 24 (1963) 457-86

Du Resnel, Jean-François Du Bellay

Richard Gilbert Knapp: *The Fortunes of Pope's 'Essay on man' in eighteenth-century France* 82 (1971)

Jürgen von Stackelberg: Pope cartésien? L'*Essay on Man* traduit, faussé, et propagé à travers l'Europe par l'abbé Du Resnel 216 (1983) 467-68

Durey de Morsan, Joseph-Marie

Jeroom Vercruysse: Joseph-Marie Durey de Morsan chroniqueur de Ferney (1769-1772) et l'édition neuchâteloise des *Questions sur l'Encyclopédie* 230 (1985) 323-91

Dyche, Thomas

Lael Ely Bradshaw: Thomas Dyche's *New general English dictionary* 194 (1981) 141-61

economics

Ellen Marie Strenski: Diderot, for and against the physiocrats 57 (1967) 1435-55

William R. Womack: Eighteenth-century themes in the *Histoire philosophique et politique des deux Indes* of Guillaume Raynal 96 (1972) 129-265

Leonard Adams: *Coyer and the Enlightenment* 123 (1974)

Thomas M. Adams: Mendicity and moral alchemy: work as rehabilitation 151 (1976) 47-76

education

— America

— and literature

Adrian P. L. Kempton: Education and the child in eighteenth-century French fiction 124 (1974) 299-362

Eugène J. Weinraub: Plays as pedagogical laboratories: *Mahomet* and Don Pèdre 140 (1975) 45-61

Jean Ehrard: La littérature française du XVIIIe siècle dans l'enseignement secondaire en France au XIXe: le manuel de Noël et La Place, 1804-1862 152 (1976) 663-75

— Austria

B. Becker-Cantarino: Joseph von Sonnenfels and the development of secular education in eighteenth-century Austria 167 (1977) 29-47

— Denmark

Carol Gold: Educational reform in Denmark, 1784-1814 167 (1977) 49-64

— England

Richard S. Tompson: English and English education in the eighteenth century 167 (1977) 65-83

Patricia A. Clancy: A French writer and educator in England: Mme Leprince de Beaumont 201 (1982) 195-208

Edward M. Jennings: Changes in English law, learning and finance, 1650-1750: time and secularisation 216 (1983) 61-62

Betty Rizzo: 'Hail, printing!': the Commonwealthman's salute to the printed word in eighteenth-century England 216 (1983) 258-59

— France

Basil J. Guy: The Chinese examination system and France, 1569-1847 25 (1963) 741-78

Kathleen Sonia Wilkins: *A study of the works of Claude Buffier* 66 (1969)

Alfred J. Bingham: Marie Joseph Chénier, ideologue and critic 94 (1972) 219-76

Leonard Adams: *Coyer and the Enlightenment* 123 (1974)

Jean Ehrard: La littérature française du XVIIIe siècle dans l'enseignement secondaire en France au XIXe: le manuel de Noël et La Place, 1804-1862 152 (1976) 663-75

Louis Trenard: L'historiographie française d'après les manuels scolaires, de Bossuet à Voltaire 155 (1976) 2083-111

Charles R. Bailey: Attempts to institute a 'system' of secular secondary education in France, 1762-1789 167 (1977) 105-24

Michèle Mat-Hasquin: Le XVIIIe siècle dans les manuels scolaires 190 (1980) 236-41

Bronislaw Baczko: 'Former l'homme nouveau': utopie et pédagogie pendant la Révolution française 191 (1980) 643-45

Jean Sareil: Le massacre de Voltaire dans les manuels scolaires 212 (1982) 83-161

J. G. Reish: France's children discover the other: Mme de Genlis's tales of travel and instruction 216 (1983) 113-15

Yves Poutet: La recherche de l'égalité dans le monde scolaire masculin de la seconde moitié du 18e siècle français 216 (1983) 213-15

Jean H. Bloch: Knowledge as a source of virtue: changes and contrasts in ideas concerning the education of boys and girls in eighteenth-century France 216 (1983) 337-38

Luís Reis Torgal et Isabel Nobre Vargues: La réception des idées pédagogiques de la Révolution française par le premier libéralisme portugais (1820-1823) 216 (1983) 433-34

Reed Benhamou: Cours publics: elective education in the eighteenth century 241 (1986) 365-76

— Germany

Charles E. McClelland: German universities in the eighteenth century: crisis and renewal 167 (1977) 169-89

Thomas E. Willey: Kant and the German theory of education 167 (1977) 543-67

Grete Klingenstein: Enlightenment and the crisis of higher education in the Habsburg monarchy 1740-1780 191 (1980) 945-53

Charlotte M. Craig: Mind and method: Sophie La Roche – a 'praeceptra filiarum Germaniae' 193 (1980) 1996-2002

Charlotte M. Craig: Patterns for a princely preparation: the duke Carl August's enlightened curriculum 216 (1983) 168-69

J. A. McCarthy: The art of reading and the goals of the German Enlightenment 216 (1983) 253-54

— Hungary

Mátyás Bajkó: The development of Hungarian formal education in the eighteenth century 167 (1977) 191-221

— Italy

Giuseppe Ricuperati and Marina Roggero: Educational policies in eighteenth-century Italy 167 (1977) 223-69

— Low Countries

Hemmo van der Laan: Influences on education and instruction in the Netherlands, especially 1750 to 1815 167 (1977) 271-311

— Poland

Grzegorz Leopold Seidler: The reform of the Polish school system in the era of the Enlightenment 167 (1977) 337-58

— Portugal

José Ferreira Carrato: The Enlightenment in Portugal and the educational reforms of the marquis of Pombal 167 (1977) 359-93

Luís Reis Torgal et Isabel Nobre Vargues: La réception des idées pédagogiques de la Révolution française par le premier libéralisme portugais (1820-1823) 216 (1983) 433-34

— Portuguese America

José Augusto Dos Santos: Education in Portuguese America in the eighteenth century 167 (1977) 395-425

— Russia

J. Laurence Black: Citizenship training and moral regeneration as the mainstay of Russian schools 167 (1977) 427-51

J. Laurence Black: The Imperial educational society for noble girls in St Petersburg (1765-1796) 191 (1980) 1003

— Scotland

R. G. Cant: The Scottish universities in the eighteenth century 58 (1967) 1953-66

Roger L. Emerson: Scottish universities in the eighteenth century, 1690-1800 167 (1977) 453-74

— Spain

George M. Addy: The first generation of academic reform in Spanish universities, 1760-1789 167 (1977) 475-89

— Spanish America

Gregorio Weinberg: The Enlightenment and some aspects of culture and higher education in Spanish America 167 (1977) 491-522

— Sweden

H. Aarnold Barton: Popular education in Sweden: theory and practice 167 (1977) 523-41

— women

Charlotte M. Craig: Mind and method: Sophie La Roche – a 'praecepta filiarum Germaniae' 193 (1980) 1996-2002

Edwards, Jonathan

Claire McGlinchee: Jonathan Edwards and Benjamin Franklin, antithetical figures 56 (1967) 813-22

Eguilles, Alexandre-Jean-Baptiste de Boyer, marquis d'

Robert S. Tate: The marquis d'Eguilles: a protégé of Bachaumont 58 (1967) 1501-14

Robert S. Tate: *Petit de Bachaumont: his circle and the 'Mémoires secrets'* 65 (1968)

Electra

Stella Gargantini Rabbi: Le mythe d'Electre dans le théâtre français du XVIIIe siècle 192 (1980) 1547-55

elitism

K. M. Baker: Scientism, elitism and liberalism: the case of Condorcet 55 (1967) 129-65

G. A. Starr: Egalitarian and elitist implications of sensibility 216 (1983) 218-20

encyclopedias

Frank A. Kafker (ed.): *Notable encyclopedias of the seventeenth and eighteenth centuries: nine precursors of the 'Encyclopédie'* 194 (1981)

Arnold Miller: Louis Moréri's *Grand dictionnaire historique* 194 (1981) 13-52

Walter W. Ross: Antoine Furetière's *Dictionnaire universel* 194 (1981) 53-67

Walter W. Ross: Thomas Corneille's *Dictionnaire des arts et des sciences* 194 (1981) 69-81

Paul Burrell: Pierre Bayle's *Dictionnaire historique et critique* 194 (1981) 83-103

Lael Ely Bradshaw: John Harris's *Lexicon technicum* 194 (1981) 107-21

Lael Ely Bradshaw: Ephraim Chambers's *Cyclopaedia* 194 (1981) 123-40

Lael Ely Bradshaw: Thomas Dyche's *New general English dictionary* 194 (1981) 141-61

Peter E. Carels and Dan Flory: Johann Heinrich Zedler's *Universal Lexicon* 194 (1981) 165-96

Silvano Garofalo: Gianfrancesco Pivati's *Nuovo dizionario* 194 (1981) 197-219

Encyclopédie

John N. Pappas: *Berthier's 'Journal de Trévoux' and the philosophes* 3 (1957)

J. Lough: Luneau de Boisjermain v. the publishers of the *Encyclopédie* 23 (1963) 115-77

Raymond Birn: The French-language press and the *Encyclopédie*, 1750-1759 55 (1967) 263-86

Paul M. Spurlin: Diderot, Alembert and the *Encyclopédie* in the United States, 1760-1800 57 (1967) 1417-33

George B. Watts: Charles Joseph Panckoucke, 'l'Atlas de la librairie française' 68 (1969) 67-205

Encyclopédie

J. Macary: L'esprit encyclopédique avant l'*Encyclopédie*: André François Deslandes 89 (1972) 975-92

Walter E. Rex: Recent British and American developments in research on the *Encyclopédie* 89 (1972) 1349-55

Dorothy B. Schlegel: Freemasonry and the *Encyclopédie* reconsidered 90 (1972) 1433-60

Ian M. Wilson: *The Influence of Hobbes and Locke in the shaping of the concept of sovereignty in eighteenth-century France* 101 (1973)

Roger Hahn: New thoughts on the origin of the *Encyclopédie* 190 (1980) 469

Frank A. Kafker (ed.): *Notable encyclopedias of the seventeenth and eighteenth centuries: nine precursors of the 'Encyclopédie'* 194 (1981)

— content

Agnes Raymond: Le problème de la population chez les encyclopédistes 26 (1963) 1379-88

Richard Switzer: America in the *Encyclopédie* 58 (1967) 1481-99

S. Werner: Diderot's *Encyclopédie* article 'Agnus Scythicus' 79 (1971) 79-92

Richard N. Schwab and Walter E. Rex: *Inventory of Diderot's 'Encyclopédie'* 80, 83, 85, 91-93 (1971-)

Hartmut Häusser: The Thomasius article in the *Encyclopédie* 81 (1971) 177-206

Kay S. Wilkins: The treatment of the supernatural in the *Encyclopédie* 90 (1972) 1757-71

Vladimir R. Rossman: L'onomancie, exemple de satire dans l'*Encyclopédie* 127 (19) 223-30

Sara Ellen Malueg: America in the *Encyclopédie* 153 (1976) 1381-94

David J. Langdon: Interpolations in the *Encyclopédie* article 'Liberté' 171 (1977) 155-88

George A. Perla: The unsigned articles and Jaucourt's bibliographical sketches in the *Encyclopédie* 171 (1977) 189-95

J. Lough: The *Encyclopédie* and Chambers's *Cyclopaedia* 185 (1980) 221-24

Robert Shackleton: The Enlightenment and the artisan 190 (1980) 53-62

Paola Vecchi: La mort dans l'*Encyclopédie* 191 (1980) 986-94

Lucia Tongiorgi Tomasi: Un problème artistique dans l'*Encyclopédie*: le débat sur les techniques en France à la moitié du XVIIIe siècle 193 (1980) 1701-1706

Jeannette Geffriaud Rosso: La représentation encyclopédiste de la femme 193 (1980) 1892-93

Lawrence Kerslake: The sources of some literary articles in the *Encyclopédie* 215 (1982) 139-61

Marc Sandoz: Les encyclopédistes et la peinture d'histoire 216 (1983) 145-46

Mariafranca Spallanzani: Notes sur le cartésianisme dans l'*Encyclopédie* 216 (1983) 326-28

Encyclopédie méthodique

D. Mimoso-Ruiz: L'*Apologie de l'Espagne* de Forner et la polémique autour de l'article 'Espagne' de la nouvelle *Encyclopédie* (1782) 216 (1983) 401-403

Marie-Hélène Cotoni: L'*Exégèse du Nouveau Testament dans la philosophie française du dix-huitième siècle* 220 (1984)

Richard N. Schwab, Walter E. Rex: *Inventory of Diderot's 'Encyclopédie': vii. Inventory of the plates* 223 (1984)

Jean-Jacques Robrieux: Jean-Philippe Rameau et l'opinion philosophique en France au dix-huitième siècle 238 (1985) 269-395

P. Swiggers: Catégories de langue et catégories de grammaire dans la théorie linguistique des Encyclopédistes 241 (1986) 339-64

Jean Viviès: Boswell, la Corse et l'*Encyclopédie* 245 (1986) 467-73

— contributors

Marta Rezler: Voltaire and the *Encyclopédie*: a re-examination 30 (1964) 147-87

J. Lough: The problem of the unsigned articles in the *Encyclopédie* 32 (1965) 327-90

Kathleen Sonia Wilkins: *A study of the works of Claude Buffier* 66 (1969)

S. Werner: Diderot's *Encyclopédie* article 'Agnus Scythicus' 79 (1971) 79-92

Richard N. Schwab and Walter E. Rex: *Inventory of Diderot's 'Encyclopédie'* 80, 83, 85, 91-93 (1971-)

Lawrence Kerslake: Johann Georg Sulzer and the supplement to the *Encyclopédie* 148 (1976) 225-47

Terence Murphy: Jean Baptiste René Robinet: the career of a man of letters 150 (1976) 183-250

Mario Longo: Illuminismo e storiografia filosofica: Brucker e l'*Encyclopédie* 191 (1980) 581-87

John Lough: The contributors to the *Encyclopédie* 223 (1984) 479-568

Paul Sadrin: *Nicolas-Antoine Boulanger (1722-1759) ou avant nous le déluge* 240 (1986)

Reed Benhamou: The sincerest form of flattery: the professional life of J. R. Lucotte 249 (1986) 381-97

— influence

John Lough: The contemporary influence of the *Encyclopédie* 26 (1963) 1071-83

Encyclopédie méthodique

Alfred J. Bingham: Voltaire and the *Encyclopédie méthodique* 6 (1958) 9-35

George B. Watts: Charles Joseph Panckoucke, 'l'Atlas de la librairie française' 68 (1969) 67-205

J.-C. Perrot: Le premier dictionnaire d'économie politique en langue française 191 (1980) 834-35

encyclopedism

Engels, Friedrich

England

— antiquaries

— booktrade

England

Calhoun Winton: Addison and Steele in the English Enlightenment 27 (1963) 1901-18

Harold Orel: Wordsworth's repudiation of Godwinism 57 (1967) 1123-45

R. M. Wiles: *Felix qui ...*: standards of happiness in eighteenth-century England 58 (1967) 1857-67

— politics

Robert Ginsberg: Early British controversy on the Declaration of Independence 152 (1976) 851-93

E. Nuzzo: La riflessione sulla storia antica nella cultura repubblicana inglese tra fine '600 e primo '700: Walter Moyle 191 (1980) 601-608

Edna Hindie Lemay: Les modèles anglais et américain à l'Assemblée constituante 191 (1980) 872-84

Michel Baridon: Le réveil du gothique et l'imaginaire politique: naissance d'un mythe créateur au siècle des Lumières 193 (1980) 1667-69

Paul Janssens: L'influence sur le continent du modèle aristocratique britannique au dix-huitième siecle 216 (1983) 183-84

Anna Maria Martellone: The myth of Germanic origins of free institutions in France and England 216 (1983) 185-87

Alain Bony: *The History of John Bull* et les comédies d'Aristophane: le modèle grec dans la propagande torie 241 (1986) 41-64

— press

Calhoun Winton: Print culture and the developing audience in England: the periodicals 216 (1983) 265-66

— religion

Günter Gawlick: Abraham's sacrifice of Isaac viewed by the English deists 56 (1967) 577-600

Norma Perry: John Vansommer of Spitalfields: Huguenot, silk-designer, and correspondent of Voltaire 60 (1968) 289-310

Günter Gawlick: The English deists' contribution to the theory of toleration 152 (1976) 823-35

Graham Gargett: *Voltaire and Protestantism* 188 (1980)

Martin Fitzpatrick: Truth and tolerance in rational dissent in late eighteenth-century England 192 (1980) 1124-26

E. R. Briggs: English Socinianism around Newton and Whiston 216 (1983) 48-50

James Flagg: Abel Boyer: a Huguenot intermediary 242 (1986) 1-73

Steve Larkin: The abbé Prévost, a convert to the Church of England? 249 (1986) 197-225

— theatre

J. Peter Verdurmen: Restoration tragedy and after: the theatre of trauma 216 (1983) 37-39

— travellers

— views of

— visitors

— Voltaire

— women

Robert Niklaus: Etude comparée de la situation de la femme en Angleterre et en France 193 (1980) 1909-18

Gae Brack: English literary ladies and the booksellers 193 (1980) 1932-39

epic

Ahmad Gunny: *Voltaire and English literature: a study of English literary influences on Voltaire* 177 (1979)

T. M. Pratt: Glittering prizes: Marmontel's theory and practice of epic 249 (1986) 341-57

Epictetus

Edward E. Malkin: Rousseau and Epictetus 106 (1973) 113-55

epicureanism

Arlette André: Recherches sur l'épicurisme de Sade: *Florville et Courval* 151 (1976) 119-29

epistemology

François Duchesneau: L'épistémologie de Maupertuis entre Leibniz et Newton 216 (1983) 312-13

Marie-Elisabeth Duchez: Valeur épistémologique de la théorie de la basse fondamental de Jean-Philippe Rameau: connaissance scientifique et représentation de la musique 245 (1986) 91-130

equality

Corrado Rosso: L'égalité du bonheur et le bonheur de l'égalité dans la pensée française du dix-huitième siècle 155 (1976) 1913-23

Vivian R. Gruder: From consensus to conflict: the élite, equality and representation, 1787-1788 216 (1983) 180-82

Wolfang Asholt: 'L'Effet Mably' et le problème de l'égalité dans le roman dialogué *Des droits et des devoirs du citoyen* 216 (1983) 191-92

G. Barthel: L'égalitarisme de dom Deschamps 216 (1983) 193-94

Glen Campbell: The search for equality of Lesage's picaresque heroes 216 (1983) 195-96

Béatrice Fink: L'égalité à table 216 (1983) 198-99

Florence Gauthier: De Mably a Robespierre: un programme économique égalitaire 1775-1793 216 (1983) 200-201

Eric Golay: Egalité populaire et égalité bourgeoise a Genève au temps de la Révolution 216 (1983) 203-204

Erasmus

eroticism

Eskimoes

ethics

C. Kiernan: Helvétius and a science of ethics 60 (1968) 229-43

Pauline Kra: *Religion in Montesquieu's 'Lettres persanes'* 72 (1970)

Anne R. Larsen: Ethical mutability in four of Diderot's tales 116 (1973) 221-34

George Klosko: Montesquieu's science of politics: absolute values and ethical relativism in *L'Esprit des lois* 189 (1980) 153-77

Johann Werner Schmidt: Diderot and Lucretius: the *De rerum natura* and Lucretius's legacy in Diderot's scientific, aesthetic, and ethical thought 208 (1982) 183-294

E. James: Voltaire and the 'Ethics' of Spinoza 228 (1984) 67-87

ethnology

Michèle Duchet: Discours ethnologique et discours historique: le texte de Lafitau 152 (1976) 607-23

Roger Mercier: Image de l'autre et image de soi-même dans le discours ethnologique au XVIIIe siècle 154 (1976) 1417-35

R. Veasey: *La Vie de mon père*: biography, autobiography, ethnography? 212 (1982) 213-24

Etudes sur le XVIIIe siècle

R. Niklaus: Review: *Etudes sur le XVIIIe siècle* 189 (1980) 401-409

Europe, central

Vilmos Gyenis: L'idéal du bonheur et la vie quotidienne dans l'Europe centrale et orientale au milieu du XVIIIe siècle: les rapports de la prose mineure 153 (1976) 1019-43

Europe, eastern

Vilmos Gyenis: L'idéal du bonheur et la vie quotidienne dans l'Europe centrale et orientale au milieu du XVIIIe siècle: les rapports de la prose mineure 153 (1976) 1019-43

Lajos Hopp: Fortune littéraire et politique du *Contrat social* en Hongrie et en Europe orientale 190 (1980) 320-26

Peter Sárközy: La funzione della poetica arcadica nella formazione del classicismo illuministico delle letterature dell'Europa centro-orientale 193 (1980) 1621-28

evil

David R. Anderson: Thomson, natural evil, and the eighteenth-century sublime 245 (1986) 489-99

evolution

Examen de la religion

exoticism

fables

fairy tales

Falconet, Etienne-Maurice

family

Irmgard A. Hartig: Réflexions sur la cellule familiale dans l'utopie sociale de Sylvain Maréchal 191 (1980) 685-87

Verena Ehrlich-Haefeli: Sécularisation, langue et structure familiale: la figure du père dans le théâtre de Lessing et de Diderot 216 (1983) 53-56

Mark Poster: Patriarchy and sexuality: Restif and the peasant family 216 (1983) 361

Farley, Felix

Norma Perry: Voltaire and Felix Farley's *Bristol journal* 62 (1968) 137-50

Farquhar, George

Retta M. Taney: The effect of Brecht's techniques in the Berliner Ensemble's *Trumpets and drums* on the staging of *The Recruiting officer* by the National Theatre of Great Britain 192 (1980) 1440-46

John McVeagh: George Farquhar and commercial England 217 (1983) 65-81

fascism

Tanguy L'Aminot: J.-J. Rousseau face à la droite française 1940-1944 242 (1985) 473-89

Fawkener, Everard

Norma Perry: *Sir Everard Fawkener, friend and correspondent of Voltaire* 133 (1975)

Fekete de Galánta, Janos

Albert Gyergyai: Un correspondant hongrois de Voltaire: le comte Fekete de Galanta 25 (1963) 779-93

Feller, François-Xavier de

John Pappas: Buffon vu par Berthier, Feller et les *Nouvelles ecclésiastiques* 216 (1983) 26-28

feminism

Madeleine Rousseau Raaphorst: Voltaire et le féminisme: un examen du théâtre et des contes 89 (1972) 1325-35

Robert F. O'Reilly: Montesquieu: anti-feminist 102 (1973) 143-56

Ellen McNiven Hine: The woman question in early eighteenth-century French literature: the influence of François Poulain de La Barre 116 (1973) 65-79

Barbara Brookes: The feminism of Condorcet and Sophie de Grouchy 189 (1980) 297-361

Maria A. Villareal: Women: their place in the sun as seen through Goldoni 192 (1980) 1517-19

Fénelon, François de Salignac de La Mothe

Ferdinand, prince

Féret, Jacques-Tranquillain

Ferguson, Adam

feudalism

Fiard, Jean-Baptiste
  Jacques Marx: L'abbé Fiard et ses sorciers 124 (1974) 253-69

Fichte, Johann Gottlieb
  Zygmunt Jedryka: Le socinianisme entre Rousseau et Fichte 192 (1980) 1101

Fielding, Henry
  Paul-Gabriel Boucé: Sex, amours and love in *Tom Jones* 228 (1984) 25-38

Filangieri, Gaetano
  Michael Suozzi: The Enlightenment in Italy: Gaetano Filangieri's *Scienza della legislazione* 155 (1976) 2049-62
  Carlo Bordini: Interpretazioni sul pensiero sociale di Gaetano Filangieri 191 (1980) 900-906

Finland
  Theodore Besterman: A provisional bibliography of Scandinavian and Finnish editions and translations of Voltaire 47 (1966) 53-92

Fiske, John
  Max I. Baym: John Fiske and Voltaire 4 (1957) 171-84

Flanders
  Luc Dhondt: La réaction nobiliaire et la révolution des notables de 1787-1789 en Flandre 216 (1983) 172-73

Flaubert, Gustave
  Theodore Besterman: Voltaire jugé par Flaubert 1 (1955) 133-58
  Colin Duckworth: Flaubert and Voltaire's *Dictionnaire philosophique* 18 (1961) 141-167
  Gustave Flaubert: *Le Théâtre de Voltaire*, edited for the first time by Theodore Besterman 50-51 (1967)

Foigny, Gabriel de
  Alberto Beretta Anguissola: Désir et utopie chez Foigny, Rétif et Casanova 191 (1980) 645-47

folklore
  Jacques Barchilon: Uses of the fairy tale in the eighteenth century 24 (1963) 111-38

Fontenelle, Bernard Le Bovier, sieur de

food

Forbes, Alexander

Formey, Jean-Henri-Samuel

Forner, Juan Pablo

Fourmont, Etienne

Franklin, Benjamin

A. O. Aldridge: Benjamin Franklin and the *philosophes* 24 (1963) 43-65

Claire McGlinchee: Jonathan Edwards and Benjamin Franklin, antithetical figures 56 (1967) 813-22

Frederick II, King of Prussia

Norma Perry: A forged letter from Frederick to Voltaire 60 (1968) 225-27

Robert Kusch: Voltaire as symbol of the eighteenth century in Carlyle's *Frederick* 79 (1971) 61-72

Jeroom Vercruysse: *L'Elégant tableau de l'Europe* ou Voltaire édité 'de main de maître' 106 (1973) 103-11

Jeroom Vercruysse: Une épigramme de Voltaire à Frédéric II 174 (1978) 59-60

Jeroom Vercruysse: L'œuvre de *Poéshie* corrigée: notes marginales de Voltaire sur les poésies de Frédéric II 176 (1979) 51-62

Valerie A. Tumins: Catherine II, Frederick II and Gustav III: three enlightened monarchs and their impact on literature 190 (1980) 350-56

Gustavo Corni: Federico II e la politica agraria dell'assolutismo 191 (1980) 943-45

Christiane Mervaud: *Voltaire et Frédéric II: une dramaturgie des Lumières 1736-1778* 234 (1985)

— works: *L'Anti-Machiavel*

Frederick II: *L'Anti-Machiavel*, éd. Charles Fleischauer 5 (1958)

— — *Art de la guerre*

Voltaire's commentary on Frederick's *L'Art de la guerre*, ed. Theodore Besterman 2 (1956) 61-206

Frederick II of Hesse-Kassel

H. A. Stavan: Landgraf Frederick II of Hesse-Kassel and Voltaire 241 (1986) 161-83

Morris Wachs: Voltaire and the landgrave of Hesse-Cassel: additions to the correspondence 241 (1986) 185-86

freemasonry

F. Weil: La Franc-maçonnerie en France jusqu'en 1755 27 (1963) 1787-815

Dorothy B. Schlegel: Freemasonry and the *Encyclopédie* reconsidered 90 (1972) 1433-60

Kay S. Wilkins: Some aspects of the irrational in 18th-century France 140 (1975) 107-201

Paul Chamley: Sir James Steuart, économiste et philosophe, ses affinités avec la franc-maçonnerie et son influence sur l'idéalisme allemand 151 (1976) 433-47

Mark Boulby: Enlightenment and Rosicrucianism 192 (1980) 1143-47

Jacques Lemaire: Un aspect de la pensée contre-révolutionnaire: la pensée antima-çonnique (1785-1805) 216 (1983) 20-21

Daniel Ligou: La sécularisation des rituels maçonniques en France au dix-huitième siècle 216 (1983) 62-65

Fréret, Nicolas

Renée Simon: *Nicolas Fréret, académicien* 17 (1961)

Fréron, Elie-Catherine

Robert L. Myers: Fréron's critique of Rémond de Saint Mard 37 (1965) 147-64

David Williams: Voltaire's guardianship of Marie Corneille and the pursuit of Fréron 98 (1972) 27-46

Marlinda Ruth Bruno: Fréron, police spy 148 (1976) 177-99

Freud, Sigmund

René Pomeau: Candide entre Marx et Freud 89 (1972) 1305-23

Friedel, Johann

Peter Horwath: Johann Friedel's Danubian journey along the Turkish border to 'Menschen wie aus dem Schoosse der lieben Mutter Natur' 191 (1980) 687-93

friendship

Blandine L. McLaughlin: *Diderot et l'amitié* 100 (1973)

Frisi, Paolo

Franco Venturi: Une lettre du baron d'Holbach 2 (1956) 285-87

Maria Grazia Sandri: Lo scienziato Paolo Frisi e la polemica sulla guglia del duomo di Milano: origine di un contrasto 216 (1983) 147-49

Furetière, Antoine

Walter W. Ross: Antoine Furetière's *Dictionnaire universel* 194 (1981) 53-67

Fuseli, Henry

Marcia Allentuck: Fuseli and Lavater: physiognomical theory and the Enlightenment 55 (1967) 89-112

Gaceta de Madrid

Daniel Henri Pageaux: La *Gaceta de Madrid* et les traductions espagnoles d'ouvrages français (1750- 1770) 57 (1967) 1147-68

Galanti, Giuseppe Maria

Anna Maria Rao: Riformismo napoletano e rivoluzione: Giuseppe Maria Galanti 190 (1980) 382-90

Galeries des Etats-Généraux

Malcolm Cook: Laclos and the *Galeries des Etats-Généraux* 228 (1984) 313-19

Galiani, Ferdinando

Rosena Davison: *Diderot et Galiani: étude d'une amitié philosophique* 237 (1985)

Galileo

A. Rupert Hall: Galileo in the eighteenth century 190 (1980) 81-100

gambling

John Dunkley: *Gambling: a social and moral problem in France, 1685-1792* 235 (1985)

Garcilaso de la Vega

Richard A. Brooks: Voltaire and Garcilaso de la Vega 30 (1964) 189-204

gardens

Norman L. Torrey: Candide's garden and the Lord's vineyard 27 (1963) 1657-66

Christopher Thacker: The misplaced garden? Voltaire, Julian and *Candide* 41 (1966) 189-202

Geoffrey Murray: *Voltaire's Candide: the protean gardener, 1755-1762* 69 (1970)

J. D. Hubert: Note malicieuse sur le jardin de Candide 70 (1970) 11-13

Christopher Thacker: Voltaire and Rousseau: eighteenth-century gardeners 90 (1972) 1595-614

Peter Willis: Rousseau, Stowe and 'le jardin anglais': speculations on visual sources for *La Nouvelle Héloïse* 90 (1972) 1791-98

Paul Ilie: The voices in Candide's garden, 1755-1759: a methodology for Voltaire's correspondence 148 (1976) 47-113

Dennis Fletcher: *Candide* and the theme of the happy husbandman 161 (1976) 137-47

Patrick Henry: Sacred and profane gardens in *Candide* 176 (1979) 133-52

R. C. Knight: Anne Dacier and gardens ancient and modern 185 (1980) 119-29

Ingrid Kisliuk: Le symbolisme du jardin et l'imagination créatrice chez Rousseau, Bernardin de Saint-Pierre et Chateaubriand 185 (1980) 297-418

Basil Guy: The prince de Ligne's *Artula hortulorum* 205 (1982) 133-39

Garrick, David

James C. Nicholls (ed.): *Mme Riccoboni's letters to David Hume, David Garrick and Sir Robert Liston, 1764-1783* 149 (1976)

V. Link: 'The little man's departure': an unnoticed literary portrait of Garrick 215 (1982) 171-74

Gauthey, Emiland-Marie

J. Guillerme: Analyse d'un mémoire inédit de 1774 intitulé 'Essai sur la langue philosophique' 216 (1983) 313-14

Gazette de Parme

Marie-Josée Latil Ferromi: *La Gazette du Parme*, véhicule de diffusion de la culture française en Italie dans la deuxième moitié du 18e siècle 216 (1983) 249-51

Gazette d'Utrecht

Jeroom Vercruysse: La Harpe et la *Gazette d'Utrecht*: une lettre inédite à Choiseul 79 (1971) 193-98

Gazette littéraire

L. A. Boiteux: Voltaire et le ménage Suard 1 (1955) 19-109

Gazette littéraire de l'Europe

Emile Lizé: Voltaire et les *Sermons de M. Yorick* 215 (1982) 99-100

Gédoyn, Nicolas

Robert S. Tate: *Petit de Bachaumont: his circle and the 'Mémoires secrets'* 65 (1968)

Geneva

Bernard Gagnebin: Le médiateur d'une petite querelle genevoise 1 (1955) 115-23

Peter Gay: Voltaire's *Idées républicaines*: a study in bibliography and interpretation 6 (1958) 67-105

Giles Barber: The Cramers of Geneva and their trade in Europe between 1755 and 1766 30 (1964) 377-413

Ronald Ian Boss: Rousseau's civil religion and the meaning of belief: an answer to Bayle's paradox 84 (1971) 123-93

R. E. Florida: *Voltaire and the socinians* 122 (1974)

John Renwick: Voltaire et les antécédents de la *Guerre civile de Genève* 185 (1980) 57-86

Eric Golay: Egalité populaire et égalité bourgeoise a Genève au temps de la Révolution 216 (1983) 203-204

Renato G. Mazzolini and Shirley A. Roe: *Science against the unbelievers: the correspondence of Bonnet and Needham, 1760-1780* 243 (1986)

Genlis, Caroline-Stéphanie-Félicité Ducrest de Mézières, comtesse de

Monique Stern: Lettres inédites de madame de Genlis à Bernardin de Saint-Pierre 169 (1977) 187-275

J. G. Reish: France's children discover the other: Mme de Genlis's tales of travel and instruction 216 (1983) 113-15

Genovesi, Antonio

Mario Agrimi: Quelques échos en France de la pensée d'Antonio Genovesi 216 (1983) 445-47

genre

Georges May: La littérature épistolaire date-t-elle du XVIIIe siècle? 56 (1967) 823-44

René Pomeau: Voyage et Lumières dans la littérature française du XVIIIe siècle 57 (1967) 1269-89

John Van Eerde: Fontenelle's *Le Tyran*: an example of mixed genre 58 (1967) 1689-705

Arthur J. Weitzmann: The oriental tale in the eighteenth century: a reconsideration 58 (1967) 1839-55

Christie Vance McDonald: *The Extravagant shepherd: a study of the pastoral vision in Rousseau's 'Nouvelle Héloïse'* 105 (1973)

Stephen Werner: Diderot, Sade and the gothic novel 114 (1973) 273-90

J. M. Blanchard: Style pastoral, style des Lumières 114 (1973) 331-46

R. J. Howells: Marivaux and the heroic 171 (1977) 115-53

Ahmad Gunny: *Voltaire and English literature: a study of English literary influences on Voltaire* 177 (1979)

Roger Clark: Aliénation et utopie: fonctions du héros dans la littérature utopique française du XVIIIe siècle 191 (1980) 661-62

Temple Maynard: Utopia and dystopia in the oriental genre in England in the eighteenth century 191 (1980) 706-11

Robert Folkenflik: Genre and the Boswellian imagination 192 (1980) 1287-95

Philip Robinson: Marivaux's poetic theatre of love: some considerations of genre 192 (1980) 1513-15

Philip Robinson: Marivaux's poetic theatre of love 199 (1981) 7-24

W. D. Howarth: Voltaire, Ninon de L'Enclos and the evolution of a dramatic genre 199 (1981) 63-72

Marc Sandoz: La peinture de l'histoire comme trait marquant du siècle des Lumières finissant 199 (1981) 263-85

Gentleman's magazine

John L. Abbott: Samuel Johnson, John Hawkesworth, and the rise of the *Gentleman's magazine*, 1738-1773 151 (1976) 31-46

geography

Sergio Moravia: Philosophie et géographie à la fin du XVIIIe siècle 57 (1967) 937-1011

geology

Marguerite Carozzi: Voltaire's geological observations in *Les Singularités de la nature* 215 (1982) 101-19

Germany

Christiane Mervaud: Voltaire, Baculard d'Arnaud et le prince Ferdinand 183 (1980) 7-33

Martin Dyck: Mathematics and literature in the German Enlightenment: Abraham Gotthelf Kästner (1719-1800) 190 (1980) 508-12

Marita Gilli: Littérature, histoire et problème national à la fin des Lumières en Allemagne 191 (1980) 564-71

Ruth P. Dawson: Women communicating: eighteenth-century German journals edited by women 216 (1983) 239-41

— booktrade

Bernhard Fabian: The importation of English books into Germany in the eighteenth-century 193 (1980) 1780-82

— education

Charles E. McClelland: German universities in the eighteenth century: crisis and renewal 167 (1977) 169-89

Thomas E. Willey: Kant and the German theory of education 167 (1977) 543-67

Grete Klingenstein: Enlightenment and the crisis of higher education in the Habsburg monarchy 1740-1780 191 (1980) 945-53

Charlotte Craig: Mind and method: Sophie La Roche – a 'praeceptra filiarum Germaniae' 193 (1980) 1996-2002

Charlotte M. Craig: Patterns for a princely preparation: the duke Carl August's enlightened curriculum 216 (1983) 168-69

J. A. McCarthy: The art of reading and the goals of the German Enlightenment 216 (1983) 253-54

— influence

Gustavo Costa: German antiquities and Gothic art in the early Italian Enlightenment 191 (1980) 559-61

— law

Mario A. Cattaneo: La discussione su Beccaria in Germania: K. F. Hommel e J. E. F. Schall 191 (1980) 935-43

— literature

Robert L. Dawson: *Baculard d'Arnaud: life and prose fiction* 141-142 (1976)

Marita Gilli: Littérature, histoire et problème national à la fin des Lumières en Allemagne 191 (1980) 564-71

Volker Hoffmann: Caraterizzazione dei sessi nei testi teoretici e letterari dell'epoca Goethiana 193 (1980) 1901-1908

Michael Ritterson: Humane ironies: the enlightenment novel and nineteenth-century realism in Germany 216 (1983) 434-35

— philosophy

Edgar Mass: *Le Marquis d'Adhémar: la correspondance inédite d'un ami des philosophes à la cour de Bayreuth* 109 (1973)

Paul Chamley: Sir James Steuart, économiste et philosophe, ses affinités avec la franc-maçonnerie et son influence sur l'idéalisme allemand 151 (1976) 433-47

Bernhard Fabian: The reception of Bernard Mandeville in eighteenth-century Germany 152 (1976) 693-722

Bruno Bianco: Piétisme et Lumières dans l'Allemagne du XVIIIe siècle 192 (1980) 1105-12

Volker Hoffmann: Caraterizzazione dei sessi nei testi teoretici e letterari dell'epoca Goethiana 193 (1980) 1901-1908

Walter Moser: L'*Aufklärung* et sa renaissance au vingtième siècle 205 (1982) 191-209

J. A. McCarthy: The art of reading and the goals of the German Enlightenment 216 (1983) 253-54

Jochen Schlobach: Les physiocrates et une tentative de réalisation de leur doctrine en Allemagne (d'après les correspondances de Mirabeau et de Du Pont de Nemours avec le margrave de Bade) 216 (1983) 293-96

Jean-François Migaud: Humanisme et surhumanisme dans *Ardinghello und die glückseligen Inseln* de Wilhelm Heinse 216 (1983) 354-56

Germany

Norbert Waszek: Bibliography of the Scottish Enlightenment in Germany 230 (1985) 283-303

— politics

Gustavo Corni: Federico II e la politica agraria dell'assolutismo 191 (1980) 943-45

Anna Maria Martellone: The myth of Germanic origins of free institutions in France and England 216 (1983) 185-87

Diethelm Klippel: The influence of the physiocrats on the development of liberal political theory in Germany 216 (1983) 284-85

Jochen Schlobach: Les physiocrates et une tentative de réalisation de leur doctrine en Allemagne (d'après les correspondances de Mirabeau et de Du Pont de Nemours avec le margrave de Bade) 216 (1983) 293-96

Hans Erich Bödeker: La conscience politique de l'*Aufklärung*: les philosophes allemands au service de l'état 216 (1983) 381-83

Giulia Cantarutti: Patriotisme et sentiment national dans les *Betrachtungen und Gedanken* (1803-1805) de F. M. Klinger, un représentant des Lumières allemandes à la cour russe 216 (1983) 383-85

Henry Lowood: Patriotism and progress: the role of the German patriotic and economic societies in the promotion of science and technology 216 (1983) 394-96

— press

François Moureau: Les journalistes de langue française dans l'Allemagne des Lumières: essai de typologie 216 (1983) 254-56

— religion

Bernard D. Weinryb: Enlightenment and German-Jewish *Haskalah* 27 (1963) 1817-47

W. Grossmann: Religious toleration in Germany, 1648-1750 192 (1980) 1103-1105

Bruno Bianco: Piétisme et Lumières dans l'Allemagne du XVIIIe siècle 192 (1980) 1105-12

Walter Grossmann: Religious toleration in Germany, 1648-1750 201 (1982) 115-41

Dominique Bourel: La sécularisation dans le judaïsme prussien dans la période post-mendelssohnienne 216 (1983) 47-48

— theatre

J. H. Tisch: Nature and function of historical reality in German early Enlightenment drama 58 (1967) 1551-75

David G. John: Women and men as equals in German comedy of the Enlightenment 216 (1983) 208-209

Gibbon, Edward

Colin Duckworth: Louis XVI and English history: a French reaction to Walpole, Hume and Gibbon on Richard III 176 (1979) 385-401

J. G. A. Pocock: Gibbon and the stages of society: progress, ambivalence and corruption in the *Decline and fall* 191 (1980) 537

Martine Watson Brownley: Gibbon's *Memoirs*: the legacy of the historian 201 (1982) 209-20

Girardin, René-Louis, marquis de

M. Molinier: Les relations de Deleyre et de Rousseau, 1753-1778, suivi de la correspondance inédite de Deleyre et du marquis de Girardin, août-décembre 1778 70 (1970) 43-176

Gladstone, William Ewart

Gladstone on *Candide*, ed. Theodore Besterman 70 (1970) 7-10

Gluck, Christoph Willibald

Karl Geiringer: Concepts of the Enlightenment as reflected in Gluck's Italian reform opera 88 (1972) 567-76

Godoy, Manuel

John Dowling: Manuel Godoy and the Spanish *ilustrados* 190 (1980) 326-34

Godwin, William

Harold Orel: Wordsworth's repudiation of Godwinism 57 (1967) 1123-45

Goethe, Johann Wolfgang von

Christine Oertel Sjögren: Pietism, pathology, or pragmatism in Goethe's *Bekenntnisse einer schönen Seele* 193 (1980) 2009-15

Goezman, Louis-Valentin

John Hampton: The literary technique of the first two *Mémoires* of Beaumarchais against Goezman 47 (1966) 177-205

Goldoni, Carlo

Colin Duckworth: Madame Denis's unpublished *Pamela*: a link between Richardson, Goldoni and Voltaire 76 (1970) 37-53

Maria A. Villareal: Women: their place in the sun as seen through Goldoni 192 (1980) 1517-19

Gozzi, Gasparo

Michel Cataudella: La polémique contre les Lumières et contre le rationalisme dans un journal peu connu de Gasparo Gozzi 216 (1983) 4-6

Graffigny, Françoise-Paule d'Issembourg d'Happoncourt Huguet de

P. M. Conlon: Two letters of Mme de Graffigny to Maupertuis 2 (1956) 279-83

English Showalter: Sensibility at Cirey: Mme Du Châtelet, Mme de Graffigny, and the *Voltairomanie* 135 (1975) 181-92

English Showalter: *Voltaire et ses amis d'après la correspondance de Mme de Graffigny* 139 (1975)

English Showalter: *Madame de Graffigny and Rousseau: between the two 'Discours'* 175 (1978)

English Showalter: Les *Lettres d'une Péruvienne*: composition, publication, suites 216 (1983) 261-62

Grafton, Augustus Henry Fitz Roy, 3rd Duke of

Samuel Taylor: The duke and duchess of Grafton with Voltaire: notes on unrecorded silhouettes by Jean Huber 135 (1975) 151-65

Graham, James

Roy Porter: Sex and the singular man: the seminal ideas of James Graham 228 (1984) 3-24

grammar

J. M. Blanchard: Grammaire(s) d'ancien régime 106 (1973) 7-20

H. Nicholas Bakalar: Language and logic: Diderot and the *grammairiens-philosophes* 132 (1975) 113-35

P. Swiggers: Studies on the French eighteenth-century grammatical tradition 219 (1983) 273-80

P. Swiggers: Catégories de langue et catégories de grammaire dans la théorie linguistique des Encyclopédistes 241 (1986) 339-64

Grasset, François

Jean Daniel Candaux: Les débuts de François Grasset 18 (1961) 197-235

Greece

C. Th. Dimaras: D. Catargi, 'philosophe' grec 25 (1963) 509-18

C. Th. Dimaras: Notes sur la présence de Voltaire en Grèce 55 (1967) 439-44

Alkis Anghelou: L'Européen et la découverte du grec moderne 216 (1983) 85-87

Roxane Argyropoulos: Patriotisme et sentiment national en Grèce au temps des Lumières 216 (1983) 377

Grimm, Friedrich Melchior

Emile Lizé: *Voltaire, Grimm et la 'Correspondance littéraire'* 180 (1979)

Georges Dulac: Grimm et la *Correspondance littéraire* envoyée à Catherine II (d'après les lettres de Dimitri Golitsyn et de F. M. Grimm au vice-chancelier Alexandre Golitsyn) 217 (1983) 207-48

Ulla Kölving et Jeanne Carriat: *Inventaire de la 'Correspondance littéraire' de Grimm et Meister* 225-227 (1984)

Guilleragues, Gabriel-Joseph de Lavergne, comte de

David L. Anderson: Abélard and Héloïse: eighteenth-century motif 84 (1971) 7-51

Guillotin, Ignace

Claudia-Anne Lopez: L'utopie americaine du dr Guillotin 191 (1980) 694-98

Gustav III, King of Sweden

G. von Proschwitz: Gustave III et les Lumières: l'affaire de *Bélisaire* 26 (1963) 1347-63

Valerie A. Tumins: Catherine II, Frederick II and Gustav III: three enlightened monarchs and their impact on literature 190 (1980) 350-56

Habsburgs

Grete Klingenstein: Enlightenment and the crisis of higher education in the Habsburg monarchy 1740-1780 191 (1980) 945-53

Helen Liebel-Weckowicz: The physiocrat tax reform of Joseph II: the challenge of modernisation in the Habsburg empire, 1780-1790 216 (1983) 287-89

Haller, Albrecht von

John Neubauer: Albrecht von Haller's philosophy of physiology 216 (1983) 320-22

Hamann, Johann Georg

Daniel Droixhe: Le cercle et le gland: linguistique et anthropologie chez Hamann 192 (1980) 1246-56

happiness

A. J. Sambrook: The English lord and the happy husbandman 57 (1967) 1357-75

R. M. Wiles: *Felix qui* ...: standards of happiness in eighteenth-century England 58 (1967) 1857-67

148

Robert Shackleton: The greatest happiness of the greatest number: the history of Bentham's phrase 90 (1972) 1461-82

Julien Offray de La Mettrie: *Discours sur le bonheur*, critical edition by John Falvey 134 (1975)

Ehrhard Bahr: The pursuit of happiness in the political writings of Lessing and Kant 151 (1976) 167-84

Colin Duckworth: D'Antraigues and the quest for happiness: nostalgia and commitment 152 (1976) 625-45

Vilmos Gyenis: L'idéal du bonheur et la vie quotidienne dans l'Europe centrale et orientale au milieu du XVIIIe siècle: les rapports de la prose mineure 153 (1976) 1019-43

Colm Kiernan: Happiness and a science of economics in the French Enlightenment 153 (1976) 1189-1200

B. Plongeron: Bonheur, et 'civilisation chrétienne': une nouvelle apologétique après 1760 154 (1976) 1637-55

Corrado Rosso: L'égalité du bonheur et le bonheur de l'égalité dans la pensée française du dix-huitième siècle 155 (1976) 1913-23

Dennis Fletcher: *Candide* and the theme of the happy husbandman 161 (1976) 137-·47

James P. Gilroy: Peace and the pursuit of happiness in the French utopian novel: Fénelon's *Télémaque* and Prévost's *Cleveland* 176 (1979) 169-87

Maria Gaetana Salvatores Scarpa: L'idée de 'bonheur' chez madame de Staël 191 (1980) 1004-1009

Alan J. Singerman: L'abbé Prévost et la quête du bonheur: lecture morale et philosophique de l'*Histoire de M. Cleveland* 228 (1984) 195-242

Harris, James

Marie-Louise Barthel: Un aspect négligé de la linguistique des Lumières: Thurot et Harris 192 (1980) 1256-63

Harris, John

Lael Ely Bradshaw: John Harris's *Lexicon technicum* 194 (1981) 107-21

Hawkesworth, John

John L. Abbott: Samuel Johnson, John Hawkesworth, and the rise of the *Gentleman's magazine*, 1738-1773 151 (1976) 31-46

Haydn, Joseph

Karl Geiringer: Joseph Haydn, protagonist of the Enlightenment 25 (1963) 683-90

hedonism

J. W. Johnson: Lord Rochester and the tradition of Cyrenaic hedonism, 1670-1790 153 (1976) 1151-67

Hegel, Georg Wilhelm Friedrich

Hernâni A. Resende: Jean-Jacques Rousseau, l'abbé Dolivier, Hegel, sur la théorie des droits naturels 190 (1980) 381

Jacques d'Hondt: Hegel et les Lumières 216 (1983) 422-23

Heinse, Wilhelm

Jean-François Migaud: Humanisme et surhumanisme dans *Ardinghello und die glückseligen Inseln* de Wilhelm Heinse 216 (1983) 354-56

Héloïse

David L. Anderson: Abélard and Héloïse: eighteenth-century motif 84 (1971) 7-51

Helvétius, Claude-Adrien

C. Kiernan: Helvétius and a science of ethics 60 (1968) 229-43

D. W. Smith: Helvétius's library 79 (1971) 153-61

David Raynor: Hume's critique of Helvétius's *De l'esprit* 215 (1982) 223-29

Franco Piva: Helvétius dans le *Giornale enciclopedico* ou les difficultés de la presse éclairée à Venise 216 (1983) 256-58

Gerhardt Stenger: Diderot lecteur de *L'Homme*: une nouvelle approche de la *Réfutation d'Helvétius* 228 (1984) 267-91

Hénault, Charles-Jean-François

Gunnar von Proschwitz: Lettres inédites de madame Du Deffand, du président Hénault et du comte de Bulkeley au baron Carl Fredrik Scheffer 1751-1756 10 (1959) 267-412

Henríquez, Camilo

A. O. Aldridge: Apostles of reason: Camilo Henriquez and the French Enlightenment 55 (1967) 65-87

Herder, Johann Gottfried

F. M. Barnard: National culture and political legitimacy: Herder and Rousseau 216 (1983) 379-81

G. A. Wells: Condillac, Rousseau and Herder on the origin of language 230 (1985) 233-46

Jeroom Vercruysse: *L'Elégant tableau de l'Europe* ou Voltaire édité 'de main de maître' 106 (1973) 103-11

Suzanne Gearhart: Rationality and the text: a study of Voltaire's historiography 140 (1975) 21-43

Michèle Duchet: Discours ethnologique et discours historique: le texte de Lafitau 152 (1976) 607-23

Karlis Racevskis: Le règne des philosophes à l'Académie française, vu par les historiens du dix-neuvième siècle 154 (1976) 1801-12

Jochen Schlobach: Pessimisme des philosophes? La théorie cyclique de l'histoire du XVIIIe siècle 155 (1976) 1971-87

Louis Trenard: L'historiographie française d'après les manuels scolaires, de Bossuet à Voltaire 155 (1976) 2083-111

C. H. Wilberger: *Voltaire's Russia: window on the east* 164 (1976)

Calvin Seerveld: The influence of periodisation upon art historiography of the Enlightenment 190 (1980) 183-89

Rosanna Albertini: Storiografia e arte della politica nel testo originale dei *Cahiers* di Barnave 191 (1980) 540-47

Gianluigi Goggi: Diderot e l'*Histoire des deux Indes*: riflessioni sulla storia 191 (1980) 571-73

Roger Ouellet: Une bataille, quatre récits: quelques mises en scène de l'histoire au XVIIIe siècle 191 (1980) 573-74

Janette Gatty: Les *Six époques* de Beaumarchais: chronique de l'histoire vue et vécue 191 (1980) 574-81

Mario Longo: Illuminismo e storiografia filosofica: Brucker e l'*Encyclopédie* 191 (1980) 581-87

Robin Price: Boulainviller and the myth of the Frankish conquest of Gaul 199 (1981) 155-85

Martine Watson Brownley: Gibbon's *Memoirs*: the legacy of the historian 201 (1982) 209-20

Nicolas Wagner: Le dix-huitième siècle de Villemain 216 (1983) 441-42

Anand C. Chitnis: Agricultural improvement, political management and civic virtue in enlightened Scotland: an historiographical critique 245 (1986) 475-88

Marie-Hélène Chabut: Diderot's *Jacques le fataliste*: a reflexion on historiography and truth 249 (1986) 333-39

history

Rémy Gilbert Saisselin: Le passé, le goût, et l'histoire 27 (1963) 1445-55

Hugh Trevor-Roper: The historical philosophy of the Enlightenment 27 (1963) 1667-87

G. Christie Wasberg: The influence of the 'enlightened' philosophy of history on Scandinavian political thought 27 (1963) 1775-85

Lionel Gossman: Time and history in Rousseau 30 (1964) 311-49

Merle L. Perkins: Rousseau on history, liberty and national survival 53 (1967) 79-169

Wolfgang Philipp: Physicotheology in the age of Enlightenment: appearance and history 57 (1967) 1233-67

J. H. Tisch: Nature and function of historical reality in German early Enlightenment drama 58 (1967) 1551-75

G. Christie Wasberg: 'Transcendence' and 'immanence' in the philosophy of history from Enlightenment to Romanticism 58 (1967) 1829-38

D. Young: Scotland and Edinburgh in the eighteenth century 58 (1967) 1967-90

N. R. Johnson: Louis XIV devant l'opinion française contemporaine: ses dernières paroles au dauphin 88 (1972) 831-43

Alfred J. Bingham: Marie Joseph Chénier, ideologue and critic 94 (1972) 219-76

Philip Stewart: L'armature historique du *Cleveland* de Prévost 137 (1975) 121-39

Sylvia Vance: History as dramatic reinforcement: Voltaire's use of history in four tragedies set in the middle ages 150 (1976) 7-31

Georges Benrekassa: Savoir politique et connaissance historique à l'aube des Lumières 151 (1976) 261-85

John Frederick Logan: Condillac, Volney, and the lessons of the past 153 (1976) 1329-35

Jean Pierre Guicciardi: Tocqueville et les Lumières 163 (1976) 203-19

Colin Duckworth: Louis XVI and English history: a French reaction to Walpole, Hume and Gibbon on Richard III 176 (1979) 385-401

Jacques Wagner: 'Comme l'eau le sucre' ou anthropologie et histoire dans le *Journal encyclopédique* (1756-1778) 183 (1980) 239-56

Franco Venturi: La prima crisi dell'antico regime: 1768-1776 190 (1980) 63-80

Doug Thompson: Writing the synthesis: a history of Italy in the Age of Enlightenment 190 (1980) 217-25

Marita Gilli: Littérature, histoire et problème national à la fin des Lumières en Allemagne 191 (1980) 564-71

Marc Sandoz: La 'peinture d'histoire' comme trait marquant du siècle des Lumières finissant 193 (1980) 1663-64

Michèle Mat-Hasquin: *Voltaire et l'antiquité grecque* 197 (1981)

Marc Sandoz: La peinture de l'histoire comme trait marquant du siècle des Lumières finissant 199 (1981) 263-85

Merle L. Perkins: *Diderot and the time-space continuum: his philosophy, aesthetics and politics* 211 (1982)

Anne Boës: *La Lanterne magique de l'histoire: essai sur le théâtre historique en France de 1750 à 1789* 213 (1982)

Marc Sandoz: Les encyclopédistes et la peinture d'histoire 216 (1983) 145-46

Rémy G. Saisselin: Le dix-huitième siècle de Paul Bourget 216 (1983) 436-37

Catherine Volpilhac-Auger: *Tacite et Montesquieu* 232 (1985)

Geraldine Sheridan: Censorship and the booktrade in France in the early eighteenth century: Lenglet Dufresnoy's *Méthode pour étudier l'histoire* 241 (1986) 95-107

— ancient

Edna Lemay: Histoire de l'antiquité et découverte du nouveau monde chez deux auteurs du XVIIIe siècle 153 (1976) 1313-28

— culture

Norman Hampson and Betty Behrens: Cultural history as infrastructure 86 (1971) 7-24

Hobbes, Thomas

Leland Thielemann: Voltaire and Hobbism 10 (1959) 237-58

Ian M. Wilson: *The Influence of Hobbes and Locke in the shaping of the concept of sovereignty in eighteenth-century France* 101 (1973)

A. Loche: Le ragioni di una polemica: Montesquieu e Hobbes 190 (1980) 334-43

Hoffmann, Friedrich

Paul Hoffmann: La théorie de l'homme dans la *Medicina rationalis systematica* de Friedrich Hoffmann 216 (1983) 314-15

Holbach, Paul Thiry, baron d'

Franco Venturi: Une lettre du baron d'Holbach 2 (1956) 285-87

J. Th. de Booy: L'abbé Coger, dit Coge Pecus, lecteur de Voltaire et de d'Holbach 18 (1961) 183-96

J. Th. de Booy: Une anecdote de Diderot sur *Le Système de la nature* 23 (1963) 105-14

Virgil W. Topazio: Holbach's moral code: social and humanistic 90 (1972) 1615-23

T. C. Newland: Holbach and religion versus morality 140 (1975) 203-18

Paulette Charbonnel: Remarques sur la futurologie politique du groupe Holbach-Diderot, 1773-1776 151 (1976) 449-66

Charles Porset: Le *Système de la nature* et la téléologie 190 (1980) 502-507

Jean-Claude David: Un théiste chez le baron d'Holbach: l'abbé Morellet 215 (1982) 253-72

Marie-Hélène Cotoni: *L'Exégèse du Nouveau Testament dans la philosophie française du dix-huitième siècle* 220 (1984)

Holland

E. R. Briggs: Pierre Cuppé's debts to England and Holland 6 (1958) 37-66

Jeroom Vercruysse: Les Provinces-Unies vues par Voltaire 27 (1963) 1715-21

Jeroom Vercruysse: *Voltaire et la Hollande* 46 (1966)

Walter Rex: 'Blasphemy' in the refuge in Holland and in the French Enlightenment 57 (1967) 1307-20

P. J. Buijnsters: Les Lumières hollandaises 87 (1972) 197-215

Jeroom Vercruysse: Bibliographie provisoire des traductions néerlandaises et flamandes de Voltaire 116 (1973) 19-64

M. P. Masterson: Montesquieu's stadholder 116 (1973) 81-107

Graham Gargett: *Voltaire and Protestantism* 188 (1980)

Camiel Hamans: Universal language and the Netherlands 192 (1980) 1218-27

Ton Broos: Johannes Allart (1754-1816): Dutch printer, publisher and bookseller 193 (1980) 1822-30

A. J. Hanou: Anglo-Dutch relations: spectators and satire in the early eighteenth century 193 (1980) 1831-32

H. M. de Blauw: The study of eighteenth-century Dutch prose fiction 193 (1980) 1832-40

A. J. Hanou: Dutch periodicals from 1697 to 1721: in imitation of the English? 199 (1981) 187-204

Tolerance in four Dutch periodicals 1714-1771: *La Bibliothèque ancienne et moderne*, Amsterdam 1714-1726: H. Bots and J. de Vet; *Le Journal britannique*, The Hague 1750-1755: U. Janssens; *Nederlandsche Letter-courant*, Leyden 1759-1763: H. Stouten; *Vaderlandsche Letter-oefeningen*, Amsterdam 1761-1771: W. van den Berg 216 (1983) 73-77

Camiel Hamans: The ape in Dutch linguistics of the 18th century 216 (1983) 108-109

C. W. Schoneveld: The Dutch translations of Pope's *Essay on Man* 216 (1983) 463-65

Peter Altena, Hans Groot, Hanna Stouten: The presentation of Dutch literary work in the *Journal encyclopédique* (1759-1793) 216 (1983) 469-71

Homer

Pamela Schwandt: Pope's tranformation of Homer's gods 193 (1980) 1586-87

Hommel, Karl Ferdinand

Mario A. Cattaneo: La discussione su Beccaria in Germania: K. F. Hommel e J. E. F. Schall 191 (1980) 935-43

honour

John Pappas: La campagne des philosophes contre l'honneur 205 (1982) 31-44

Maria Evelina Zoltowska: La démocratisation de l'idée de l'honneur dans le *Manuscrit trouvé à Saragosse* de Jean Potocki 216 (1983) 224-26

Hooker, Richard

Sheila Mason: An essentialist inheritance: from Hooker to Montesquieu 242 (1986) 83-124

Horace

Arnold Ages: Voltaire and Horace: the testimony of the correspondence 120 (1974) 199-221

Houdon, Jean-Antoine

Theodore Besterman: The terra-cotta statue of Voltaire made by Houdon for Beaumarchais 12 (1960) 21-27

Huber, Jean

Samuel Taylor: The duke and duchess of Grafton with Voltaire: notes on unrecorded silhouettes by Jean Huber 135 (1975) 151-65

Hugo, Victor

H. Temple Patterson: *Poetic genesis: Sébastien Mercier into Victor Hugo* 11 (1960)

Arnold Ages: Hugo and the *philosophes* 87 (1972) 37-64

Huguenots

Walter Rex: 'Blasphemy' in the refuge in Holland and in the French Enlightenment 57 (1967) 1307-20

Norma Perry: John Vansommer of Spitalfields: Huguenot, silk-designer, and correspondent of Voltaire 60 (1968) 289-310

Norma Perry: Voltaire's London agents for the *Henriade*: Simond and Bénézet, Huguenot merchants 102 (1973) 265-99

G. Gargett: Voltaire, Gilbert de Voisins's *Mémoires* and the problem of Huguenot civil rights (1767-1768) 174 (1978) 7-57

G. Gargett: Voltaire, Richelieu and the problem of Huguenot emancipation in the reign of Louis XV 176 (1979) 97-132

Margaret D. Thomas: Michel de La Roche: a Huguenot critic of Calvin 238 (1985) 97-195

James Flagg: Abel Boyer: a Huguenot intermediary 242 (1986) 1-73

humanism

Lester G. Crocker: Voltaire's struggle for humanism 4 (1957) 137-69

Norman Suckling: The unfulfilled Renaissance: an essay on the fortunes of enlightened humanism in the eighteenth century 86 (1971) 25-136

Virgil W. Topazio: Holbach's moral code: social and humanistic 90 (1972) 1615-23

Marie-Hélène Cotoni: Dénigrement de la providence et défense des valeurs humaines dans les manuscrits clandestins de la première moitié du dix-huitième siècle 152 (1976) 497-513

Jean-François Migaud: Humanisme et surhumanisme dans *Ardinghello und die glückse-ligen Inseln* de Wilhelm Heinse 216 (1983) 354-56

humanitarianism

Renata Carocci: Dom Pernety polémiste humanitaire 216 (1983) 196-98

L'Humanité

Jean Biou: Les 'Lumières' de *L'Humanité* en 1977 et 1978 190 (1980) 241

Hume, David

Robert Ginsberg: David Hume and the Enlightenment 88 (1972) 599-650

James C. Nicholls (ed.): *Mme Riccoboni's letters to David Hume, David Garrick and Sir Robert Liston, 1764-1783* 149 (1976)

Richard H. Popkin: Isaac de Pinto's criticism of Mandeville and Hume on luxury 154 (1976) 1705-14

Colin Duckworth: Louis XVI and English history: a French reaction to Walpole, Hume and Gibbon on Richard III 176 (1979) 385-401

Christiane Lanau: 'Je tiens Jean-Jacques Rousseau': un point de l'affaire Rousseau-Hume 182 (1979) 29-34

Jeffrey Barnouw: Johnson and Hume considered as the core of a new 'period conception' of the Enlightenment 190 (1980) 189-96

Reinhard Brandt: L'identità della persona (Locke et Hume) 190 (1980) 445-49

J. I. Biró: Description and explanation in Hume's science of man 190 (1980) 449-57

Nadia Boccara Postigliola: Il 'craving for employment' nella scienza dell'uomo e della società di David Hume 191 (1980) 753-60

Bruno Morcavallo: Influenza del pensiero religioso di John Toland su David Hume 192 (1980) 1119-23

Christine Battersby: An enquiry concerning the Humean woman 193 (1980) 1964-67

David Raynor: Hume's critique of Helvétius's *De l'esprit* 215 (1982) 223-29

Stanley Tweyman: An 'inconvenience' of anthropomorphism 216 (1983) 79

Seizo Hotta: Quesnay or Hume: Beccaria between France and Britain 216 (1983) 281-83

Nadia Boccara Postigliola: 'Passions égoïstes' et 'passions altruistes' chez David Hume (*avarice, ambition, bienveillance*) 216 (1983) 338-40

Seizo Hotta: Quesnay or Hume: Beccaria between France and Britain 245 (1986) 457-65

Hungary

Albert Gyergyai: Un correspondant hongrois de Voltaire: le comte Fekete de Galanta 25 (1963) 779-93

Mátyás Bajkó: The development of Hungarian formal education in the eighteenth century 167 (1977) 191-221

Lajos Hopp: Fortune littéraire et politique du *Contrat social* en Hongrie et en Europe orientale 190 (1980) 320-26

Ferenc Biró: L'apparition de la mentalité sentimentale dans la vie littéraire de la Hongrie des Lumières 191 (1980) 997-1003

Eduard Bene: La rénovation de l'abbaye des Prémontrés de Csorna à la fin du XVIIIe siècle 192 (1980) 1112-18

István Szathmári: Les Lumières et les débuts de la linguistique en Hongrie 192 (1980) 1227-33

Dóra Csanak: L'*Essai sur la foiblesse des esprits-forts* du comte Joseph Teleki 216 (1983) 9-10

László Ferenczi: Les ennemis hongrois des Lumières avant et après la Révolution 216 (1983) 12-13

Janos Barta: Enlightened Hungarian noblemen for and against the enlightened absolutism/despotism of Joseph II 216 (1983) 163-64

Domokos Kosáry: La presse hongroise et les Lumières, 1764-1795 216 (1983) 248-49

Eva H. Balázs: Physiocrates et pseudophysiocrates dans la Hongrie des Lumières 216 (1983) 275-77

Hutcheson, Francis

David Fate Norton: Francis Hutcheson in America 154 (1976) 1547-68

Eugenio Lecaldano: Il metodo della 'scienza dell'uomo' nell'Illuminismo scozzese da Hutcheson a Smith 190 (1980) 457-67

idealism

Marguerite Marie D. Stevens: L'idéalisme et le réalisme dans *Les Egarements du cœur et de l'esprit* de Crébillon fils 47 (1966) 157-76

Paul Chamley: Sir James Steuart, économiste et philosophe, ses affinités avec la franc-maçonnerie et son influence sur l'idéalisme allemand 151 (1976) 433-47

ideas

Theodore Besterman: Review: Lester G. Crocker, *An age of crisis* 12 (1960) 116-19

R. Mortier: Unité ou scission du siècle des Lumières? 26 (1963) 1207-21

Sallustio Bandini: pensée française et politique locale dans la Toscane des Médicis 242 (1986) 233-42

— atheism

Jean Wahl: *Cours sur l'athéisme éclairé de dom Deschamps* 52 (1967)

— bureaucracy

G. L. Seidler: The concept of bureaucracy in the Enlightenment 216 (1983) 70-72

— Cartesianism

Mariafranca Spallanzani: Notes sur le cartésianisme dans l'*Encyclopédie* 216 (1983) 326-28

Jürgen von Stackelberg: Pope cartésien? L'*Essay on Man* traduit, faussé, et propagé à travers l'Europe par l'abbé Du Resnel 216 (1983) 467-68

— causality

Georges Benrekassa: Théorie et mise en œuvre du concept de cause dans les *Considérations* de Montesquieu 191 (1980) 539

— civilisation

B. Plongeron: Bonheur, et 'civilisation chrétienne': une nouvelle apologétique après 1760 154 (1976) 1637-55

Alexandru Dutu: Structures mentales et communication internationale: l'image de la civilisation européene chez Vico, Montesquieu, et Dimitrie Cantemir 191 (1980) 601

— climate

Michael Cardy: Discussion of the theory of climate in the *querelle des anciens et des modernes* 163 (1976) 73-88

— conscience

Philip Robinson: 'La conscience': a perceptual problem in Rousseau 90 (1972) 1377-94

— continuity

Giorgio Tonelli: The law of continuity in the eighteenth century 27 (1963) 1619-38

— dialectics

Hernâni A. Resende: Sur l'étude des prémisses théoriques de la pensée dialectique au sein des doctrines sociales en France au siècle des Lumières: remarques de méthode 216 (1983) 69-70

— dogmatism

Louise Marcil-Lacoste: Le 'dogmatisme' des philosophes: l'origine d'une distortion 190 (1980) 209-14

— élite

Françoise Aubert: Elite et Lumières: approche lexicologique de la notion d'*élite* dans la langue française du XVIIIe siècle 192 (1980) 1263-68

— encyclopedism

J. Macary: L'esprit encyclopédique avant l'*Encyclopédie*: André François Deslandes 89 (1972) 975-92

— equality

Corrado Rosso: L'égalité du bonheur et le bonheur de l'égalité dans la pensée française du dix-huitième siècle 155 (1976) 1913-23

— essentialism

Sheila Mason: An essentialist inheritance: from Hooker to Montesquieu 242 (1986) 83-124

— evolution

Geoffrey Bremner: The impossibility of a theory of evolution in eighteenth-century French thought 216 (1983) 309-11

— freemasonry

Jacques Lemaire: Un aspect de la pensée contre-révolutionnaire: la pensée antimaçonnique (1785-1805) 216 (1983) 20-21

— Germany

Janine Buenzod: De l'*Aufklärung* au *Sturm und Drang*: continuité ou rupture? 24 (1963) 289-313

— happiness

R. M. Wiles: *Felix qui* ...: standards of happiness in eighteenth-century England 58 (1967) 1857-67

Corrado Rosso: L'égalité du bonheur et le bonheur de l'égalité dans la pensée française du dix-huitième siècle 155 (1976) 1913-23

Maria Gaetana Salvatores Scarpa: L'idée de 'bonheur' chez madame de Staël 191 (1980) 1004-1009

— hedonism

J. W. Johnson: Lord Rochester and the tradition of Cyrenaic hedonism, 1670-1790 153 (1976) 1151-67

— hierarchy

Paul H. Meyer: The breakdown of hierarchial concepts in 18th-century French society, literature, and art 216 (1983) 210-11

— history

Hugh Trevor-Roper: The historical philosophy of the Enlightenment 27 (1963) 1667-87

G. C. Wasberg: The influence of the 'enlightened' philosophy of history on Scandinavian political thought 27 (1963) 1775-85

Wolfgang Philipp: Physicotheology in the age of Enlightenment: appearance and history 57 (1967) 1233-67

G. Christie Wasberg: 'Transcendence' and 'immanence' in the philosophy of history from Enlightenment to Romanticism 58 (1967) 1829-38

Norman Hampson and Betty Behrens: Cultural history as infrastructure 86 (1971) 7-24

— honour

John Pappas: La campagne des philosophes contre l'honneur 205 (1982) 31-44

Maria Evelina Zoltowska: La démocratisation de l'idée de l'honneur dans le *Manuscrit trouvé à Saragosse* de Jean Potocki 216 (1983) 224-26

— humanism

Lester G. Crocker: Voltaire's struggle for humanism 4 (1957) 137-69

Norman Suckling: The unfulfilled Renaissance: an essay on the fortunes of enlightened humanism in the eighteenth century 86 (1971) 25-136

Jean-François Migaud: Humanisme et surhumanisme dans *Ardinghello und die glückseligen Inseln* de Wilhelm Heinse 216 (1983) 354-56

— Ideologues

Brian W. Head: The origin of 'idéologue' and 'idéologie' 183 (1980) 257-64

— innocence

Vera Lee: Innocence and initiation in the eighteenth-century French novel 153 (1976) 1307-12

— Jansenism

Robert Shackleton: Jansenism and the Enlightenment 57 (1967) 1387-97

Charles H. O'Brien: Jansenists and *philosophes* 1760-1790 216 (1983) 66-68

— language

Ronald Grimsley: Some aspects of 'nature' and 'language' in the French Enlightenment 56 (1967) 659-77

— law

G. Benrekassa: Loi naturelle et loi civile: l'idéologie des Lumières et la prohibition de l'inceste 87 (1972) 115-44

— legitimacy

M. L. Perkins: Liberty and the concept of legitimacy in the *Discours sur l'inégalité* 89 (1972) 1293-304

— liberalism

Dorothy Medlin: André Morellet, translator of liberal thought 174 (1978) 189-201

— libertarianism

Durand Echeverria: The emergence of American libertarianism into French thought and literature before 1776 152 (1976) 647-62

— literary history

Basil Guy: La notion de l'histoire littéraire du XVIIIe siècle 153 (1976) 1001-18

— luxury

M. R. de Labriolle-Rutherford: L'évolution de la notion de luxe depuis Mandeville jusqu'à la révolution 26 (1963) 1025-36

Hans Kortum: Frugalité et luxe à travers la querelle des anciens et des modernes 56 (1967) 765-75

Michael Cardy: Le 'nécessaire' et le 'superflu': antithèse des Lumières 205 (1982) 183-90

— mankind

Florence Gauthier: L'universalité du genre humain chez Robespierre 190 (1980) 377-80

Ann Thomson: From 'l'histoire naturelle de l'homme' to the natural history of mankind 216 (1983) 121-22

Paul Hoffmann: La théorie de l'homme dans la *Medicina rationalis systematica* de Friedrich Hoffmann 216 (1983) 314-15

Igor Smirnov: Le problème de l'homme dans l'œuvre d'Alexandre Radichtchev 216 (1983) 324-26

Michel Delon: *Homo sum, humani nihil a me alienum puto*: sur le vers de Térence comme devise des Lumières 216 (1983) 344-46

— materialism

Charles Rihs: L'influence du siècle des Lumières sur la formation du matérialisme historique 26 (1963) 1389-416

— modernisation

Arthur M. Wilson: The *philosophes* in the light of present-day theories of modernisation 58 (1967) 1893-913

Harriet Branson Applewhite and Darline Gay Levy: The concept of modernisation and the French Enlightenment 84 (1971) 53-98

— nationalism

Alexandru Dutu: National and European consciousness in the Romanian Enlightenment 55 (1967) 463-79

— natural law

Ronald Grimsley: Quelques aspects de la théorie du droit naturel au siècle des Lumières 25 (1963) 721-40

— nature

J. Robert Loy: Nature, reason and enlightenment, Voltaire, Rousseau and Diderot 26 (1963) 1085-107

Ronald Grimsley: Some aspects of 'nature' and 'language' in the French Enlightenment 56 (1967) 659-77

Maurice Crosland: 'Nature' and measurement in eighteenth-century France 87 (1972) 277-309

A. Owen Aldridge: The state of nature: an undiscovered country in the history of ideas 98 (1972) 7-26

C. Joel Block: The 'unnatural' versus the 'natural' in *La Religieuse* and *Le Supplément au Voyage de Bougainville* 124 (1974) 249-52

Giulio Barsanti: Linné et Buffon: deux images différentes de la nature et de l'histoire naturelle 216 (1983) 306-307

— Newtonianism

Dennis J. Fletcher: Bolingbroke and the diffusion of Newtonianism in France 53 (1967) 29-46

— optimism

R. A. Leigh: Rousseau's letter to Voltaire on optimism (18 August 1756) 30 (1964) 247-309

Barbara W. Maggs: Eighteenth-century Russian reflections on the Lisbon earthquake, Voltaire and optimism 137 (1975) 7-29

— pacifism

Jean Daniel Candaux: Charles Borde et la première crise d'antimilitarisme de l'opinion publique européenne 24 (1963) 315-44

— perfectibility

Peter Horwath: *Austriacus perfectus*: the ideal man of the Austrian literature of the Enlightenment 216 (1983) 59-61

— *philosophe*

Charles G. Stricklen: The *philosophe*'s political mission: the creation of an idea, 1750-1789 86 (1971) 137-228

Maurice Colgan: Prophecy against reason: Ireland and the Apocalypse 216 (1983) 6-7

— reason of state

Grzegorz Leopold Seidler: The concept 'reason of state' and the Polish Enlightenment 155 (1976) 2015-32

— reform

Ronald Ian Boss: Linguet: the reformer as anti-*philosophe* 151 (1976) 333-51

— relativism

Isaiah Berlin: A note on alleged relativism in eighteenth-century European thought 191 (1980) 561-64

— science

Colm Kiernan: *The Enlightenment and science in eighteenth-century France.* Second edition revised and enlarged 59A (1973)

Alberto Gil Novales: Il concetto di accademia delle scienze in Spagna, secolo XVIII 190 (1980) 470-71

— scientism

K. M. Baker: Scientism, elitism and liberalism: the case of Condorcet 55 (1967) 129-65

— sovereignty

Ian M. Wilson: *The Influence of Hobbes and Locke in the shaping of the concept of sovereignty in eighteenth-century France* 101 (1973)

— supernatural

Kay S. Wilkins: The treatment of the supernatural in the *Encyclopédie* 90 (1972) 1757-71

— teleology

Marie-Luise Spieckermann: The idea of teleology and the theory of scientific progress at the beginning of the eighteenth century 216 (1983) 328-29

— time

Lionel Gossman: Time and history in Rousseau 30 (1964) 311-49

— toleration

Elisabeth Labrousse: Note à propos de la conception de la tolérance au XVIIIe siècle 56 (1967) 799-811

— utopianism

J. L. Lecercle: Utopie et réalisme politique chez Mably 26 (1963) 1049-70

Charles Rihs: Les utopistes contre les Lumières 57 (1967) 1321-55

Philip Stewart: Du sauvage au colon anglais: l'Américain au dix-huitième siècle 216 (1983) 120-21

Robert Toupin: Pierre Potier, jésuite belge chez les Hurons du Détroit (1744-1781): les chemins d'un espace nouveau à explorer 216 (1983) 122-24

Françoise Weil: La découverte des Indiens du Canada et des Esquimaux au début du dix-huitième siècle par Antoine Raudot 216 (1983) 124-25

industrial revolution

David Irwin: The industrial revolution and the dissemination of neoclassical taste 153 (1976) 1087-98

inequality

Charles Porset: Discours d'un anonyme sur l'inégalité 1754 182 (1979) 7-27

initiation

Vera Lee: Innocence and initiation in the eighteenth-century French novel 153 (1976) 1307-12

innocence

Vera Lee: Innocence and initiation in the eighteenth-century French novel 153 (1976) 1307-12

inoculation

Anne Lacombe: La lettre sur l'insertion de la petite vérole et les *Lettres philosophiques* 117 (1974) 113-31

Institut et musée Voltaire

Theodore Besterman: The manuscripts of the Institut et musée Voltaire 6 (1958) 293-95

Jennifer Montagu: Inventaire des tableaux, sculptures, estampes, etc. de l'Institut et musée Voltaire 20 (1962) 223-47

institutions

Merle L. Perkins: Voltaire on the source of national power 20 (1962) 141-73

David Y. Jacobson: Trial by jury and criticism of the old régime 153 (1976) 1099-111

Hans-Jürgen Lüsebrink: L'affaire Cléreaux (Rouen 1785-1790): affrontements idéologiques et tensions institutionnelles sur la scène judiciaire de la fin du XVIIIe siècle 191 (1980) 892-900

Piero Del Negro: Venezia allo specchio: la crisi delle istituzioni repubblicane negli scritti del patriziato (1670-1797) 191 (1980) 920-26

Anna Maria Martellone: The myth of Germanic origins of free institutions in France and England 216 (1983) 185-87

international relations

Merle L. Perkins: Voltaire and the abbé de Saint-Pierre on world peace 18 (1961) 9-34

Merle L. Perkins: Voltaire's concept of international order 26 (1963) 1291-306

Merle L. Perkins: *Voltaire's concept of international order* 36 (1965)

Ireland

Maurice Colgan: An Enlightenment solution of the Irish problem 152 (1967) 485-96

Maurice Colgan: Prophecy against reason: Ireland and the Apocalypse 216 (1983) 6-7

David Nokes: The radical conservatism of Swift's Irish pamphlets 216 (1983) 25-26

Simon Davies: The idea of nationalism in late eighteenth-century Ireland: the case of Belfast 216 (1983) 385-86

Robert and Catherine Ward: Charles O'Conor: historian, reformer, patriot 216 (1983) 412-13

irony

Jean A. Perkins: Irony and candour in certain libertine novels 60 (1968) 245-59

Irving Wohlfarth: The irony of criticism and the criticism of irony: a study of Laclos criticism 120 (1974) 269-317

Hans P. Braendlin: The dilemma of luxury and the ironic structures of Lessing's *Emilia Galotti* and Lenz's *The Soldiers* 151 (1976) 353-62

irrationalism

Kay S. Wilkins: Some aspects of the irrational in 18th-century France 140 (1975) 107-201

Enrico Fubini: Razionalismo e irrazionalismo nelle concezioni musicali del tardo Illuminismo 193 (1980) 1710-16

Islam

Magdy Gabriel Badir: *Voltaire et l'Islam* 125 (1974)

A. Gunny: Montesquieu's view of Islam in the *Lettres persanes* 174 (1978) 151-66

O. H. Bonnerot: L'Islam devant les Lumières: le marquis de Pastoret 192 (1980) 1142-43

Italy

— archaeology

Françoise Waquet: Les souscriptions au *Museum etruscum* et la diffusion de l'étruscologie au dix-huitième siècle 208 (1982) 305-13

— architecture

Giuliana Ricci: L'architettura del neoclassicismo e i sui rapporti con le preesistenze gotiche a Milano nella seconda metà del '700 216 (1983) 141-43

Maria Grazia Sandri: Lo scienziato Paolo Frisi e la polemica sulla guglia del duomo di Milano: origine di un contrasto 216 (1983) 147-49

— art

Gustavo Costa: German antiquities and Gothic art in the early Italian Enlightenment 191 (1980) 559-61

David Irwin: The Italian Renaissance viewed by an 18th-century sculptor 193 (1980) 1664-67

Roberta Roani Villani: Lo scultore pistoiese Francesco Carradori 193 (1980) 1707-10

Georges Festa: Images du Bernin au dix-huitième siècle: l'œuvre du sculpteur jugée par les voyageurs français en Italie 241 (1986) 87-94

— bibliography

Theodore Besterman: A provisional bibliography of Italian editions and translations of Voltaire 18 (1961) 263-310

— booktrade

Anne Machet: Librairie et commerce du livre en Italie dans la deuxième moitié du XVIIIe siècle 153 (1976) 1347-80

Franco Piva: Le livre français dans les bibliothèques vicentines du dix-huitième siècle 193 (1980) 1791-98

Anne Machet: Edition populaire et colporteurs italiens dans la deuxième moitié du XVIIIe siècle 193 (1980) 1852-57

— commerce

Georges Festa: Images et réalités de la vie commerciale italienne à travers le *Voyage d'Italie* de Sade 217 (1983) 23-26

— cosmopolitanism

Anna Vittoria Migliorini: Spunti di cosmopolitismo in Francesco Algarotti 190 (1980) 395-402

— diplomacy

Harriet Dorothy Rothschild: Benoît de Maillet's Leghorn letters 30 (1964) 351-75

— economics

Anna Li Donni: La teoria della popolazione negli scrittori italiani del Settecento 191 (1980) 835-42

Luigi Cajani: L'assistenza ai poveri nell'Italia del Settecento 191 (1980) 914-20

— education

Giuseppe Ricuperati and Marina Roggero: Educational policies in eighteenth-century Italy 167 (1977) 223-69

— history

Doug Thompson: Writing the synthesis: a history of Italy in the Age of Enlightenment 190 (1980) 217-25

— influence

Gustavo Costa: German antiquities and Gothic art in the early Italian Enlightenment 191 (1980) 559-61

Mario Agrimi: Quelques échos en France de la pensée d'Antonio Genovesi 216 (1983) 445-47

Jean Claude Waquet: La composition du *Discorso sopra la Maremma di Siena* de Sallustio Bandini: pensée française et politique locale dans la Toscane des Médicis 242 (1986) 233-42

— literature

Renzo de Felice: Trois prises de position italiennes à propos de *Mahomet* 10 (1959) 259-66

— music

Karl Geiringer: Concepts of the Enlightenment as reflected in Gluck's Italian reform opera 88 (1972) 567-76

— philosophy

Roland Mortier: Un adversaire vénitien des 'Lumières', le comte de Cataneo 32 (1965) 91-268

Aldo Vallone: Aspetti dell'Illuminismo salentino 190 (1980) 214-17

Carla Pellandra Cazzoli: La polémique antiphilosophique dans la prédication des ordres religieux de la seconde moitié du dix-huitième siècle en Italie du Nord 216 (1983) 28-29

— politics

Anna Maria Rao: Riformismo napoletano e rivoluzione: Giuseppe Maria Galanti 190 (1980) 382-90

Piero Del Negro: Venezia allo specchio: la crisi delle istituzioni repubblicane negli scritti del patriziato (1670-1797) 191 (1980) 920-26

Jean Claude Waquet: La composition du *Discorso sopra la Maremma di Siena* de Sallustio Bandini: pensée française et politique locale dans la Toscane des Médicis 242 (1986) 233-42

— press

Marie-Josée Latil Ferromi: *La Gazette du Parme*, véhicule de diffusion de la culture française en Italie dans la deuxième moitié du 18e siècle 216 (1983) 249-51

Franco Piva: Helvétius dans le *Giornale enciclopedico* ou les difficultés de la presse éclairée à Venise 216 (1983) 256-58

Stella Gargantini Rabbi: Les Lumières dans la presse milanaise du 19e siècle (*Il Conciliatore* 1818-1819, *Il Politecnico* 1839-1845, 1860-1865): réception et débat 216 (1983) 423-24

— religion

Marina Caffiero Trincia: Il problema della riforma della Chiesa e le istanze cattoliche de rinnovamento culturale in Italia nel XVIII secolo 192 (1980) 1135-41

Carla Pellandra Cazzoli: La polémique antiphilosophique dans la prédication des ordres religieux de la seconde moitié du dix-huitième siècle en Italie du Nord 216 (1983) 28-29

— social history

Vittorio E. Giuntella: La città dell'Illuminismo 191 (1980) 927-35

— theatre

Maria Ines Aliverti et Marco Alderigi: Théâtre et spectacle à Pise au temps de Léopold Ier (1765-1790) 192 (1980) 1432-40

Letizia Norci Cagiano de Azevedo: Elementi illuministici nelle scenografie fantastiche del primo Settecento italiano 193 (1980) 1670-80

Milena Montanile: Morale et vertu dans la tragédie jacobine en Italie (1796-1799) 216 (1983) 356-57

— travel

Giuliana Toso Rodinis: Vivant Denon e le sue note al *Voyage di H. Swinburne dans les deux Siciles* 193 (1980) 1669

— visitors

Micheline Fort Harris: Le séjour de Montesquieu en Italie (août 1728 - juillet 1729): chronologie et commentaires 127 (1974) 65-197

Georges Festa: Images et réalités de la vie commerciale italienne à travers le *Voyage d'Italie* de Sade 217 (1983) 23-26

Mireille Gille: La 'Lettre d'Italie' au dix-huitième siècle: forme et signification 219 (1983) 257-72

Georges Festa: Images du Bernin au dix-huitième siècle: l'œuvre du sculpteur jugée par les voyageurs français en Italie 241 (1986) 87-94

— Voltaire

P. M. Conlon: Voltaire's election to the Accademia della Crusca 6 (1958) 133-39

Renzo de Felice: Trois prises de position italiennes à propos de *Mahomet* 10 (1959) 259-66

Theodore Besterman: A provisional bibliography of Italian editions and translations of Voltaire 18 (1961) 263-310

Jacobi, Friedrich Heinrich

Les Années de formation de F. H. Jacobi, d'après ses lettres inédites à M. M. Rey (1763-1771) avec Le Noble, de madame de Charrière, textes présentées par J. Th. de Booy et Roland Mortier 45 (1966)

Jacobinism

Françoise Brunel et Myriam Revault d'Allonnes: Jacobinisme et libéralisme: de la politique des principes à l'art de la politique 190 (1980) 377

Ida Cappiello: I Giacobini e le scienze sociali 191 (1980) 781-88

Jansenism

Robert Shackleton: Jansenism and the Enlightenment 57 (1967) 1387-97

Hélène Himelfarb: Saint Simon et le jansénisme des Lumières 88 (1972) 749-68

Charles H. O'Brien: Jansenists and *philosophes* 1760-1790 216 (1983) 66-68

Japan

Masao Okamoto: The Enlightenment in Japan 26 (1963) 1263-73

Jaucourt, Louis, chevalier de

George A. Perla: The unsigned articles and Jaucourt's bibliographical sketches in the *Encyclopédie* 171 (1977) 189-95

Jean-Paul

Alain Montandon: Jean-Paul et les philosophes 216 (1983) 460-62

Jenyns, Soame

Donald T. Siebert: The uses of adversity: Soame Jenyns's debt to Johnson 143 (1975) 181-87

Jesuits

Jews

Joan of Arc

Jodin, Marie-Madeleine

P. Vernière: Marie Madeleine Jodin, amie de Diderot et témoin des Lumières 58 (1967) 1765-75

Johnson, Samuel

Clarence Tracy: Johnson's *Journey to the western islands of Scotland*: a reconsideration 58 (1967) 1593-606

Rebecca Price Parkin: Neoclassic defensive techniques in the verse of Swift and Johnson dealing with the theme of *Christianus perfectus* 89 (1972) 1255-75

Donald T. Siebert: The uses of adversity: Soame Jenyns's debt to Johnson 143 (1975) 181-87

John L. Abbott: Samuel Johnson, John Hawkesworth, and the rise of the *Gentleman's magazine*, 1738-1773 151 (1976) 31-46

Jeffrey Barnouw: Johnson and Hume considered as the core of a new 'period conception' of the Enlightenment 190 (1980) 189-96

Joseph II, Emperor of Austria-Hungary

Peter Horwath: Literature in the service of enlightened absolutism: the age of Joseph II (1780-1790) 56 (1967) 707-34

Adrienne D. Hytier: Joseph II, la cour de Vienne et les philosophes 106 (1973) 225-51

Janos Barta: Enlightened Hungarian noblemen for and against the enlightened absolutism/despotism of Joseph II 216 (1983) 163-64

Helen Liebel-Weckowicz: The physiocrat tax reform of Joseph II: the challenge of modernisation in the Habsburg empire, 1780-1790 216 (1983) 287-89

Journal des dames

Nina Gelbart: The *Journal des dames* and the *frondeur* press in the *ancien régime* 216 (1983) 244-46

Journal des savants

George B. Watts: Charles Joseph Panckoucke, 'l'Atlas de la librairie française' 68 (1969) 67-205

Journal de Trévoux

John N. Pappas: *Berthier's 'Journal de Trévoux' and the philosophes* 3 (1957)

Journal encyclopédique

Raymond F. Birn: The *Journal encyclopédique* and the old régime 24 (1963) 219-40

Raymond F. Birn: *Pierre Rousseau and the philosophes of Bouillon* 29 (1964)

Jullien de La Drôme

Jacques Wagner: 'Comme l'eau le sucre' ou anthropologie et histoire dans le *Journal encyclopédique* (1756-1778) 183 (1980) 239-56

Jacques Wagner: Le rôle du *Journal encyclopédique* dans la diffusion de la culture 193 (1980) 1805-12

Peter Altena, Hans Groot, Hanna Stouten: The presentation of Dutch literary work in the *Journal encyclopédique* (1759-1793) 216 (1983) 469-71

Journal étranger

Marie Rose de Labriolle: Le *Journal étranger* dans l'histoire du cosmopolitisme littéraire 56 (1967) 783-97

Peter Lester Smith: The launching of the *Journal étranger* (1752-1754): the problem of audience 163 (1976) 117-27

journalism

Madeleine Fields: Voltaire et le *Mercure de France* 20 (1962) 175-215

Marie-Rose de Labriolle: *'Le Pour et contre' et son temps* 34-35 (1965)

Raymond Birn: The French-language press and the *Encyclopédie*, 1750-1759 55 (1967) 263-86

Peter Lester Smith: The launching of the *Journal étranger* (1752-1754): the problem of audience 163 (1976) 117-27

Ruth P. Dawson: Women communicating: eighteenth-century German journals edited by women 216 (1983) 239-41

François Moureau: Les journalistes de langue française dans l'Allemagne des Lumières: essai de typologie 216 (1983) 254-56

Margarete G. Smith: J. H. S. Formey, assiduous journalist and discreet propagandist of new scientific discoveries and philosophical trends 216 (1983) 262-64

Jugoslavia

Gabrijela Vidan: Les tergiversations d'un déraciné: Stjepan Zanović, écrivain d'aventure 216 (1983) 472-73

Julian

Christopher Thacker: The misplaced garden? Voltaire, Julian and *Candide* 41 (1966) 189-202

J. S. Spink: The Reputation of Julian the 'apostate' in the Enlightenment 57 (1967) 1399-415

Jullien de La Drôme, Marc-Antoine

R. Galliani: Quelques lettres inédites de Mably 98 (1972) 183-97

Jung, Carl Gustav

James Maurice Kaplan: *'La Neuvaine de Cythère': une démarmontélisation de Marmontel* 113 (1973)

Kant, Immanuel

A. C. Genova: Kant's Enlightenment 88 (1972) 577-98

M. W. Beal: Condillac as precursor of Kant 102 (1973) 193-229

Ehrhard Bahr: The pursuit of happiness in the political writings of Lessing and Kant 151 (1976) 167-84

Thomas E. Willey: Kant and the German theory of education 167 (1977) 543-67

James L. Larson: Kant's principle of formal purposiveness 190 (1980) 507-508

Stefano Poggi: Le categorie dell'esperienza scientifica nella prima ricezione del kantismo 190 (1980) 513-17

Giuseppe Micheli: Kant et la storia della filosofia 191 (1980) 587-95

Alain-Marc Rieu: Kant: critique du 'Cosmologisme' et fin des Lumières 216 (1983) 324

Kantemir, Antioch

I. Serman: Kantemir et le problème du contexte dans le mouvement littéraire russe du XVIIIe siècle 193 (1980) 1644-46

Karamzin, Nicholas

J. L. Black: Nicholas Karamzin and the dilemma of luxury in eighteenth-century Russia 151 (1976) 313-22

Kästner, Abraham Gotthelf

Martin Dyck: Mathematics and literature in the German Enlightenment: Abraham Gotthelf Kästner (1719-1800) 190 (1980) 508-12

Keats, John

Harold Orel: *English Romantic poets and the Enlightenment: nine essays on a literary relationship* 103 (1973)

Klinger, Friedrich Maximilian

Giulia Cantarutti: Patriotisme et sentiment national dans les *Betrachtungen und Gedanken* (1803-1805) de F. M. Klinger, un représentant des Lumières allemandes à la cour russe 216 (1983) 383-85

Knigge, Adolph Freiherr

Joachim Schmitt-Sasse: J. M. v. Loen and A. Freiherr Knigge: bourgeois ideals in the writings of German aristocrats 216 (1983) 187-88

Kotzwara, Franz

Richard J. Wolfe: The hang-up of Franz Kotzwara and its relationship to sexual quackery in late 18th-century London 228 (1984) 47-66

La Barre, François Poulain de

Ellen McNiven Hine: The woman question in early eighteenth-century French literature: the influence of François Poulain de La Barre 116 (1973) 65-79

labour

Thomas M. Adams: Mendicity and moral alchemy: work as rehabilitation 151 (1976) 47-76

Jacques Rychner: A l'ombre des Lumières: coup d'œil sur la main d'œuvre de quelques imprimeurs du XVIIIe siècle 155 (1976) 1925-55

Nadia Boccara Postigliola: Il 'craving for employment' nella scienza dell'uomo e della società di David Hume 191 (1980) 753-60

Laclos, Pierre-Antoine-François Choderlos de

David Coward: Laclos et la sensibilité 87 (1972) 235-51

James S. Munro: Studies in sub-conscious motivation in Laclos and Marivaux 89 (1972) 1053-68

R. P. Thomas: *Jacques le fataliste, Les Liaisons dangereuses*, and the autonomy of the novel 117 (1974) 239-49

Jenny H. Batlay: Amour et métaphore: analyse de la lettre 23 des *Liaisons dangereuses* 117 (1974) 251-57

Irving Wohlfarth: The irony of criticism and the criticism of irony: a study of Laclos criticism 120 (1974) 269-317

Lloyd R. Free: Laclos and the myth of courtly love 148 (1976) 201-23

Jacques Bourgeacq: A partir de la lettre XLVIII des *Liaisons dangereuses*: analyse stylistique 183 (1980) 177-88

Graham E. Rodmell: Laclos, Brissot, and the petition of the Champ de Mars 183 (1980) 189-222

Madelyn Gutwirth: Laclos and 'Le sexe': the rack of ambivalence 189 (1980) 247-96

Jeannette Geffriaud Rosso: Libertinage et 'surcompensation' dans les rapports entre les sexes au dix-huitième siècle', d'après Laclos, Diderot et Crébillon fils 216 (1983) 348-49

La Mettrie

John Falvey: The aesthetics of La Mettrie 87 (1972) 397-479

Julien Offray de La Mettrie: *Discours sur le bonheur*, critical edition by John Falvey 134 (1975)

Aram Vartanian: Cabanis and La Mettrie 155 (1976) 2149-66

Lionel P. Honoré: The philosophical satire of La Mettrie 215 (1982) 175-222

Lionel P. Honoré: The philosophical satire of La Mettrie: part II 241 (1986) 203-36

landscape

Maurice Colgan: The language of landscape: truth or pleasing delusion? 193 (1980) 1736-41

David Irwin: Death in the landscape: the neo-classic tomb 216 (1983) 132-33

language

M. L. Dufrenoy: Maupertuis et le progrès scientifique 25 (1963) 519-87

Ronald Grimsley: Some aspects of 'nature' and 'language' in the French Enlightenment 56 (1967) 659-77

Werner Krauss: La néologie dans la littérature du XVIIIe siècle 56 (1967) 777-82

David Williams: Voltaire and the language of the gods 62 (1968) 57-81

Alfred J. Bingham: Marie Joseph Chénier, ideologue and critic 94 (1972) 219-76

J. M. Blanchard: Grammaire(s) d'ancien régime 106 (1973) 7-20

H. Nicholas Bakalar: Language and logic: Diderot and the *grammairiens-philosophes* 132 (1975) 113-35

Robert C. Carroll: Muse and Narcissus: Rousseau's *Lettres à Sara* 137 (1975) 81-107

Maureen F. O'Meara: *Le Taureau blanc* and the activity of language 148 (1976) 115-75

M. B. Therrien: Rousseau: lucidité et sincérité 155 (1976) 2071-82

Dennis F. Essar: *The Language theory, epistemology, and aesthetics of Jean Lerond d'Alembert* 159 (1976)

Massimo Mugnai: Linguaggio e teoria nella concezione della scienza di J. Heinrich Lambert 190 (1980) 517

Robert Wokler: The ape debates in Enlightenment anthropology 192 (1980) 1164-75

Antonio Verri: Antropologia e linguistica in Rousseau 192 (1980) 1205-18

Camiel Hamans: Universal language and the Netherlands 192 (1980) 1218-27

István Szathmári: Les Lumières et les débuts de la linguistique en Hongrie 192 (1980) 1227-33

I. Gopnik: Universal language schemes and the linguistic relativity hypothesis 192 (1980) 1233-36

Sylvain Auroux: Le concept de détermination: Port-Royal et Beauzée 192 (1980) 1236-45

Daniel Droixhe: Le cercle et le gland: linguistique et anthropologie chez Hamann 192 (1980) 1246-56

Marie-Louise Barthel: Un aspect négligé de la linguistique des Lumières: Thurot et Harris 192 (1980) 1256-63

Françoise Aubert: Elite et Lumières: approche lexicologique de la notion d'*élite* dans la langue française du XVIIIe siècle 192 (1980) 1263-68

Rémy G. Saisselin: Langage et peinture: la dialectique du regard 193 (1980) 1735-36

Maurice Colgan: The language of landscape: truth or pleasing delusion? 193 (1980) 1736-41

Micheline Coulaud: Les *Mémoires sur la matière étymologique* de Charles de Brosses 199 (1981) 287-352

Verena Ehrlich-Haefeli: Sécularisation, langue et structure familiale: la figure du père dans le théâtre de Lessing et de Diderot 216 (1983) 53-56

Julie Andresen: L'image des langues américaines au dix-huitième siècle 216 (1983) 88-89

Camiel Hamans: The ape in Dutch linguistics of the 18th century 216 (1983) 108-109

J. Guillerme: Analyse d'un mémoire inédit de 1774 intitulé 'Essai sur la langue philosophique' 216 (1983) 313-14

Sylvain Auroux: Réception et critique de la linguistique des Lumières chez les auteurs français du dix-neuvième siècle 216 (1983) 417-18

Maureen F. O'Meara: Linguistic power-play: Voltaire's considerations on the evolution, use, and abuse of language 219 (1983) 93-103

P. Swiggers: Studies on the French eighteenth-century grammatical tradition 219 (1983) 273-80

P. Swiggers: Catégories de langue et catégories de grammaire dans la théorie linguistique des Encyclopédistes 241 (1986) 339-64

David Beeson: Maupertuis at the crossroads: dating the *Réflexions philosophiques* 249 (1986) 241-50

— origin

Ronald Grimsley: Maupertuis, Turgot and Maine de Biran on the origin of language 62 (1968) 285-307

Ellen McNiven Hine: Condillac and the problem of language 106 (1973) 21-62

Robert Wokler: Rameau, Rousseau, and the *Essai sur l'origine des langues* 117 (1974) 179-238

Charles Porset: L'inquiétante étrangeté de l'*Essai sur l'origine des langues*: Rousseau et ses exégètes 154 (1976) 1715-58

Antonio Verri: On the Porset edition of Rousseau's *Essai sur l'origine des langues* 155 (1976) 2167-71

Romano Baldi: Louis-Claude de Saint-Martin et la question de l'origine des langues 193 (1980) 1650-58

P. Swiggers: Maupertuis sur l'origine du langage 215 (1982) 163-69

G. A. Wells: Condillac, Rousseau and Herder on the origin of language 230 (1985) 233-46

— semantics

Horst Günther: Sémantique philosophique et histoire des concepts 190 (1980) 518-26

— semiotics

Karlis Racevskis: Le discours philosophique à l'Académie française: une sémiotique de la démagogie et de l'arrivisme 190 (1980) 343-50

La Noue, Jean-Baptiste Sauvé de, *called*

Spire Pitou: Sauvé de La Noue: actor, author, producer 117 (1974) 89-112

Larcher, Pierre-Henry

Jean-Claude David: Documents inédits concernant l'*Histoire d'Hérodote* de Pierre Henry Larcher (1786) 219 (1983) 195-210

La Roche, Michel de

Margaret D. Thomas: Michel de La Roche: a Huguenot critic of Calvin 238 (1985) 97-195

La Roche, Sophie

Charlotte Craig: Mind and method: Sophie La Roche – a 'praecepta filiarum Germaniae' 193 (1980) 1996-2002

Lavater, Johann Caspar

Marcia Allentuck: Fuseli and Lavater: physiognomical theory and the Enlightenment 55 (1967) 89-112

Lavoisier, Antoine-Laurent

Louis S. Greenbaum: The humanitarianism of Antoine Laurent Lavoisier 88 (1972) 651-75

law

Paul M. Spurlin: Beccaria's *Essay on crimes and punishments* in eighteenth-century America 27 (1963) 1489-504

Diana Guiragossian: *Manon Lescaut* et la justice criminelle sous l'ancien régime 56 (1967) 679-91

Darline Gay Levy: Simon Linguet's sociological system: an exhortation to patience and invitation to revolution 70 (1970) 219-93

Pauline Kra: *Religion in Montesquieu's 'Lettres persanes'* 72 (1970)

G. Benrekassa: Loi naturelle et loi civile: l'idéologie des Lumières et la prohibition de l'inceste 87 (1972) 115-44

Paolo Casini: La loi naturelle: réflexion politique et sciences exactes 151 (1976) 417-32

David Y. Jacobson: Trial by jury and criticism of the old régime 153 (1976) 1099-111

Michael Suozzi: The Enlightenment in Italy: Gaetano Filangieri's *Scienza della legislazione* 155 (1976) 2049-62

Alan Williams: The police and the poor in Paris 155 (1976) 2285-300

Hernâni A. Resende: Jean-Jacques Rousseau, l'abbé Dolivier, Hegel, sur la théorie des droits naturels 190 (1980) 381

William Doyle: Reforming the French criminal law at the end of the old regime: the example of president Dupaty 191 (1980) 866-72

Hans-Jürgen Lüsebrink: L'affaire Cléreaux (Rouen 1785-1790): affrontements idéologiques et tensions institutionnelles sur la scène judiciaire de la fin du XVIIIe siècle 191 (1980) 892-900

Mario A. Cattaneo: La discussione su Beccaria in Germania: K. F. Hommel e J. E. F. Schall 191 (1980) 935-43

Hans-Jürgen Lüsebrink: *Mémoire pour la fille Cléreaux* (Rouen 1785) 208 (1982) 323-72

Edward M. Jennings: Changes in English law, learning and finance, 1650-1750: time and secularisation 216 (1983) 61-62

Colby H. Kullman: James Boswell, compassionate lawyer and harsh criminologist: a divided self 217 (1983) 199-205

Iris Cox: *Montesquieu and the history of French laws* 218 (1983)

William Doyle: Dupaty (1746-1788): a career in the late Enlightenment 230 (1985) 1-125

John Dunkley: *Gambling: a social and moral problem in France, 1685-1792* 235 (1985)

Magdy Gabriel Badir: Législation et définition de la prostitution au dix-huitième siècle 249 (1986) 447-66

Le Bret, Alexis-Jean

H. T. Mason: Voltaire and Le Bret's digest of Bayle 20 (1962) 217-21

Lebrun-Pindare, Ponce-Denis Ecouchard Lebrun, *called*

Emile Lizé: Une lettre oubliée de Lebrun-Pindare à Voltaire 174 (1978) 113-20

Le Clerc, Jean

Marie-Hélène Cotoni: *L'Exégèse du Nouveau Testament dans la philosophie française du dix-huitième siècle* 220 (1984)

Ledoux, Claude-Nicolas

Monique Nemer: Ledoux et Boullée: une écriture monumentale 216 (1983) 137-38

Helen Rosenau-Carmi: Ledoux's *L'Architecture* 230 (1985) 393-459

Leibniz, Gottfried Wilhelm von

Theodore Besterman: Review: W. H. Barber, *Leibniz in France from Arnauld to Voltaire* 2 (1956) 317-18

Oscar A. Haac: Voltaire and Leibniz: two aspects of rationalism 25 (1963) 795-809

R. Galliani: A propos de Voltaire, de Leibniz et de la *Théodicée* 189 (1980) 7-17

Michelangelo Ghio: I progetti di pace perpetua dell'abate di St Pierre nei giudizi di Rousseau, Leibniz e Voltaire 190 (1980) 307-18

Paul Hoffmann: La controverse entre Leibniz et Stahl sur la nature de l'âme 190 (1980) 492-94

Paul Hoffmann: La controverse entre Leibniz et Stahl sur la nature de l'âme 199 (1981) 237-49

François Duchesneau: L'épistémologie de Maupertuis entre Leibniz et Newton 216 (1983) 312-13

Le Mascrier, Jean-Baptiste

Miguel Benítez: Benoît de Maillet et la littérature clandestine: étude de sa correspondance avec l'abbé Le Mascrier 183 (1980) 133-59

Lemercier, Louis-Jean-Népomucène

Edouard Guitton: Un thème 'philosophique': 'l'invention' des poètes de Louis Racine à Népomucène Lemercier 88 (1972) 677-709

Le Mierre, Antoine-Marin

John Van Eerde: The people in eighteenth-century tragedy from *Œdipe* to *Guillaume Tell* 27 (1963) 1703-13

Lenclos, Ninon de

A. C. Keys: Bret, Douxménil and the *Mémoires* of Ninon de Lanclos 12 (1960) 43-54

A. C. Keys: The vicissitudes of the *Mémoires* of Ninon de Lanclos 18 (1961) 129-39

W. D. Howarth: Voltaire, Ninon de L'Enclos and the evolution of a dramatic genre 199 (1981) 63-72

Lenglet Du Fresnoy, Nicolas

Lester A. Segal: Nicolas Lenglet Du Fresnoy: tradition and change in French historiographical thought of the early eighteenth century 98 (1972) 69-117

Lester A. Segal: Lenglet Du Fresnoy: the treason of a cleric in eighteenth-century France 116 (1973) 251-79

Geraldine Sheridan: Censorship and the booktrade in France in the early eighteenth century: Lenglet Dufresnoy's *Méthode pour étudier l'histoire* 241 (1986) 95-107

Lenz, Siegfried

Hans P. Braendlin: The dilemma of luxury and the ironic structures of Lessing's *Emilia Galotti* and Lenz's *The Soldiers* 151 (1976) 353-62

Leopold I, Grand Duke of Tuscany

Maria Ines Aliverti et Marco Alderigi: Théâtre et spectacle à Pise au temps de Léopold Ier (1765-1790) 192 (1980) 1432-40

Le Prince de Beaumont, Jeanne-Marie

Patricia A. Clancy: A French writer and educator in England: Mme Leprince de Beaumont 201 (1982) 195-208

Leroux, Pierre

Charles Porset: Ambiguïtés de la philosophie de Voltaire: sa réception par Pierre Leroux 216 (1983) 433

Lesage, Alain-René

Katharine Whitman Carson: *Aspects of contemporary society in 'Gil Blas'* 110 (1973)

Jenny H. Batlay: L'art du portrait dans *Gil Blas*: effet d'esthétique à travers le mouvement 124 (1974) 181-89

Richard L. Frautschi et Roberta Hackel: Le comportement verbal du narrateur dans *Gil Blas*: quelques observations quantitatives 192 (1980) 1340-52

Glen Campbell: The search for equality of Lesage's picaresque heroes 216 (1983) 195-96

Lessing, Gotthold Ephraim

Ehrhard Bahr: The pursuit of happiness in the political writings of Lessing and Kant 151 (1976) 167-84

Hans P. Braendlin: The dilemma of luxury and the ironic structures of Lessing's *Emilia Galotti* and Lenz's *The Soldiers* 151 (1976) 353-62

Verena Ehrlich-Haefeli: Sécularisation, langue et structure familiale: la figure du père dans le théâtre de Lessing et de Diderot 216 (1983) 53-56

John Boening: Carlyle versus the Enlightenment: the curious case of Lessing 216 (1983) 419-21

Steven D. Martinson: Lessing and the European Enlightenment: problems and perspective 216 (1983) 458-60

lexicology

Françoise Aubert: Elite et Lumières: approche lexicologique de la notion d'*élite* dans la langue française du XVIIIe siècle 192 (1980) 1263-68

liberalism

K. M. Baker: Scientism, elitism and liberalism: the case of Condorcet 55 (1967) 129-65

Dorothy Medlin: André Morellet, translator of liberal thought 174 (1978) 189-201

Françoise Brunel et Myriam Revault d'Allonnes: Jacobinisme et libéralisme: de la politique des principes à l'art de la politique 190 (1980) 377

Alain Tichoux: Théorie et pratique du libéralisme réformateur: le paradoxe canadien (1760-1765) 191 (1980) 971-79

Luís Reis Torgal et Isabel Nobre Vargues: La réception des idées pédagogiques de la Révolution française par le premier libéralisme portugais (1820-1823) 216 (1983) 433-34

libertarianism

Durand Echeverria: The emergence of American libertarianism into French thought and literature before 1776 152 (1976) 647-62

libertinism

Jean A. Perkins: Irony and candour in certain libertine novels 60 (1968) 245-59

Barry Ivker: Towards a definition of libertinism in 18th-century French fiction 73 (1970) 221-39

Gabrijela Vidan: Style libertin et imagination ludique dans la correspondance de Diderot 90 (1972) 1731-45

Irving Wohlfarth: The irony of criticism and the criticism of irony: a study of Laclos criticism 120 (1974) 269-317

E. Thompsett: Love and libertinism in the novels of Duclos 137 (1975) 109-19

Gregorio Piaia: Dal libertinismo erudito all'illuminismo: l'*Histoire critique de la philosophie* di A.-F. Boureau-Deslandes 191 (1980) 595-601

P. L. M. Fein: The role of women in certain eighteenth-century French *libertin* novels 193 (1980) 1925-32

Andrzej Siemek: *La Recherche morale et esthétique dans le roman de Crébillon fils* 200 (1981)

Jeannette Geffriaud Rosso: Libertinage et 'surcompensation' dans les rapports entre les sexes au dix-huitième siècle', d'après Laclos, Diderot et Crébillon fils 216 (1983) 348-49

liberty

M. L. Perkins: Rousseau on history, liberty and national survival 53 (1967) 79-169

M. L. Perkins: Jean Jacques Rousseau, liberté et état de guerre 57 (1967) 1217-31

Paul Hoffmann: L'idée de liberté dans la philosophie médicale de Théophile de Bordeu 88 (1972) 769-87

M. L. Perkins: Liberty and the concept of legitimacy in the *Discours sur l'inégalité* 89 (1972) 1293-304

Huguette Cohen: *La Figure dialogique dans 'Jacques le fataliste'* 162 (1976)

David J. Langdon: Interpolations in the *Encyclopédie* article 'Liberté' 171 (1977) 155-88

Catherine Volpilhac-Auger: *Tacite et Montesquieu* 232 (1985)

James E. Crimmins: 'The study of true politics': John Brown on manners and liberty 241 (1986) 65-86

libraries

J. Vercruysse: Notes sur les imprimés et les manuscrits du collection Launoit 20 (1962) 249-59

Jean-Pierre Le Bouler, Catherine Lafarge: Les emprunts de Mme Dupin à la Bibliothèque du roi dans les années 1748-1750 182 (1979) 107-85

Andrew Brown: Voltaire at the Bibliothèque nationale [review of *Catalogue générale des livres imprimés de la Bibliothèque nationale: auteurs* (Paris 1978), t.ccxiv] 199 (1981) 375-79

Richard L. Frautschi: La diffusion du roman francophone au dix-huitième siècle: relevé provisoire de quelques collections en Europe centrale 216 (1983) 243-44

Iacob Mârza: Horizon livresque des Lumières dans les bibliothèques roumaines de Transylvanie depuis le milieu du 18e siècle jusqu'aux premières décennies du 19e 216 (1983) 251-52

James M. Kaplan: The Stockholm manuscript of Marmontel's *Les Incas* 249 (1986) 359-72

Liège

B. Demoulin: La réaction de la noblesse et la défense de ses privilèges dans la principauté de Liège au début du dix-huitième siècle 216 (1983) 170-71

Ligne, Charles-Joseph, prince de

Basil Guy: The prince de Ligne's *Artula hortulorum* 205 (1982) 133-39

Lillo, George

J. Chouillet: Images continentales du *Marchand de Londres* 217 (1983) 3-10

Linguet, Simon-Nicolas-Henri

Darline Gay Levy: Simon Linguet's sociological system: an exhortation to patience and invitation to revolution 70 (1970) 219-93

Spire Pitou: Voltaire, Linguet, and China 98 (1972) 61-68

Ronald Ian Boss: Linguet: the reformer as anti-*philosophe* 151 (1976) 333-51

Roger Barny: Un anti-philosophe dans la Révolution: Simon Nicolas Henri Linguet, de 1788 à 1794 190 (1980) 381-82

Darline Gay Levy: Despotism in Simon-Nicolas-Henri Linguet's science of society: theory and application 191 (1980) 761-68

Linnaeus, Carl

Giulio Barsanti: Linné et Buffon: deux images différentes de la nature et de l'histoire naturelle 216 (1983) 306-307

Liotard, Jean-Etienne

Erich Bachmann: An unknown portrait of Voltaire by Jean Etienne Liotard? 62 (1968) 123-36

Liston, Sir Robert

James C. Nicholls (ed.): *Mme Riccoboni's letters to David Hume, David Garrick and Sir Robert Liston, 1764-1783* 149 (1976)

literary criticism

Oscar A. Haac: Theories of literary criticism and Marivaux 88 (1972) 711-34

Emilie P. Kostoroski: *The Eagle and the dove: Corneille and Racine in the literary criticism of eighteenth-century France* 95 (1972)

Henri Mydlarski: Vauvenargues, juge littéraire de son siècle 150 (1976) 149-81

René Wellek: The price of progress in eighteenth-century reflections on literature 155 (1976) 2265-84

Gregory Ludlow: Eighteenth-century literature and the French new criticism 190 (1980) 258-60

literary history

Theodore Besterman: Review: J. Vier, *Histoire de la littérature française, XVIIIe siècle* 47 (1966) 257-63

Marie Rose de Labriolle: Le *Journal étranger* dans l'histoire du cosmopolitisme littéraire 56 (1967) 783-97

Basil Guy: La notion de l'histoire littéraire du XVIIIe siècle 153 (1976) 1001-18

Basil Guy: Toward a history of eighteenth-century French literature in the nineteenth century: 1810-1894 176 (1979) 403-28

W. Schröder: La Révolution française de 1789 – une césure d'époque de l'histoire de la littérature? 190 (1980) 160-66

literary technique

John Hampton: The literary technique of the first two *Mémoires* of Beaumarchais against Goezman 47 (1966) 177-205

Pierre Haffter: L'usage satirique des causales dans les contes de Voltaire 53 (1967) 7-28

Herbert Dieckmann: Diderot's *Promenade du sceptique*: a study in the relationship of thought and form 55 (1967) 417-38

Vivienne Mylne: Literary techniques and methods in Voltaire's *contes philosophiques* 57 (1967) 1055-80

Jeanne R. Monty: *Les Romans de l'abbé Prévost: procédés littéraires et pensée morale* 78 (1970)

Irwin L. Greenberg: Narrative technique and literary intent in Diderot's *Les Bijoux indiscrets* and *Jacques le fataliste* 79 (1971) 93-101

Barry Ivker: On the darker side of the Enlightenment: a comparison of the literary techniques of Sade and Restif 79 (1971) 199-218

Peter V. Conroy: *Crébillon fils: techniques of the novel* 99 (1972)

D. Berry: The technique of literary digression in the fiction of Diderot 118 (1974) 115-272

Stephen Werner: *Diderot's great scroll: narrative art in 'Jacques le fataliste'* 128 (1975)

Lloyd R. Free: Point of view and narrative space in Vivant Denon's *Point de lendemain* 163 (1976) 89-115

Ninette Boothroyd: *Les Lettres de la Marquise de M*** au Comte de R**** – le discours de la passion: structure et modulations 185 (1980) 199-220

Colette G. Levin: *Gulliver* and *Candide*: a comparative study of narrative techniques 192 (1980) 1317-24

Vivienne Mylne: Chapters as a structural device in the *conte* and the novel 192 (1980) 1332-33

Bernard Bray: Structures en série dans *Manon Lescaut* et *Histoire d'une Grecque moderne* de l'abbé Prévost 192 (1980) 1333-40

Aurelio Principato: Rhétorique et technique narrative chez l'abbé Prévost 192 (1980) 1352-59

literary theory

Réal Ouellet: La théorie du roman épistolaire en France au XVIIIe siècle 89 (1972) 1209-27

François Jost: *Ut sculptura poesis*: littérature et arts plastiques 193 (1980) 1722-29

Michael Cardy: *The Literary doctrines of Jean-François Marmontel* 210 (1982)

Teresa Kostkiewiczowa: Les doctrines littéraires dans la Pologne des 'Lumières' et leurs relations avec l'esthétique française 216 (1983) 457-58

Loaisel de Tréogate, Joseph-Marie

Townsend Whelen Bowling: *The Life, works and literary career of Loaisel de Tréogate* 196 (1981)

Locke, John

Peter D. Jimack: *La Genèse et la rédaction de l''Emile' de J.-J. Rousseau* 13 (1960)

Ian M. Wilson: *The Influence of Hobbes and Locke in the shaping of the concept of sovereignty in eighteenth-century France* 101 (1973)

Ralph S. Pomeroy: Locke, Alembert, and the anti-rhetoric of the Enlightenment 154 (1976) 1657-75

Reinhard Brandt: L'identità della persona (Locke et Hume) 190 (1980) 445-49

Malcolm Carroll: *Jacques le fataliste*: essay in Lockian epistemology? 190 (1980) 468-69

Loen, Johann Michael von

Joachim Schmitt-Sasse: J. M. v. Loen and A. Freiherr Knigge: bourgeois ideals in the writings of German aristocrats 216 (1983) 187-88

logic

H. Nicholas Bakalar: Language and logic: Diderot and the *grammairiens-philosophes* 132 (1975) 113-35

Louis, Antoine

Paola Vecchi: Mort apparente et procédés de 'ressuscitation' dans la littérature médicale du 18e siècle (Bruhier, Louis, Réaumur, Menuret de Chambaud) 216 (1983) 330-32

Louis XIV

N. R. Johnson: Louis XIV devant l'opinion française contemporaine: ses dernières paroles au dauphin 88 (1972) 831-43

N. R. Johnson: *Louis XIV and the age of the Enlightenment: the myth of the Sun King from 1715 to 1789* 172 (1978)

Colin Duckworth: Louis XVI and English history: a French reaction to Walpole, Hume and Gibbon on Richard III 176 (1979) 385-401

Louis XV

G. Gargett: Voltaire, Richelieu and the problem of Huguenot emancipation in the reign of Louis XV 176 (1979) 97-132

Louise-Dorothée, duchesse de Gotha

H. A. Stavan: Voltaire et la duchesse de Gotha 185 (1980) 27-56

Louvet de Couvray, Jean-Baptiste

S. F. Davies: Louvet as social critic: *Les Amours du Chevalier de Faublas* 183 (1980) 223-37

love

Oscar A. Haac: L'amour dans les collèges jésuites: une satire anonyme du dix-huitième siècle 18 (1961) 95-111

Jenny H. Batlay: Amour et métaphore: analyse de la lettre 23 des *Liaisons dangereuses* 117 (1974) 251-57

E. Thompsett: Love and libertinism in the novels of Duclos 137 (1975) 109-19

Lloyd R. Free: Laclos and the myth of courtly love 148 (1976) 201-23

Philip Robinson: Marivaux's poetic theatre of love: some considerations of genre 192 (1980) 1513-15

Robert M. Cammarrota: *Così fan tutte*: Mozart's rhetoric of love and reason 193 (1980) 1719-20

Mildred Greene: 'A chimera of her own creating': love and fantasy in novels from madame de Lafayette to Jane Austen 193 (1980) 1940-42

Philip Robinson: Marivaux's poetic theatre of love 199 (1981) 7-24

Andrzej Siemek: *La Recherche morale et esthétique dans le roman de Crébillon fils* 200 (1981)

Paul-Gabriel Boucé: Sex, amours and love in *Tom Jones* 228 (1984) 25-38

R. J. Howells: Deux histoires, un discours: *La Nouvelle Héloïse* et le récit des amours d'Emile et Sophie dans l'*Emile* 249 (1986) 267-94

Low Countries

Lucian

Lucotte, J. R.

Lucretius

Luneau de Boisjermain, Pierre-Joseph-François

Luther, Martin

Graham Gargett: *Voltaire and Protestantism* 188 (1980)

luxury

M. R. de Labriolle-Rutherford: L'évolution de la notion de luxe depuis Mandeville jusqu'à la révolution 26 (1963) 1025-36

Hans Kortum: Frugalité et luxe à travers la querelle des anciens et des modernes 56 (1967) 765-75

Roger Bauer: Le dilemme du luxe dans les lettres autrichiennes du XVIIIe siècle 151 (1976) 235-47

J. L. Black: Nicholas Karamzin and the dilemma of luxury in eighteenth-century Russia 151 (1976) 313-22

Hans P. Braendlin: The dilemma of luxury and the ironic structures of Lessing's *Emilia Galotti* and Lenz's *The Soldiers* 151 (1976) 353-62

Michael Cartwright: Luxe, goût et l'ivresse de l'objet: un problème moral et esthétique chez Diderot 151 (1976) 405-15

Philip Pinkus: Mandeville's paradox 154 (1976) 1629-35

Richard H. Popkin: Isaac de Pinto's criticism of Mandeville and Hume on luxury 154 (1976) 1705-14

Ellen Ross: Mandeville, Melon, and Voltaire: the origins of the luxury controversy in France 155 (1976) 1897-912

R. G. Saisselin: Architecture in the age of Louis XVI: from private luxury to public power 155 (1976) 1957-70

R. Galliani: Le débat en France sur le luxe: Voltaire ou Rousseau? 161 (1976) 205-17

Michael Cardy: Le 'nécessaire' et le 'superflu': antithèse des Lumières 191 (1980) 749-50

Michael Cardy: Le 'nécessaire' et le 'superflu': antithèse des Lumières 205 (1982) 183-90

R. Galliani: L'idéologie de la noblesse dans le débat sur le luxe (1699-1756) 216 (1983) 173-74

Anthony Strugnell: Diderot on luxury, commerce and the merchant 217 (1983) 83-93

Philippe Bonolas: Fénelon et le luxe dans *Télémaque* 249 (1986) 81-90

Mably, Gabriel Bonnot de

J. L. Lecercle: Utopie et réalisme politique chez Mably 26 (1963) 1049-70

Renato Galliani: Quelques aspects de la fortune de Mably au XXe siècle 88 (1972) 549-65

J. L. Lecercle: Mably et la théorie de la diplomatie 88 (1972) 899-913

R. Galliani: Quelques lettres inédites de Mably 98 (1972) 183-97

J. L. Lecercle: Mably devant la révolution américaine 153 (1976) 1287-1306

Wolfang Asholt: 'L'Effet Mably' et le problème de l'égalité dans le roman dialogué *Des droits et des devoirs du citoyen* 216 (1983) 191-92

Florence Gauthier: De Mably a Robespierre: un programme économique égalitaire 1775-1793 216 (1983) 200-201

S. Baudiffier: La notion d'évidence: Le Mercier de La Rivière, Diderot, Mably 216 (1983) 278-80

Machiavelli, Niccolò

Frederick II: *L'Anti-Machiavel*, éd. Charles Fleischauer 5 (1958)

Maillet, Benoît de

Harriet Dorothy Rothschild: Benoît de Maillet's Leghorn letters 30 (1964) 351-75

Harriet Dorothy Rothschild: Benoît de Maillet's Marseilles letters 37 (1965) 109-45

Harriet Dorothy Rothschild: Benoît de Maillet's letters to the marquis de Caumont 60 (1968) 311-38

Harriet Dorothy Rothschild: Benoît de Maillet's Cairo letters 169 (1977) 115-85

Miguel Benítez: Benoît de Maillet et la littérature clandestine: étude de sa correspondance avec l'abbé Le Mascrier 183 (1980) 133-59

Miguel Benítez: Entre le mythe et la science: Benoît de Maillet et l'origine des êtres dans la mer 216 (1983) 307-309

Maine de Biran, Marie-François-Pierre Gonthier de Biran, *called*

Ronald Grimsley: Maupertuis, Turgot and Maine de Biran on the origin of language 62 (1968) 285-307

Maistre, Joseph de

Richard A. Lebrun: Joseph de Maistre and Rousseau 88 (1972) 881-98

J. Marx: Joseph de Maistre contre Voltaire 89 (1972) 1017-48

Robert H. McDonald: A forgotten Voltairean poem: *Voltaire et le comte de Maistre* by Anne Bignan 102 (1973) 231-64

Michel Fuchs: Edmund Burke vu par Joseph de Maistre 216 (1983) 14-15

Malebranche, Nicolas de

Robert Challe: *Difficultés sur la religion proposées au père Malebranche*. Edition critique d'après un manuscrit inédit par Frédéric Deloffre et Melâhat Menemencioglu 209 (1982)

Malesherbes, Chrétien-Guillaume de Lamoignan de

Emile Lizé: Quand Malesherbes entrait à l'Académie ... 183 (1980) 89-90

Mandeville, Bernard

M. R. de Labriolle-Rutherford: L'évolution de la notion de luxe depuis Mandeville jusqu'à la révolution 26 (1963) 1025-36

H. T. Dickinson: Bernard Mandeville: an independent Whig 152 (1976) 559-70

Bernhard Fabian: The reception of Bernard Mandeville in eighteenth-century Germany 152 (1976) 693-722

Philip Pinkus: Mandeville's paradox 154 (1976) 1629-35

Richard H. Popkin: Isaac de Pinto's criticism of Mandeville and Hume on luxury 154 (1976) 1705-14

Ellen Ross: Mandeville, Melon, and Voltaire: the origins of the luxury controversy in France 155 (1976) 1897-912

Manichean dualism

Haydn T. Mason: Voltaire and Manichean dualism 26 (1963) 1143-60

Marchand, Prosper

J. D. Woodbridge: The Parisian book trade in the early Enlightenment: an update on the Prosper Marchand project 193 (1980) 1763-72

Steve Larkin: *Correspondance entre Prosper Marchand et le marquis d'Argens* 222 (1984)

Maréchal, Sylvain

Irmgard A. Hartig: Réflexions sur la cellule familiale dans l'utopie sociale de Sylvain Maréchal 191 (1980) 685-87

Marivaux, Pierre Carlet de Chamblain de

Harry Redman: Marivaux's reputation among his contemporaries 47 (1966) 137-55

Oscar A. Haac: Paradox and levels of understanding in Marivaux 56 (1967) 693-706

William H. Trapnell: The 'philosophical' implications of Marivaux's *Dispute* 73 (1970) 193-219

Lubbe Levin: Masque et identité dans *Le Paysan parvenu* 79 (1971) 177-92

Ronald C. Rosbottom: Parody and truth in Mme Riccoboni's continuation of *La Vie de Marianne* 81 (1971) 163-75

Lester G. Crocker: Portrait de l'homme dans le *Paysan parvenu* 87 (1972) 253-76

Oscar A. Haac: Theories of literary criticism and Marivaux 88 (1972) 711-34

Emita B. Hill: Sincerity and self-awareness in the *Paysan parvenu* 88 (1972) 735-48

Marmontel, Jean-François

mathematics

Maurice Crosland: The development of chemistry in the eighteenth century 24 (1963) 369-441

John Pappas: L'esprit de finesse contre l'esprit de géométrie: un débat entre Diderot et Alembert 89 (1972) 1229-53

Martin Dyck: Mathematics and literature in the German Enlightenment: Abraham Gotthelf Kästner (1719-1800) 190 (1980) 508-12

Pietro Giustini: Le 'machines arithmétiques' nella cultura illuministica 190 (1980) 518

Maupertuis, Pierre-Louis Moreau de

P. M. Conlon: Two letters of Mme de Graffigny to Maupertuis 2 (1956) 279-83

Harcourt Brown: Maupertuis *philosophe*: Enlightenment and the Berlin academy 24 (1963) 255-69

M. L. Dufrenoy: Maupertuis et le progrès scientifique 25 (1963) 519-87

Ronald Grimsley: Maupertuis, Turgot and Maine de Biran on the origin of language 62 (1968) 285-307

Aram Vartanian: Maupertuis's brother and the man-machine 190 (1980) 490-92

P. Swiggers: Maupertuis sur l'origine du langage 215 (1982) 163-69

François Duchesneau: L'épistémologie de Maupertuis entre Leibniz et Newton 216 (1983) 312-13

David Beeson (ed.): Maupertuis, *Lettre d'un horloger anglois à un astronome de Pékin* 230 (1985) 189-222

David Beeson: Maupertuis at the crossroads: dating the *Réflexions philosophiques* 249 (1986) 241-50

medicine

Jean Starobinski: La nostalgie: théories médicales et expression littéraire 27 (1963) 1505-18

Renée Waldinger: Voltaire and medicine 58 (1967) 1777-806

Paul Hoffmann: L'idée de liberté dans la philosophie médicale de Théophile de Bordeu 88 (1972) 769-87

Hélène Monod-Cassidy: Le mesmérisme: opinions contemporaines 89 (1972) 1077-87

S. Moravia: Philosophie et médecine en France à la fin du XVIIIe siècle 89 (1972) 1089-151

A. Magnan: Un épisode oublié de la lutte des médecins parisiens contre Théodore Tronchin: à propos de deux lettres de Voltaire 94 (1972) 417-29

Katharine Whitman Carson: *Aspects of contemporary society in 'Gil Blas'* 110 (1973)

Anne Lacombe: La lettre sur l'insertion de la petite vérole et les *Lettres philosophiques* 117 (1974) 113-31

Louis S. Greenbaum: Health-care and hospital-building in eighteenth-century France: reform proposals of Du Pont de Nemours and Condorcet 152 (1976) 895-930

Lester S. King: Theory and practice in eighteenth-century medicine 153 (1976) 1201-18

Carmelina Imbroscio: Recherches et réflexions de la médecine française du dix-huitième siècle sur les phénomènes psychosomatiques 190 (1980) 494-501

Paul Hoffmann: La théorie de l'homme dans la *Medicina rationalis systematica* de Friedrich Hoffmann 216 (1983) 314-15

Carmelina Imbroscio: La musique comme thérapie des maladies de nerfs à travers des ouvrages de vulgarisation et des traités médicaux de la seconde moitié du 18e siècle 216 (1983) 317-18

Paola Vecchi: Mort apparente et procédés de 'ressuscitation' dans la littérature médicale du 18e siècle (Bruhier, Louis, Réaumur, Menuret de Chambaud) 216 (1983) 330-32

R. Galliani: Voltaire, Astruc, et la maladie vénérienne 219 (1983) 19-36

Roy Porter: Sex and the singular man: the seminal ideas of James Graham 228 (1984) 3-24

Richard J. Wolfe: The hang-up of Franz Kotzwara and its relationship to sexual quackery in late 18th-century London 228 (1984) 47-66

Meister, Johann Heinrich

J. Th. de Booy: Henri Meister et la première édition de la *Correspondance littéraire* (1812- 1813) 23 (1963) 215-69

Ulla Kölving et Jeanne Carriat: *Inventaire de la 'Correspondance littéraire' de Grimm et Meister* 225-227 (1984)

melancholy

Wolf Wucherpfennig: 'Die unvergnügte Seele': mélancolie et idylle dans le siècle des Lumières 216 (1983) 372-73

melodrama

W. D. Howarth: Tragedy into melodrama: the fortunes of the Calas affair on the stage 174 (1978) 121-50

Melon, Jean-François

Ellen Ross: Mandeville, Melon, and Voltaire: the origins of the luxury controversy in France 155 (1976) 1897-912

Mémoires secrets

Robert S. Tate: *Petit de Bachaumont: his circle and the 'Mémoires secrets'* 65 (1968)

Michèle Mat-Hasquin: L'image de Voltaire dans les *Mémoires secrets* 182 (1979) 319-29

Mendelssohn, Moses

David Dowdey: Secularisation in Moses Mendelssohn's thinking: harmony between the world of Judaism and Enlightenment? 216 (1983) 52-53

mentalities

Ferenc Biró: L'apparition de la mentalité sentimentale dans la vie littéraire de la Hongrie des Lumières 191 (1980) 997-1003

Neal R. Johnson: Almanachs français et les mentalités collectives au dix-huitième siècle 191 (1980) 1023-30

Menuret de Chambaud, Jean-Jacques

Paola Vecchi: Mort apparente et procédés de 'ressuscitation' dans la littérature médicale du 18e siècle (Bruhier, Louis, Réaumur, Menuret de Chambaud) 216 (1983) 330-32

Mercier, Louis Sébastien

H. Temple Patterson: *Poetic genesis: Sébastien Mercier into Victor Hugo* 11 (1960)

Catherine Lafarge: Londres en 1781: une utopie inédite de L. S. Mercier 191 (1980) 693-94

Mercier de La Rivière, Paul-Pierre

S. Baudiffier: La notion d'évidence: Le Mercier de La Rivière, Diderot, Mably 216 (1983) 278-80

Mercure de France

Madeleine Fields: Voltaire et le *Mercure de France* 20 (1962) 175-215

George B. Watts: Charles Joseph Panckoucke, 'l'Atlas de la librairie française' 68 (1969) 67-205

Douglas A. Bonneville: Glanures du *Mercure* 1739-1748: Diderot et Marivaux 98 (1972) 165-68

Angus Martin: The origins of the *Contes moraux*: Marmontel and other authors of short fiction in the *Mercure de France* (1750-1761) 171 (1977) 197-210

Angus Martin: Marmontel's successors: short fiction in the *Mercure de France* (1760-1789) 201 (1982) 221-31

Mercure galant

François Moureau: Le '*Mercure galant*' *de Dufresny 1710-1714* 206 (1982)

Mercure suisse

Claire-Eliane Engel: L'abbé Prévost collaborateur d'une revue neuchâteloise 2 (1956) 225-32

Mérimée, Prosper

Arnold Ages: Merimée and the *philosophes* 161 (1976) 245-52

Meslier, Jean

Jean Deprun: Jean Meslier et l'héritage cartésien 24 (1963) 443-55

Mesmer, Anton

Hélène Monod-Cassidy: Le mesmérisme: opinions contemporaines 89 (1972) 1077-87

Messerschmidt, Franz Xaver

Gerhard Charles Rump: The so-called 'Charakterköpfe' (characteristic heads) of Franz Xaver Messerschmidt (1736-1783) 216 (1983) 143-45

metaphysics

Otis Fellows: Metaphysics and the *Bijoux indiscrets*: Diderot's debt to Prior 56 (1967) 509-40

Paul Hoffmann: La controverse entre Leibniz et Stahl sur la nature de l'âme 190 (1980) 492-94

Linda Gardiner Janik: Searching for the metaphysics of science: the structure and composition of Mme Du Châtelet's *Institutions de physique*, 1737-1740 201 (1982) 85-113

Metastasio, Pietro

Elena Sala di Felice: Vertu et bonheur à la cour de Vienne: les livrets d'Apostolo Zeno et Pietro Metastasio 216 (1983) 361-63

methodology

Maurice Crosland: 'Nature' and measurement in eighteenth-century France 87 (1972) 277-309

J. I. Biró: Description and explanation in Hume's science of man 190 (1980) 449-57

Maria Teresa Marcialis: Pirronismo e perfettibilità della scienza nell'*Histoire de l'Académie royale des sciences* (1676-1776) 190 (1980) 472-80

Gianni Nicoletti: Méthodologies pour Sade 192 (1980) 1403-1409

Hernâni A. Resende: Sur l'étude des prémisses théoriques de la pensée dialectique au sein des doctrines sociales en France au siècle des Lumières: remarques de méthode 216 (1983) 69-70

Mexico

Giovanni Marchetti: Cultura e nazione in Clavijero 190 (1980) 402-11

Mey, Mathieu

Alexander A. Sokalski: Le poète Mey et son double 212 (1982) 163-81

Middle ages

François Pupil: Aux sources du néo-gothique français: la représentation du moyen âge au dix-huitième siècle 216 (1983) 139-41

militarism

Jean Daniel Candaux: Charles Borde et la première crise d'antimilitarisme de l'opinion publique européenne 24 (1963) 315-44

Hubert C. Johnson: The *philosophes* as militarists 216 (1983) 387-88

Milton, John

Olivier Lutaud: D'*Areopagitica* à la *Lettre à un premier commis* et de l'*Agreement* au *Contrat social* 26 (1963) 1109-27

Yvonne Noble: *Clarissa*: paradise irredeemably lost 154 (1976) 1529-45

mimesis

Thomas M. Kavanagh: *The Vacant mirror: a study of mimesis through Diderot's 'Jacques le fataliste'* 104 (1973)

Minet, Jean-Baptiste

Sylvie Chevalley: Le 'sieur Minet' 62 (1968) 273-83

minor writers

Werner Krauss: L'étude des écrivains obscurs du siècle des Lumières 26 (1963) 1019-24

Mirabeau, Honoré-Gabriel Riqueti, comte de

Jochen Schlobach: Les physiocrates et une tentative de réalisation de leur doctrine en Allemagne (d'après les correspondances de Mirabeau et de Du Pont de Nemours avec le margrave de Bade) 216 (1983) 293-96

missionaries

Michael Cartwright: A curious attraction: missionary zeal and tribal androgyny in Jesuit and American Indian relations during the Enlightenment 216 (1983) 100-102

Robert Toupin: Pierre Potier, jésuite belge chez les Hurons du Détroit (1744-1781): les chemins d'un espace nouveau à explorer 216 (1983) 122-24

Missy, César de

J. Patrick Lee: Voltaire and César de Missy 163 (1976) 57-72

modernisation

Arthur M. Wilson: The *philosophes* in the light of present-day theories of modernisation 58 (1967) 1893-913

Harriet Branson Applewhite and Darline Gay Levy: The concept of modernisation and the French Enlightenment 84 (1971) 53-98

Helen Liebel-Weckowicz: The physiocrat tax reform of Joseph II: the challenge of modernisation in the Habsburg empire, 1780-1790 216 (1983) 287-89

Molière

Samuel S. B. Taylor: Le développement du genre comique en France de Molière à Beaumarchais 90 (1972) 1545-66

A. C. Keys: An eighteenth-century editor of Molière: Antoine Bret 98 (1972) 219-30

Monique Wagner: *Molière and the age of Enlightenment* 112 (1973)

monarchy

Theodore Besterman: Voltaire, absolute monarchy, and the enlightened monarch 32 (1965) 7-21

M. G. Carroll: Sénac de Meilhan's *Les Deux cousins*: a monarchist paradox at the end of the *ancien régime* 171 (1977) 211-21

Valerie A. Tumins: Catherine II, Frederick II and Gustav III: three enlightened monarchs and their impact on literature 190 (1980) 350-56

Monbron, Fougeret de

J. H. Broome: 'L'homme au cœur velu': the turbulent career of Fougeret de Monbron 23 (1963) 179-213

Sheila Mason: An essentialist inheritance: from Hooker to Montesquieu 242 (1986) 83-124

— politics

D. J. Fletcher: Montesquieu's conception of patriotism 56 (1967) 541-55

— works: *Considérations*

Georges Benrekassa: Théorie et mise en œuvre du concept de cause dans les *Considérations* de Montesquieu 191 (1980) 539

— — *L'Esprit des lois*

R. Galliani (ed.): Quelques notes inédites de Voltaire à l'*Esprit des lois* 163 (1976) 7-18

George Klosko: Montesquieu's science of politics: absolute values and ethical relativism in *L'Esprit des lois* 189 (1980) 153-77

Alberto Postigliola: Dal *monde* alla *nature*: gli scritti scientifici di Montesquieu e la genesi epistemologica dell'*Esprit des lois* 190 (1980) 480-90

— — *Lettres persanes*

Pauline Kra: The invisible chain of the *Lettres persanes* 23 (1963) 7-60

Patrick Brady: The *Lettres persanes*: rococo or neo-classical? 53 (1967) 47-77

J. L. Carr: The secret chain of the *Lettres persanes* 55 (1967) 333-44

Robert F. O'Reilly: The structure and meaning of the *Lettres persanes* 67 (1969) 91-131

Pauline Kra: *Religion in Montesquieu's 'Lettres persanes'* 72 (1970)

Michel Gaulin: Montesquieu et l'attribution de la lettre XXXIV des *Lettres persanes* 79 (1971) 73-78

David L. Anderson: Abélard and Héloïse: eighteenth-century motif 84 (1971) 7-51

Agnes G. Raymond: Encore quelques réflexions sur la 'chaîne secrète' des *Lettres persanes* 89 (1972) 1337-47

Mary M. Crumpacker: The secret chain of the *Lettres persanes*, and the mystery of the B edition 102 (1973) 121-41

A. Gunny: Montesquieu's view of Islam in the *Lettres persanes* 174 (1978) 151-66

Pauline Kra: The role of the harem in imitations of Montesquieu's *Lettres persanes* 182 (1979) 273-83

Alan J. Singerman: Réflexions sur une métaphore: le sérail dans les *Lettres persanes* 185 (1980) 181-98

Susan C. Strong: Why a *secret* chain?: oriental *topoi* and the essential mystery of the *Lettres persanes* 230 (1985) 167-79

C. J. Betts: Some doubtful passages in the text of Montesquieu's *Lettres persanes* 230 (1985) 181-88

with Classical, Christian and Enlightenment moralities 191 (1980) 1031-33

Marialuisa Lussu: Critica della religione e autonomia della morale in alcune figure dell'Illuminismo francese 192 (1980) 1085-93

Martin Staum: The Class of moral and political sciences, 1795-1803 192 (1980) 1183-89

Monique Moser-Verrey: Le drame bourgeois ou l'édification du public 192 (1980) 1534-35

Emmet Kennedy: The French revolutionary catechisms: ruptures and continuities with Classical, Christian, and Enlightenment moralities 199 (1981) 353-62

Andrzej Siemek: *La Recherche morale et esthétique dans le roman de Crébillon fils* 200 (1981)

Johann Werner Schmidt: Diderot and Lucretius: the *De rerum natura* and Lucretius's legacy in Diderot's scientific, aesthetic, and ethical thought 208 (1982) 183-294

Simon Davies: *Paris and the provinces in prose fiction* 214 (1982)

Henri Mydlarski: La sécularisation de la pensée chez les moralistes de dix-huitième siècle 216 (1983) 65-66

Takaho Ando: Mme de Condorcet et la philosophie de la 'sympathie' 216 (1983) 335-36

Jean H. Bloch: Knowledge as a source of virtue: changes and contrasts in ideas concerning the education of boys and girls in eighteenth-century France 216 (1983) 337-38

Nadia Boccara Postigliola: 'Passions égoïstes' et 'passions altruistes' chez David Hume (*avarice, ambition, bienveillance*) 216 (1983) 338-40

Valentini Brady: *La Religieuse* de Diderot: métaphorisation spatiale d'une situation morale 216 (1983) 340

Jean Dagen: Formes de l'irresponsabilité dans l'œuvre de Diderot 216 (1983) 340-43

James H. Davis: Morality, virtue, and children's theatre in eighteenth-century France 216 (1983) 343-44

Willem Elias: La 'vertu' dans l'œuvre de Adriaan Beverland 216 (1983) 347-48

Alberto Gil Novales: Vertu et morale: Saint-Evremond en Espagne: Jaime Sicre 216 (1983) 349-50

Anne-Marie Jaton: Morale et vertu: histoire parallèle du costume et de la cosmétique 216 (1983) 351-52

J. Robert Loy: Saint-Lambert, moralist: philosophy at second hand; Enlightenment among the titled 216 (1983) 353-54

Milena Montanile: Morale et vertu dans la tragédie jacobine en Italie (1796-1799) 216 (1983) 356-57

R. Niklaus: L'idée de vertu chez Beaumarchais et la morale implicite dans ses pièces de théâtre 216 (1983) 358-59

Yvonne Noble: 'Virgins are like The Fair Flower in its Lustre': the fortunes of one text in the Augustan age 216 (1983) 359

Morangiés, Jean François Charles, comte de

Morellet, André

Morelly

Aldo Maffey: Morelly-Diderot: un'amicizia nascosta 191 (1980) 701-706

N. Wagner: Utopie et littérature: la *Basiliade* de Morelly 191 (1980) 731-32

Moréri, Louis

Arnold Miller: Louis Moréri's *Grand dictionnaire historique* 194 (1981) 13-52

Moritz, Karl Philipp

Erdmann Waniek: Rousseau's *Confessions* and Moritz's *Anton Reiser*: narrative strategies for presenting the self 192 (1980) 1307-13

Möser, Justus

Virgil Nemoianu: Textual and political recentralisation in Möser and Rivarol 216 (1983) 23-25

motifs

John Van Eerde: The people in eighteenth-century tragedy from *Œdipe* to *Guillaume Tell* 27 (1963) 1703-13

David L. Anderson: Abélard and Héloïse: eighteenth-century motif 84 (1971) 7-51

Claire McGlinchee: 'The smile of reason': its metamorphosis in late 18th-century architecture and literature 89 (1972) 993-1001

Jeroom Vercruysse: Jeanne d'Arc au siècle des Lumières 90 (1972) 1659-729

David L. Anderson: Aspects of motif in *La Nouvelle Héloïse* 94 (1972) 25-72

Adrian P. L. Kempton: The theme of childhood in French eighteenth-century memoir novels 132 (1975) 205-25

Bernard Bray: Héloïse et Abélard au XVIIIe siècle en France: une imagerie épistolaire 151 (1976) 385-404

Beatrice C. Fink: The banquet as phenomenon or structure in selected eighteenth-century French novels 152 (1976) 729-40

Vera Lee: Innocence and initiation in the eighteenth-century French novel 153 (1976) 1307-12

Raymonde Robert: Le comte de Caylus et l'orient: la littérature aux prises avec le même et l'autre 154 (1976) 1825-53

Pauline Kra: The role of the harem in imitations of Montesquieu's *Lettres persanes* 182 (1979) 273-83

Edward A. Bloom: Eden betray'd: city motifs in satire 191 (1980) 956-62

Carminella Biondi: L'image du noir dans la littérature française du dix-huitième siècle 192 (1980) 1175-81

Timothy M. Scanlan: Patterns of imagery in Rousseau's *Emile* 192 (1980) 1381-87

Moyle, Walter

Mozart, Wolfgang Amadeus

music

— exotic

music

— instruments

Sylvette Milliot: Influence des progrès de la lutherie sur la technique des violonistes et violoncellistes au XVIIIe siècle 193 (1980) 1717-18

Sylvette Milliot: L'évolution du violon et du violoncelle au dix-huitième siècle 219 (1983) 211-24

— opera

Marquis d'Argenson: *Notices sur les œuvres de théâtre*, éd. H. Lagrave 42-43 (1966)

Karl Geiringer: Concepts of the Enlightenment as reflected in Gluck's Italian reform opera 88 (1972) 567-76

Richard Switzer: Voltaire, Rousseau et l'opéra 90 (1972) 1519-28

Spire Pitou: Rameau's *Dardanus* at Fontainebleau in 1763 116 (1973) 281-305

Spire Pitou: The *opéra-ballet* and *Scanderberg* at Fontainebleau in 1763 129 (1975) 27-66

R. S. Ridgway: Voltaire's operas 189 (1980) 119-51

Robert M. Cammarrota: *Così fan tutte*: Mozart's rhetoric of love and reason 193 (1980) 1719-20

Donald C. Spinelli: Beaumarchais's opera *Tarare* 193 (1980) 1721

James M. Kaplan: *Marmontel et 'Polymnie'* 229 (1984)

R. S. Ridgway: Voltairian bel canto: operatic adaptations of Voltaire's tragedies 241 (1986) 125-54

Donald Schier: Prima le parole? Chastellux on the aesthetics of opera 245 (1986) 351-57

— technique

Sylvette Milliot: Influence des progrès de la lutherie sur la technique des violonistes et violoncellistes au XVIIIe siècle 193 (1980) 1717-18

— theory

Karl Geiringer: Joseph Haydn, protagonist of the Enlightenment 25 (1963) 683-90

Karl Geiringer: The impact of the Enlightenment on the artistic concepts of Johann Sebastian Bach 56 (1967) 601-10

Enrico Fubini: Razionalismo e irrazionalismo nelle concezioni musicali del tardo Illuminismo 193 (1980) 1710-16

Marie-Elisabeth Duchez: Valeur épistémologique de la théorie de la basse fondamental de Jean-Philippe Rameau: connaissance scientifique et représentation de la musique 245 (1986) 91-130

— therapy

Carmelina Imbroscio: La musique comme thérapie des maladies de nerfs à travers des ouvrages de vulgarisation et des traités médicaux de la seconde moitié du 18e siècle 216 (1983) 317-18

mysticism

E. R. Briggs: Mysticism and rationalism in the debate upon eternal punishment 24 (1963) 241-54

Valerie A. Tumins: Enlightenment and mysticism in eighteenth-century Russia 58 (1967) 1671-88

Lawrence J. Forno: The cosmic mysticism of Diderot 143 (1975) 113-40

Nadia Minerva: Des Lumières à l'Illuminisme: Cazotte et son monde 191 (1980) 1015-22

mythology

J. Deshayes: De l'abbé Pluche au citoyen Dupuis: à la recherche de la clef des fables 24 (1963) 457-86

René Etiemble: Le mythe taoïste au XVIIIe siècle 25 (1963) 589-602

Lester G. Crocker: When myths die 151 (1976) 19-29

James King and Bernadette Lynn: The *Metamorphoses* in English eighteenth-century mythological handbooks and translations 185 (1980) 131-79

David L. Anderson: Structures mythologiques et religieuses dans le roman épistolaire du XVIIIe siècle 192 (1980) 1273-75

Stella Gargantini Rabbi: Le mythe d'Electre dans le théâtre français du XVIIIe siècle 192 (1980) 1547-55

Pamela Schwandt: Pope's tranformation of Homer's gods 193 (1980) 1586-87

Barbara Bianco Wojciechowska: Le mythe de Narcisse au XVIIIe siècle – instrument d'analyse du rapport avec autrui 193 (1980) 1621

Michèle Mat-Hasquin: *Voltaire et l'antiquité grecque* 197 (1981)

K. K. Simonsuuri: Thomas Blackwell and the study of classical mythology 216 (1983) 117-18

Miguel Benítez: Entre le mythe et la science: Benoît de Maillet et l'origine des êtres dans la mer 216 (1983) 307-309

Narcissus

Barbara Bianco Wojciechowska: Le mythe de Narcisse au XVIIIe siècle – instrument d'analyse du rapport avec autrui 193 (1980) 1621

nationalism

Merle L. Perkins: Rousseau on history, liberty and national survival 53 (1967) 79-169

Werner Bahner: Le Mot et la notion de 'peuple' dans l'œuvre de Rousseau 55 (1967) 113-27

Alexandru Dutu: National and European consciousness in the Romanian Enlightenment 55 (1967) 463-79

James A. Leith: Nationalism and the fine arts in France, 1750-1789 89 (1972) 919-37

Louis Trenard: Patriotisme et nationalisme dans les Pays-Bas français au XVIIIe siècle 90 (1972) 1625-57

Marita Gilli: Littérature, histoire et problème national à la fin des Lumières en Allemagne 191 (1980) 564-71

Seymour Howard: Blake, classicism, gothicism, and nationalism 216 (1983) 132

Roxane Argyropoulos: Patriotisme et sentiment national en Grèce au temps des Lumières 216 (1983) 377

F. M. Barnard: National culture and political legitimacy: Herder and Rousseau 216 (1983) 379-81

Giulia Cantarutti: Patriotisme et sentiment national dans les *Betrachtungen und Gedanken* (1803-1805) de F. M. Klinger, un représentant des Lumières allemandes à la cour russe 216 (1983) 383-85

Simon Davies: The idea of nationalism in late eighteenth-century Ireland: the case of Belfast 216 (1983) 385-86

Jože Koruza: L'éveil de la conscience nationale et les idées du siècle des Lumières dans la littérature slovène de la deuxième moitié du dix-huitième siècle 216 (1983) 390-92

N. Liu: Les Lumières et l'orientation nationale de la culture Roumaine 216 (1983) 392-94

Raymond Mas: Recherches sur les Gaulois et sentiment national en France au dix-huitième siècle (1700-1789) 216 (1983) 398-400

Mona Scheuermann: The ethos of productivity: citizenship and national feeling in the eighteenth-century English novel 216 (1983) 405-406

Dominique Triaire: Jean Potocki et l'indépendance nationale pendant la Grande Diète polonaise (1788-1792) 216 (1983) 408-409

Georg Wacha: Nationale Eigenheiten der europäischen Völker: die Einschätzung der anderen in Berichten, Spott und Schimpfnamen 216 (1983) 409-12

Merle L. Perkins: Montesquieu on national power and international rivalry 238 (1985) 1-95

natural disasters

Bruna Ombretta Ranzani: Représentation, étiologie et prophylaxie des catastrophes naturelles au dix-huitième siècle 191 (1980) 1033-40

natural history

Maurice Crosland: The development of chemistry in the eighteenth century 24 (1963) 369-441

Otis Fellows: Buffon's place in the Enlightenment 25 (1963) 603-29

Elizabeth Anderson: La collaboration de Sonnini de Manoncourt à l'*Histoire naturelle* de Buffon 120 (1974) 329-58

naturalism

natural law

nature

neologism

Nerciat, Andréa de

Newton, Isaac

New World

Edouard Guitton: L'architecture d'un nouveau monde dans *Les Mois* de Roucher 153 (1976) 937-49

Edna Lemay: Histoire de l'antiquité et découverte du nouveau monde chez deux auteurs du XVIIIe siècle 153 (1976) 1313-28

Mathé Allain: The coloniser's viewpoint: Louisiana Indians as seen by the French 216 (1983) 87-88

Townsend W. Bowling: European man encounters the New World native in the French novel 1751-1800 216 (1983) 95-97

C. P. Hanlon: Some observations on French contacts with aboriginal society (1801-1803) 216 (1983) 109-10

Nietzsche, Friedrich

Lester G. Crocker: Hidden affinities: Nietzsche and Rousseau 190 (1980) 119-41

Nieuwentydt, Bernard

J. Vercruysse: La fortune de Bernard Nieuwentydt en France au XVIIIe siècle et les notes marginales de Voltaire 30 (1964) 223-46

nobility

A. J. Sambrook: The English lord and the happy husbandman 57 (1967) 1357-75

Katharine Whitman Carson: *Aspects of contemporary society in 'Gil Blas'* 110 (1973)

Robin Price: Boulainviller and the myth of the Frankish conquest of Gaul 199 (1981) 155-85

P. J. Buijnsters: The tutor/governess between nobility and bourgeoisie: some considerations with reference to an essay of 1734 by Justus van Effen 216 (1983) 164-66

Maurice Colin: Peut-on parler d'une idéologie nobiliaire en Russie? 216 (1983) 166-68

B. Demoulin: La réaction de la noblesse et la défense de ses privilèges dans la principauté de Liège au début du dix-huitième siècle 216 (1983) 170-71

Luc Dhondt: La réaction nobiliaire et la révolution des notables de 1787-1789 en Flandre 216 (1983) 172-73

R. Galliani: L'idéologie de la noblesse dans le débat sur le luxe (1699-1756) 216 (1983) 173-74

Jean Garagnon: La sensibilité comme idéologie de substitution de la noblesse dans *Aline et Valcour* 216 (1983) 174-77

G. Gerhardi: L'idéologie du sang chez Boulainvilliers et sa réception au dix-huitième siècle 216 (1983) 177-79

Léa et Arié Gilon: La thalimanie 216 (1983) 179-80

Vivian R. Gruder: From consensus to conflict: the élite, equality and representation, 1787-1788 216 (1983) 180-82

Paul Janssens: L'influence sur le continent du modèle aristocratique britannique au dix-huitième siecle 216 (1983) 183-84

Joachim Schmitt-Sasse: J. M. v. Loen and A. Freiherr Knigge: bourgeois ideals in the writings of German aristocrats 216 (1983) 187-88

J. Robert Loy: Saint-Lambert, moralist: philosophy at second hand; Enlightenment among the titled 216 (1983) 353-54

Margaret Östman: Caractère et position sociale des personnages de quelques romans français, 1699-1742 216 (1983) 359-61

Robert E. Jones: Patriotism and the opposition to war and expansion among the Russian nobility during the second half of the eighteenth century 216 (1983) 388-90

Nodier, Charles

Raymond Setbon: Voltaire jugé par Charles Nodier 137 (1975) 55-71

nostalgia

Jean Starobinski: La nostalgie: théories médicales et expression littéraire 27 (1963) 1505-18

Nouvelles ecclésiastiques

John Pappas: Buffon vu par Berthier, Feller et les *Nouvelles ecclésiastiques* 216 (1983) 26-28

novel

Lawrence J. Forno: The fictional letter in the memoir novel: Robert Challe's *Illustres Françoises* 81 (1971) 149-61

Ahmad Gunny: Voltaire and the novel: Sterne 124 (1974) 149-61

David Williams: Voltaire on the sentimental novel 135 (1975) 115-34

Ahmad Gunny: Voltaire's thoughts on prose fiction 140 (1975) 7-20

J. Robert Loy: Rococo and the novel as guide to periodisation in the eighteenth century 190 (1980) 166-76

Wulf Koepke: The epistolary novel: from self-assertion to alienation 192 (1980) 1275-84

John Neubauer: Narrative uses of time in the eighteenth-century novel 192 (1980) 1284-86

Frederick M. Keener: The philosophical tale, the novel, and *Gulliver's travels* 192 (1980) 1315-17

Vivienne Mylne: Chapters as a structural device in the *conte* and the novel 192 (1980) 1332-33

Marie-Laure Girou-Swiderski: Fonctions de la femme du peuple dans le roman du XVIIIe siècle 193 (1980) 1925

Mildred Greene: 'A chimera of her own creating': love and fantasy in novels from madame de Lafayette to Jane Austen 193 (1980) 1940-42

Elizabeth Fox-Genovese: Female identity: symbol and structure of bourgeois domesticity 193 (1980) 2016

Lois A. Chaber: 'This intricate labyrinth': order and contingency in eighteenth-century fictions 212 (1982) 183-212

Henri Coulet: Le roman anti-révolutionnaire en France à l'époque de la Révolution (1789-1800) 216 (1983) 7-9

Michael Ritterson: Humane ironies: the enlightenment novel and nineteenth-century realism in Germany 216 (1983) 434-35

— criticism

Marie-Rose de Labriolle: *'Le Pour et contre' et son temps* 34-35 (1965)

— England

Mona Scheuermann: Social protest in the eighteenth-century English novel 191 (1980) 962-65

Denis Douglas: Inchworm's antecedents: caricatures of the Enlightenment in the English novel of the eighteenth century 216 (1983) 11-12

P. Hunter: Print culture and the developing audience in England: fiction 216 (1983) 266-67

Mona Scheuermann: The ethos of productivity: citizenship and national feeling in the eighteenth-century English novel 216 (1983) 405-406

— epistolary

Georges May: La littérature épistolaire date-t-elle du XVIIIe siècle? 56 (1967) 823-44

Arnold Ages: The private Voltaire: three studies in the correspondence 81 (1971) 7-125

Réal Ouellet: La théorie du roman épistolaire en France au XVIIIe siècle 89 (1972) 1209-27

Emile Lizé: *La Religieuse*, un roman épistolaire? 98 (1972) 143-63

Bernard Bray: Héloïse et Abélard au XVIIIe siècle en France: une imagerie épistolaire 151 (1976) 385-404

David L. Anderson: Structures mythologiques et religieuses dans le roman épistolaire du XVIIIe siècle 192 (1980) 1273-75

Wulf Koepke: The epistolary novel: from self-assertion to alienation 192 (1980) 1275-84

— France

A. Kibédi Varga: La désagrégation de l'idéal classique dans le roman français de la première moitié du XVIIIe siècle 26 (1963) 965-98

Barry Ivker: Towards a definition of libertinism in 18th-century French fiction 73 (1970) 221-39

Jeanne R. Monty: *Les Romans de l'abbé Prévost: procédés littéraires et pensée morale* 78 (1970)

Richard L. Frautschi: Some eighteenth-century French stances of silence 79 (1971) 219-34

Richard L. Frautschi: Style de roman et style de censure dans la seconde moitié du dix-huitième siècle français 88 (1972) 513-47

Raymond Joly: Entre *Le Père de famille* et *Le Neveu de Rameau*: conscience morale et réalisme romanesque dans *La Religieuse* 88 (1972) 845-57

Réal Ouellet: La théorie du roman épistolaire en France au XVIIIe siècle 89 (1972) 1209-27

Marie Laure Swiderski: L'image de la femme dans le roman au début du XVIIIe siècle: les *Illustres Françaises* de Robert Challe 90 (1972) 1505-18

Emile Lizé: *La Religieuse*, un roman épistolaire? 98 (1972) 143-63

Peter V. Conroy: *Crébillon fils: techniques of the novel* 99 (1972)

R. P. Thomas: *Jacques le fataliste*, *Les Liaisons dangereuses*, and the autonomy of the novel 117 (1974) 239-49

Anne Lacombe: Du théâtre au roman: Sade 129 (1975) 115-43

Adrian P. L. Kempton: The theme of childhood in French eighteenth-century memoir novels 132 (1975) 205-25

E. Thompsett: Love and libertinism in the novels of Duclos 137 (1975) 109-19

Manfred Kusch: *Manon Lescaut*, or voyage du chevalier Des Grieux dans la basse Romancie 143 (1975) 141-60

Beatrice C. Fink: The banquet as phenomenon or structure in selected eighteenth-century French novels 152 (1976) 729-40

Richard L. Frautschi: Quelques paramètres de la production romanesque de 1751 à 1800 152 (1976) 741-52

Vera Lee: Innocence and initiation in the eighteenth-century French novel 153 (1976) 1307-12

Douglas A. Bonneville: *Voltaire and the form of the novel* 158 (1976)

Huguette Cohen: *La Figure dialogique dans 'Jacques le fataliste'* 162 (1976)

Lloyd R. Free: Point of view and narrative space in Vivant Denon's *Point de lendemain* 163 (1976) 89-115

James P. Gilroy: Peace and the pursuit of happiness in the French utopian novel: Fénelon's *Télémaque* and Prévost's *Cleveland* 176 (1979) 169-87

Jean Ehrard: De Meilcour à Adolphe, ou la suite des *Egarements* 190 (1980) 101-17

Sarah Simmons: Héroïne ou figurante? La femme dans le roman du XVIIIe siècle en France 193 (1980) 1918-24

occultism

O'Conor, Charles

opera

optimism

Oratorians

Anne Boës: *La Lanterne magique de l'histoire: essai sur le théâtre historique en France de 1750 à 1789* 213 (1982)

order

Charles Jacques Beyer: Montesquieu et la philosophie de l'ordre 87 (1972) 145-66

Orient

Francis J. Carmody: Voltaire et la renaissance indo-iranienne 24 (1963) 345-54

René Etiemble: Le mythe taoïste au XVIIIe siècle 25 (1963) 589-602

Arthur J. Weitzmann: The oriental tale in the eighteenth century: a reconsideration 58 (1967) 1839-55

Raymonde Robert: Le comte de Caylus et l'orient: la littérature aux prises avec le même et l'autre 154 (1976) 1825-53

Temple Maynard: Utopia and dystopia in the oriental genre in England in the eighteenth century 191 (1980) 706-11

Malcolm C. Cook: Politics in the fiction of the French Revolution, 1789-1794 201 (1982) 233-340

Christophe Balaÿ: François Pétis de La Croix et les *Mille et un jours* 215 (1982) 9-43

J. Chupeau: Le voyageur philosophe ou Robert Challe au miroir du *Journal d'un voyage aux Indes* 215 (1982) 45-61

Barbara Widenor Maggs: *Russia and 'le rêve chinois': China in eighteenth-century Russian literature* 224 (1984)

Susan C. Strong: Why a *secret* chain?: oriental *topoi* and the essential mystery of the *Lettres persanes* 230 (1985) 167-79

David Beeson (ed.): Maupertuis, *Lettre d'un horloger anglois à un astronome de Pékin* 230 (1985) 189-222

Claudine Hunting: Les mille et une sources du *Diable amoureux* de Cazotte 230 (1985) 247-71

Ottoboni, Pietro

Edward J. Olszewski: A repudiation of baroque extravagance: cardinal Pietro Ottoboni's project for the tomb of Alexander VIII in St Peter's 216 (1983) 138-39

Ovid

James King and Bernadette Lynn: The *Metamorphoses* in English eighteenth-century mythological handbooks and translations 185 (1980) 131-79

Pacific

Alan Frost: The Pacific Ocean: the eighteenth century's 'new world' 152 (1976) 779-822

Paolo Casini: Tahiti, Diderot e l'utopia 191 (1980) 653-60

Urs Bitterli: Visiteurs du pacifique en Europe au siècle des Lumières 216 (1983) 93-95

pacifism

Jean Daniel Candaux: Charles Borde et la première crise d'antimilitarisme de l'opinion publique européenne 24 (1963) 315-44

Robert E. Jones: Patriotism and the opposition to war and expansion among the Russian nobility during the second half of the eighteenth century 216 (1983) 388-90

Paine, Thomas

A. Owen Aldridge: Thomas Paine and the *idéologues* 151 (1976) 109-17

painting

Warren Ramsey: Voltaire et 'l'art de peindre' 26 (1963) 1365-77

Marianne Roland Michel: Représentations de l'exotisme dans la peinture en France dans la première moitié du XVIIIe siècle 154 (1976) 1437-57

Leslie Carr: Painting and the paradox of the spectator in Diderot's art criticism 193 (1980) 1690-98

Thomas R. Cleary: Illusion in late baroque painting and complex perspective in Enlightenment satire 216 (1983) 131

Edward J. Sullivan: The revival of classical themes in painting and the academic style at the Court of Madrid in the 18th century 216 (1983) 155-57

Rémy G. Saisselin: Painting, writing and primitive purity: from expression to sign in eighteenth-century French painting and architecture 217 (1983) 257-369

Palissot de Montenoy, Charles

Colin Duckworth: Voltaire's *L'Ecossaise* and Palissot's *Les Philosophes*: a strategic battle in a major war 87 (1972) 333-51

Panard, Charles-François

Stefania Spada: Osservazioni su due commedie inedite di Charles-François Panard 192 (1980) 1486-96

Panckoucke, Charles-Joseph

George B. Watts: Charles Joseph Panckoucke, 'l'Atlas de la librairie française' 68 (1969) 67-205

Parfaict, frères

Philip Koch: L'*Histoire de l'ancien Théâtre-Italien*: la part des frères Parfaict 192 (1980) 1460-63

Philip Koch: L'*Histoire de l'Ancien Théâtre-Italien*: la part des frères Parfaict 199 (1981) 25-46

Parini, Giuseppe

Pierre Van Bever: Néo-classicisme et Lumières: Parini 216 (1983) 157-58

Paris

Simon Davies: *Paris and the provinces in prose fiction* 214 (1982)

parliaments

Robert S. Tate: Voltaire and the *parlements*: a reconsideration 90 (1972) 1529-43

Paolo Alatri: Parlements et lutte politique en France au XVIIIe siècle 151 (1976) 77-108

Martha Fletcher, Nadine Labbé, A. de Laforcade et Christian Desplat: Le rétablissement des anciens parlements (1774-1775) vu de la correspondance inédite de Théophile de Bordeu 174 (1978) 203-67

William Doyle: Dupaty (1746-1788): a career in the late Enlightenment 230 (1985) 1-125

Parnell, Thomas

Richard Waller: Voltaire, Parnell and the hermit 191 (1980) 994-96

parody

Ronald C. Rosbottom: Parody and truth in Mme Riccoboni's continuation of *La Vie de Marianne* 81 (1971) 163-75

Jürgen von Stackelberg: La parodie dramatique au XVIIIe siècle: formes et fonctions 192 (1980) 1519-26

Pascal, Blaise

Richard A. Brooks: Condorcet and Pascal 55 (1967) 297-307

Harcourt Brown: Pascal *philosophe* 55 (1967) 309-20

Rémy G. Saisselin: The transformation of art into culture: from Pascal to Diderot 70 (1970) 193-218

M. Alcover: La casuistique du père Tout à tous et *Les Provinciales* 81 (1971) 127-32

Mara Vamos: Pascal's *Pensées* and the Enlightenment: the roots of a misunderstanding 97 (1972) 7-145

Dorothy R. Thelander: The oak and the thinking reed 102 (1973) 53-63

Jerolyn Scull: Voltaire's reading of Pascal: his quotations compared to early texts 161 (1976) 19-41

Ralph Arthur Nablow: Addison's indebtedness to Pascal in *Spectator* no.420 217 (1983) 183-85

Marie Souviron: Les *Pensées philosophiques* de Diderot ou les 'Provinciales' de l'athéisme 238 (1985) 197-267

pastoral

Christie Vance McDonald: *The Extravagant shepherd: a study of the pastoral vision in Rousseau's 'Nouvelle Héloïse'* 105 (1973)

J. M. Blanchard: Style pastoral, style des Lumières 114 (1973) 331-46

Pastoret, Claude-Emmanuel-Joseph-Pierre, marquis de

O. H. Bonnerot: L'Islam devant les Lumières: le marquis de Pastoret 192 (1980) 1142-43

patriotism

D. J. Fletcher: Montesquieu's conception of patriotism 56 (1967) 541-55

Louis Trenard: Patriotisme et nationalisme dans les Pays-Bas français au XVIIIe siècle 90 (1972) 1625-57

Andrew Hunwick: Le patriotisme de Voltaire 116 (1973) 7-18

John Renwick: Chamfort, patriote en coulisses: réflexions sur une lettre inédite à Roland 183 (1980) 165-76

Roxane Argyropoulos: Patriotisme et sentiment national en Grèce au temps des Lumières 216 (1983) 377

Giulia Cantarutti: Patriotisme et sentiment national dans les *Betrachtungen und Gedanken* (1803-1805) de F. M. Klinger, un représentant des Lumières allemandes à la cour russe 216 (1983) 383-85

Robert E. Jones: Patriotism and the opposition to war and expansion among the Russian nobility during the second half of the eighteenth century 216 (1983) 388-90

Henry Lowood: Patriotism and progress: the role of the German patriotic and economic societies in the promotion of science and technology 216 (1983) 394-96

Mona Scheuermann: The ethos of productivity: citizenship and national feeling in the eighteenth-century English novel 216 (1983) 405-406

Joyce Seltzer: The French citizen's catechism: a *philosophe*'s moral vision in 1793 216 (1983) 406-407

Robert and Catherine Ward: Charles O'Conor: historian, reformer, patriot 216 (1983) 412-13

perfectibility

periodisation

Pernety, Antoine-Joseph

pessimism

Peter the Great

Pétis de La Croix, François

Petty, William

Paola Bora: Sir William Petty: macchina e organismo alle origini dell'economia politica 191 (1980) 804-11

philosophy

Theodore Besterman: Review: Lester G. Crocker, *An age of crisis* 12 (1960) 116-19

Wolfgang Bernard Fleischmann: The debt of the Enlightenment to Lucretius 25 (1963) 631-43

A. C. Genova: Kant's Enlightenment 88 (1972) 577-98

M. W. Beal: Condillac as precursor of Kant 102 (1973) 193-229

Arthur Donovan: Chemistry in the Scottish Enlightenment 152 (1976) 587-605

Walter Moser: Pour et contre la Bible: croire et savoir au XVIIIe siècle 154 (1976) 1509-28

Krzysztof Pomian: Médailles/coquilles = érudition/philosophie 154 (1976) 1677-1703

Jacques Marx: *Charles Bonnet contre les Lumières* 156-157 (1976)

Etienne Bonnot de Condillac: *Les Monades*, edited with and introduction and notes by Laurence L. Bongie 187 (1980)

Horst Günther: Sémantique philosophique et histoire des concepts 190 (1980) 518-26

Gregorio Piaia: Dal libertinismo erudito all'illuminismo: l'*Histoire critique de la philosophie* di A.-F. Boureau-Deslandes 191 (1980) 595-601

Pierre Malandain: *Delisle de Sales: philosophe de la nature 1741-1816* 203-204 (1982)

Miguel Benítez: Naturalisme et atomisme: le refus des atomes et du vide dans la littérature clandestine 215 (1982) 121-38

Lionel Honoré: The philosophical satire of La Mettrie 215 (1982) 175-222

John Neubauer: Albrecht von Haller's philosophy of physiology 216 (1983) 320-22

Marie-Hélène Cotoni: *L'Exégèse du Nouveau Testament dans la philosophie française du dix-huitième siècle* 220 (1984)

Roger L. Emerson: Natural philosophy and the problem of the Scottish Enlightenment 242 (1986) 243-91

Renato G. Mazzolini and Shirley A. Roe: *Science against the unbelievers: the correspondence of Bonnet and Needham, 1760-1780* 243 (1986)

— Cartesianism

Jean Deprun: Jean Meslier et l'héritage cartésien 24 (1963) 443-55

Mariafranca Spallanzani: Notes sur le cartésianisme dans l'*Encyclopédie* 216 (1983) 326-28

— deontology

Paul H. Meyer: Politics and morals in the thought of Montesquieu 56 (1967) 845-91

C. Kiernan: Helvétius and a science of ethics 60 (1968) 229-43

Jeanne R. Monty: *Les Romans de l'abbé Prévost: procédés littéraires et pensée morale* 78 (1970)

J. P. de Beaumarchais: Les *Mémoires contre Goezman* et la morale rousseauiste de l'intention 87 (1972) 101-13

Virgil W. Topazio: Holbach's moral code: social and humanistic 90 (1972) 1615-23

James F. Hamilton: Virtue in Rousseau's first discourse 98 (1972) 119-29

Anne R. Larsen: Ethical mutability in four of Diderot's tales 116 (1973) 221-34

T. C. Newland: Holbach and religion versus morality 140 (1975) 203-18

Michael Cartwright: Luxe, goût et l'ivresse de l'objet: un problème moral et esthétique chez Diderot 151 (1976) 405-15

Marialuisa Lussu: Critica della religione e autonomia della morale in alcune figure dell'Illuminismo francese 192 (1980) 1085-93

Martin Staum: The Class of moral and political sciences, 1795-1803 192 (1980) 1183-89

Henri Laboucheix: *Richard Price as moral philosopher and political theorist*, translated by Sylvia and David Raphael 207 (1982)

Johann Werner Schmidt: Diderot and Lucretius: the *De rerum natura* and Lucretius's legacy in Diderot's scientific, aesthetic, and ethical thought 208 (1982) 183-294

Henri Mydlarski: La sécularisation de la pensée chez les moralistes de dix-huitième siècle 216 (1983) 65-66

Takaho Ando: Mme de Condorcet et la philosophie de la 'sympathie' 216 (1983) 335-36

J. Robert Loy: Saint-Lambert, moralist: philosophy at second hand; Enlightenment among the titled 216 (1983) 353-54

Ursula Winter: Philosophie des sciences et morale 'matérialiste': le troisième dialogue du *Rêve de d'Alembert* 216 (1983) 370-72

Joyce Seltzer: The French citizen's catechism: a *philosophe*'s moral vision in 1793 216 (1983) 406-407

Martin Staum: The prize contests in moral and political sciences 216 (1983) 437-39

— determinism

Judith McFadden: *Les Bijoux indiscrets*: a deterministic interpretation 116 (1973) 109-35

— epistemology

Giorgio Tonelli: The law of continuity in the eighteenth century 27 (1963) 1619-38

Sergio Moravia: Philosophie et géographie à la fin du XVIIIe siècle 57 (1967) 937-1011

Charles Jacques Beyer: Montesquieu et la philosophie de l'ordre 87 (1972) 145-66

— language

J. Guillerme: Analyse d'un mémoire inédit de 1774 intitulé 'Essai sur la langue philosophique' 216 (1983) 313-14

— materialism

Charles Rihs: L'influence du siècle des Lumières sur la formation du matérialisme historique 26 (1963) 1389-416

Henri Laboucheix: Chimie, matérialisme et théologie chez Joseph Priestley 153 (1976) 1219-44

Aram Vartanian: Maupertuis's brother and the man-machine 190 (1980) 490-92

Miguel Benítez: Anatomie de la matière: matière et mouvement dans le naturalisme clandestin du XVIIIe siècle en France 205 (1982) 7-30

Lionel P. Honoré: The philosophical satire of La Mettrie: part II 241 (1986) 203-36

— metaphysics

Otis Fellows: Metaphysics and the *Bijoux indiscrets*: Diderot's debt to Prior 56 (1967) 509-40

— natural law

Ronald Grimsley: Quelques aspects de la théorie du droit naturel au siècle des Lumières 25 (1963) 721-40

G. Benrekassa: Loi naturelle et loi civile: l'idéologie des Lumières et la prohibition de l'inceste 87 (1972) 115-44

Paolo Casini: La loi naturelle: réflexion politique et sciences exactes 151 (1976) 417-32

Hernâni A. Resende: Jean-Jacques Rousseau, l'abbé Dolivier, Hegel, sur la théorie des droits naturels 190 (1980) 381

Colette Verger Michael: Condorcet and the inherent contradiction in the American affirmation of natural rights and slaveholding 191 (1980) 768-74

— of history

Hugh Trevor-Roper: The historical philosophy of the Enlightenment 27 (1963) 1667-87

G. Christie Wasberg: The influence of the 'enlightened' philosophy of history on Scandinavian political thought 27 (1963) 1775-85

G. Christie Wasberg: 'Transcendence' and 'immanence' in the philosophy of history from Enlightenment to Romanticism 58 (1967) 1829-38

— of medicine

Paul Hoffmann: L'idée de liberté dans la philosophie médicale de Théophile de Bordeu 88 (1972) 769-87

S. Moravia: Philosophie et médecine en France à la fin du XVIIIe siècle 89 (1972) 1089-151

philosophy

— ontology

P. D. Jimack: Rousseau and the primacy of self 32 (1965) 73-90

William H. Trapnell: The 'philosophical' implications of Marivaux's *Dispute* 73 (1970) 193-219

Robert C. Carroll: Rousseau's bookish ontology 79 (1971) 103-52

Reinhard Brandt: L'identità della persona (Locke et Hume) 190 (1980) 445-49

Paul Hoffmann: La controverse entre Leibniz et Stahl sur la nature de l'âme 199 (1981) 237-49

— optimism

Theodore Besterman: Voltaire et le désastre de Lisbonne: ou, la mort de l'optimisme 2 (1956) 7-24

Rita Falke: Eldorado: le meilleur des mondes possibles 2 (1956) 25-41

R. A. Leigh: Rousseau's letter to Voltaire on optimism (18 August 1756) 30 (1964) 247-309

Jerry L. Curtis: La providence: vicissitudes du dieu voltairien 118 (1974) 7-114

Barbara W. Maggs: Eighteenth-century Russian reflections on the Lisbon earthquake, Voltaire and optimism 137 (1975) 7-29

— pessimism

Jochen Schlobach: Pessimisme des philosophes? La théorie cyclique de l'histoire du XVIIIe siècle 155 (1976) 1971-87

— political

Lester G. Crocker: Voltaire and the political philosophers 219 (1983) 1-17

— propaganda

P. Laubriet: Les guides de voyages au début du XVIIIe siècle et la propagande philosophique 32 (1965) 269-325

— rationalism

Theodore Besterman: Reason and progress 24 (1963) 27-41

E. R. Briggs: Mysticism and rationalism in the debate upon eternal punishment 24 (1963) 241-54

Oscar A. Haac: Voltaire and Leibniz: two aspects of rationalism 25 (1963) 795-809

Elisabeth Labrousse: Obscurantisme et Lumières chez Pierre Bayle 26 (1963) 1037-48

J. Robert Loy: Nature, reason and enlightenment, Voltaire, Rousseau and Diderot 26 (1963) 1085-107

Henry Pettit: The limits of reason as literary theme in the English enlightenment 26 (1963) 1307-19

Sven Stelling-Michaud: Lumières et politique 27 (1963) 1519-43

philosophy

Robert Voitle: The reason of the English Enlightenment 27 (1963) 1735-74

Roland Mortier: Un adversaire vénitien des 'Lumières', le comte de Cataneo 32 (1965) 91-268

A. O. Aldridge: Apostles of reason: Camilo Henriquez and the French Enlightenment 55 (1967) 65-87

Hugh Trevor-Roper: The Scottish Enlightenment 58 (1967) 1635-58

Robert Ginsberg: David Hume and the Enlightenment 88 (1972) 599-650

Patrick Henry: *Voltaire and Camus: the limits of reason and the awareness of absurdity* 138 (1975)

Suzanne Gearhart: Rationality and the text: a study of Voltaire's historiography 140 (1975) 21-43

Georges Gusdorf: Déclin de la providence? 153 (1976) 951-99

Henry F. May: The decline of providence? 154 (1976) 1401-16

Michel Cataudella: La polémique contre les Lumières et contre le rationalisme dans un journal peu connu de Gasparo Gozzi 216 (1983) 4-6

— realism

Marguerite Marie D. Stevens: L'idéalisme et le réalisme dans *Les Egarements du cœur et de l'esprit* de Crébillon fils 47 (1966) 157-76

— rhetoric

R. Ginsberg: The argument of Voltaire's *L'Homme aux quarante écus*: a study in philosophic rhetoric 56 (1967) 611-579

— scepticism

Richard H. Popkin: Scepticism in the Enlightenment 26 (1963) 1321-45

Martin S. Staum: Newton and Voltaire: constructive sceptics 62 (1968) 29-56

— sensationalism

M. L. Perkins: The crisis of sensationalism in Diderot's *Lettre sur les aveugles* 174 (1978) 167-88

— sensualism

Walter Moser: De la signification d'une poésie insignifiante: examen de la poésie fugitive au XVIIIe siècle et de ses rapports avec la pensée sensualiste en France 94 (19) 277-415

— society

R. J. Howells: The metaphysic of nature: basic values and their application in the social philosophy of Rousseau 60 (1968) 109-200

— teleology

Charles Porset: Le *Système de la nature* et la téléologie 190 (1980) 502-507 *philosophy*

— utilitarianism

Robert Shackleton: The greatest happiness of the greatest number: the history of Bentham's phrase 90 (1972) 1461-82

physics

Linda Gardiner Janik: Searching for the metaphysics of science: the structure and composition of Mme Du Châtelet's *Institutions de physique*, 1737-1740 201 (1982) 85-113

physiocrats

Ellen Marie Strenski: Diderot, for and against the physiocrats 57 (1967) 1435-55

Lazaros Houmanidis: Introduzione [to a collection of papers on economics] 191 (1980) 793-804

Mario Mirri: Analisi della realtà ed elaborazione teorica nei fisiocratici: a proposito della definizione di 'arti sterili' 191 (1980) 828

Roberto Finzi: Turgot fra fisiocrazia e pensiero classico 191 (1980) 828-29

Marco Minerbi: Libertà economica, prezzo e profitto nell'analisi fisiocratica 191 (1980) 829-34

Eva H. Balázs: Physiocrates et pseudophysiocrates dans la Hongrie des Lumières 216 (1983) 275-77

S. Baudiffier: La notion d'évidence: Le Mercier de La Rivière, Diderot, Mably 216 (1983) 278-80

Elizabeth Fox-Genovese: The internationalisation of physiocracy 216 (1983) 280-81

Diethelm Klippel: The influence of the physiocrats on the development of liberal political theory in Germany 216 (1983) 284-85

Edna Hindie Lemay: Physiocratie et renouveau à l'Assemblée constituante 1789-1791 216 (1983) 285-87

Helen Liebel-Weckowicz: The physiocrat tax reform of Joseph II: the challenge of modernisation in the Habsburg empire, 1780-1790 216 (1983) 287-89

J. Nagels: Objectifs et instruments de la politique économique et sociale de la physiocratie 216 (1983) 289-92

Ian Ross: The physiocrats and Adam Smith 216 (1983) 292-93

Jochen Schlobach: Les physiocrates et une tentative de réalisation de leur doctrine en Allemagne (d'après les correspondances de Mirabeau et de Du Pont de Nemours avec le margrave de Bade) 216 (1983) 293-96

Janis Spurlock: The Physiocrats, the people and public economic policy: debates for and against a non-interventionist state 216 (1983) 296-99

Larissa L. Albina: Les sources du conte antiphysiocratique *L'Homme aux quarante écus* d'après les données nouvelles provenant de la bibliothèque personnelle de Voltaire 242 (1986) 159-68

Seizo Hotta: Quesnay or Hume: Beccaria between France and Britain 245 (1986) 457-65

physiognomy

Marcia Allentuck: Fuseli and Lavater: physiognomical theory and the Enlightenment 55 (1967) 89-112

physiology

François Azouvi: Quelques jalons dans la préhistoire de la cénesthésie 216 (1983) 303-305

John Neubauer: Albrecht von Haller's philosophy of physiology 216 (1983) 320-22

picaresque

Glen Campbell: The search for equality of Lesage's picaresque heroes 216 (1983) 195-96

pietism

Bruno Bianco: Piétisme et Lumières dans l'Allemagne du XVIIIe siècle 192 (1980) 1105-12

Christine Oertel Sjögren: Pietism, pathology, or pragmatism in Goethe's *Bekenntnisse einer schönen Seele* 193 (1980) 2009-15

Pigalle, Jean-Baptiste

Judith Colton: Pigalle's *Voltaire*: realist manifesto or tribute *all'antica*? 193 (1980) 1680-87

Pilati, Carlo Antonio

J. Th. de Booy: La traduction française de *Di una riforma d'Italia*, de Pilati di Tassulo 12 (1960) 29-42

Pinto, Isaac de

Richard H. Popkin: Isaac de Pinto's criticism of Mandeville and Hume on luxury 154 (1976) 1705-14

Pirandello, Luigi

Virgil W. Topazio: Rousseau and Pirandello: a quest for identity and dignity 58 (1967) 1577-92

Piron, Alexis

H. Gaston Hall: From extravagant poet to the writer as hero: Piron's *La Métromanie* and Pierre Cerou's *L'Amant auteur et valet* 183 (1980) 117-32

Pierre Gobin: L'*Arlequin-Deucalion* de Piron: pertinence de l'impertinence 192 (1980) 1478-86

Pivati, Gianfrancesco

Silvano Garofalo: Gianfrancesco Pivati's *Nuovo dizionario* 194 (1981) 197-219

Plato

Joseph Gallanar: Argenson's 'Platonic republics' 56 (1967) 557-75

M. J. Silverthorne: Rousseau's Plato 116 (1973) 235-49

Pluche, Noël-Antoine

J. Deshayes: De l'abbé Pluche au citoyen Dupuis: à la recherche de la clef des fables 24 (1963) 457-86

Bertram Eugene Schwarzbach: Coincé entre Pluche et Lucrèce: Voltaire et la théologie naturelle 192 (1980) 1072-84

pluralism

Paul Cornea: Polygenèse et pluralisme des 'Lumières' 190 (1980) 203-208

Plutarch

Peter D. Jimack: *La Genèse et la rédaction de l'"Emile' de J.-J. Rousseau* 13 (1960)

poetics

Warren Ramsey: Voltaire et 'l'art de peindre' 26 (1963) 1365-77

Edouard Guitton: Un thème 'philosophique': 'l'invention' des poètes de Louis Racine à Népomucène Lemercier 88 (1972) 677-709

Renata Carocci: Les héroïdes: une contribution à la poétique du XVIIIe siècle 193 (1980) 1596-1604

Garry Retzleff: *Ut pictura poesis* once again: picturesque aesthetics and imagism 193 (1980) 1614-21

Peter Sárközy: La funzione della poetica arcadica nella formazione del classicismo illuministico delle letterature dell'Europa centro-orientale 193 (1980) 1621-28

Jay Martin: Three phases of American enlightenment poetry: from the literature of anxiety to visionary poetics 216 (1983) 396-98

Julie C. Hayes: Sophistry and displacement: the poetics of Sade's ciphers 242 (1986) 335-43

André G. Bourassa: Polémique et propagande dans *Rome sauvée* et *Les Triumvirs* de Voltaire 60 (1968) 73-103

Gérard Luciani: L'œuvre de Carlo Gozzi et les polémiques théâtrales contre les Lumières 89 (1972) 939-74

Carla Pellandra Cazzoli: La polémique antiphilosophique dans la prédication des ordres religieux de la seconde moitié du dix-huitième siècle en Italie du Nord 216 (1983) 28-29

Renata Carocci: Dom Pernety polémiste humanitaire 216 (1983) 196-98

B. E. Schwarzbach: The sacred genealogy of a Voltairean polemic: the development of critical hypotheses regarding the composition of the canonical and apocryphal gospels 245 (1986) 303-50

police

Marlinda Ruth Bruno: Fréron, police spy 148 (1976) 177-99

Alan Williams: The police and the poor in Paris 155 (1976) 2285-300

Polier de Bottens, Georges

J. Marx: Autour des *Pensées philosophiques*: une lettre inédite de Georges Polier de Bottens 84 (1971) 99-108

politics

Theodore Besterman: Review: Lester G. Crocker, *An age of crisis* 12 (1960) 116-19

Olivier Lutaud: D'*Areopagitica* à la *Lettre à un premier commis* et de l'*Agreement* au *Contrat social* 26 (1963) 1109-27

Sven Stelling-Michaud: Lumières et politique 27 (1963) 1519-43

Lionello Sozzi: Interprétations de Rousseau pendant la Révolution 64 (1968) 187-223

Charles G. Stricklen: The *philosophe*'s political mission: the creation of an idea, 1750-1789 86 (1971) 137-228

Robert Ginsberg: David Hume and the Enlightenment 88 (1972) 599-650

M. L. Perkins: Liberty and the concept of legitimacy in the *Discours sur l'inégalité* 89 (1972) 1293-304

James F. Hamilton: Parallel interpretations, religious and political, of Rousseau's *Discours sur l'inégalité* 94 (1972) 7-16

M. P. Masterson: Montesquieu's stadholder 116 (1973) 81-107

Georges Benrekassa: Savoir politique et connaissance historique à l'aube des Lumières 151 (1976) 261-85

Paolo Casini: La loi naturelle: réflexion politique et sciences exactes 151 (1976) 417-32

Paulette Charbonnel: Remarques sur la futurologie politique du groupe Holbach-Diderot, 1773-1776 151 (1976) 449-66

politics

Corrado Rosso: L'égalité du bonheur et le bonheur de l'égalité dans la pensée française du dix-huitième siècle 155 (1976) 1913-23

Grzegorz Leopold Seidler: The concept 'reason of state' and the Polish Enlightenment 155 (1976) 2015-32

William Hanley: The policing of thought: censorship in eighteenth-century France 183 (1980) 265-95

George Klosko: Montesquieu's science of politics: absolute values and ethical relativism in *L'Esprit des lois* 189 (1980) 153-77

Rosanna Albertini: Storiografia e arte della politica nel testo originale dei *Cahiers* di Barnave 191 (1980) 540-47

Monique Mosser et Jean-Pierre Mouilleseaux: Architecture, politique et utopie: vers une *Foederapolis europeana*: les monuments à la paix de Louis Combes 191 (1980) 712-16

Antonio Paoluzzi: L'utopia dalla scienza politica alla letteratura 191 (1980) 717-22

Martin Staum: The Class of moral and political sciences, 1795-1803 192 (1980) 1183-89

Malcolm C. Cook: Politics in the fiction of the French Revolution, 1789-1794 201 (1982) 233-340

John Pappas: La campagne des philosophes contre l'honneur 205 (1982) 31-44

Merle L. Perkins: *Diderot and the time-space continuum: his philosophy, aesthetics and politics* 211 (1982)

Virgil Nemoianu: Textual and political recentralisation in Möser and Rivarol 216 (1983) 23-25

J. Peter Verdurmen: Restoration tragedy and after: the theatre of trauma 216 (1983) 37-39

Vivian R. Gruder: From consensus to conflict: the élite, equality and representation, 1787-1788 216 (1983) 180-82

Cécile Douxchamps-Lefèvre: La correspondance politique secrète sur la cour de France: 1er juillet 1774 – 22 décembre 1779 216 (1983) 241-42

J. Nagels: Objectifs et instruments de la politique économique et sociale de la physiocratie 216 (1983) 289-92

Janis Spurlock: The Physiocrats, the people and public economic policy: debates for and against a non-interventionist state 216 (1983) 296-99

F. M. Barnard: National culture and political legitimacy: Herder and Rousseau 216 (1983) 379-81

Marco Guidi: State, society and the purposes of politics: David Ricardo's theory of economic policy and its origins 216 (1983) 425-26

Iris Cox: *Montesquieu and the history of French laws* 218 (1983)

Catherine Volpilhac-Auger: *Tacite et Montesquieu* 232 (1985)

Rosena Davison: *Diderot et Galiani: étude d'une amitié philosophique* 237 (1985)

Merle L. Perkins: Montesquieu on national power and international rivalry 238 (1985) 1-95

James E. Crimmins: 'The study of true politics': John Brown on manners and liberty 241 (1986) 65-86

Anand C. Chitnis: Agricultural improvement, political management and civic virtue in enlightened Scotland: an historiographical critique 245 (1986) 475-88

— absolutism

Theodore Besterman: Voltaire, absolute monarchy, and the enlightened monarch 32 (1965) 7-21

Merle L. Perkins: *Voltaire's concept of international order* 36 (1965)

Peter Horwath: Literature in the service of enlightened absolutism: the age of Joseph II (1780-1790) 56 (1967) 707-34

Béla Köpeczi: L'absolutisme éclairé et les philosophes 190 (1980) 292-98

Gustavo Corni: Federico II e la politica agraria dell'assolutismo 191 (1980) 943-45

— anarchism

Alberto Andreatta: Alle origini dell'anarchismo moderno: Dom Deschamps: la metafisica al servizio dell'utopia 191 (1980) 637-43

Maria Ludassy: Tendances autoritaires et tendances anarchiques dans les utopies du XVIIIe siècle 191 (1980) 699-701

— aristocracy

Adrienne Koch: The contest of democracy and aristocracy in the American Enlightenment 26 (1963) 999-1018

— authoritarianism

Maria Ludassy: Tendances autoritaires et tendances anarchiques dans les utopies du XVIIIe siècle 191 (1980) 699-701

— democracy

Adrienne Koch: The contest of democracy and aristocracy in the American Enlightenment 26 (1963) 999-1018

Maria Evelina Zoltowska: La démocratisation de l'idée de l'honneur dans le *Manuscrit trouvé à Saragosse* de Jean Potocki 216 (1983) 224-26

— despotism

Orest Ranum: D'Alembert, Tacitus and the political sociology of despotism 191 (1980) 547-58

Darline Gay Levy: Despotism in Simon-Nicolas-Henri Linguet's science of society: theory and application 191 (1980) 761-68

— England

Paul Janssens: L'influence sur le continent du modèle aristocratique britannique au dix-huitième siècle 216 (1983) 183-84

Alain Bony: *The History of John Bull* et les comédies d'Aristophane: le modèle grec dans la propagande torie 241 (1986) 41-64

— France

Colm Kiernan: *The Enlightenment and science in eighteenth-century France*. Second edition revised and enlarged 59A (1973)

Paolo Alatri: Parlements et lutte politique en France au XVIIIe siècle 151 (1976) 77-108

N. R. Johnson: *Louis XIV and the age of the Enlightenment: the myth of the Sun King from 1715 to 1789* 172 (1978)

Franco Venturi: La prima crisi dell'antico regime: 1768-1776 190 (1980) 63-80

Elspeth M. Horsman: The abbé de Saint-Pierre and domestic politics 190 (1980) 284-90

Girolamo Imbruglia et Paolo Viola: Sur le problème du pouvoir chez les républicains révolutionnaires 190 (1980) 370-77

Françoise Brunel et Myriam Revault d'Allonnes: Jacobinisme et libéralisme: de la politique des principes à l'art de la politique 190 (1980) 377

John M. J. Rogister: The question of the refusal of the sacraments and the crisis in France in 1756-1757 191 (1980) 885

Vivian R. Gruder: Paths to political consciousness: the Assembly of notables, 1787 191 (1980) 886-91

David M. Klinck: An examination of the *notes de lecture* of Louis de Bonald: at the origins of the ideology of the radical right in France 216 (1983) 18-19

N. Johnson: L'idéologie politique du marquis d'Argenson, d'après ses œuvres inédites 216 (1983) 185

— Germany

Ehrhard Bahr: The pursuit of happiness in the political writings of Lessing and Kant 151 (1976) 167-84

Diethelm Klippel: The influence of the physiocrats on the development of liberal political theory in Germany 216 (1983) 284-85

Hans Erich Bödeker: La conscience politique de l'*Aufklärung*: les philosophes allemands au service de l'état 216 (1983) 381-83

— institutions

Merle L. Perkins: Voltaire on the source of national power 20 (1962) 141-73

Piero Del Negro: Venezia allo specchio: la crisi delle istituzioni repubblicane negli scritti del patriziato (1670-1797) 191 (1980) 920-26

— international relations

Merle L. Perkins: Voltaire and the abbé de Saint-Pierre on world peace 18 (1961) 9-34

D. J. Fletcher: Montesquieu's conception of patriotism 56 (1967) 541-55

Louis Trenard: Patriotisme et nationalisme dans les Pays-Bas français au XVIIIe siècle 90 (1972) 1625-57

Marita Gilli: Littérature, histoire et problème national à la fin des Lumières en Allemagne 191 (1980) 564-71

— pacifism

Jean Daniel Candaux: Charles Borde et la première crise d'antimilitarisme de l'opinion publique européenne 24 (1963) 315-44

— patriotism

Andrew Hunwick: Le patriotisme de Voltaire 116 (1973) 7-18

— Poland

Emanuel Rostworowski: Républicanisme 'sarmate' et les Lumières 26 (1963) 1417-38

— power

Alberto Postigliola: Sur quelques interprétations de la 'séparation des pouvoirs' chez Montesquieu 154 (1976) 1759-75

— realism

Eric Cahm: Review: Peter Gay, *Voltaire's politics: the poet as realist* 12 (1960) 111-16

J. L. Lecercle: Utopie et réalisme politique chez Mably 26 (1963) 1049-70

— religion

Pauline Kra: *Religion in Montesquieu's 'Lettres persanes'* 72 (1970)

— republicanism

Joseph Gallanar: Argenson's 'Platonic republics' 56 (1967) 557-75

— Romania

Adrian Marino: Aspects et idées politiques des Lumières roumaines 190 (1980) 356-64

— Scandinavia

G. C. Wasberg: The influence of the 'enlightened' philosophy of history on Scandinavian political thought 27 (1963) 1775-85

— Scotland

Istvan Hont: Equality and the structure of needs in eighteenth-century Scottish political economy 216 (1983) 204-207

246

Port-Royal

Sylvain Auroux: Le concept de détermination: Port-Royal et Beauzée 192 (1980) 1236-45

Portugal

Theodore Besterman: Provisional bibliography of Portuguese editions of Voltaire 76 (1970) 15-35

José Ferreira Carrato: The Enlightenment in Portugal and the educational reforms of the marquis of Pombal 167 (1977) 359-93

David Higgs: The impact of counter-revolutionary literature in late eighteenth-century Portugal 216 (1983) 15-18

Manuel Augusto Rodrigues: La sécularisation au Portugal 216 (1983) 70

Luís Reis Torgal et Isabel Nobre Vargues: La réception des idées pédagogiques de la Révolution française par le premier libéralisme portugais (1820-1823) 216 (1983) 433-34

Potier, Pierre

Robert Toupin: Pierre Potier, jésuite belge chez les Hurons du Détroit (1744-1781): les chemins d'un espace nouveau à explorer 216 (1983) 122-24

Potocki, Jean

B. Didier: L'exotisme et la mise en question du système familial et moral dans le roman à la fin du XVIIIe siècle: Beckford, Sade, Potocki 152 (1976) 571-86

Maria Evelina Zoltowska: La démocratisation de l'idée de l'honneur dans le *Manuscrit trouvé à Saragosse* de Jean Potocki 216 (1983) 224-26

Dominique Triaire: Jean Potocki et l'indépendance nationale pendant la Grande Diète polonaise (1788-1792) 216 (1983) 408-409

poverty

Thomas M. Adams: Mendicity and moral alchemy: work as rehabilitation 151 (1976) 47-76

Harry C. Payne: *Pauvreté, misère*, and the aims of enlightened economics 154 (1976) 1581-92

Alan Williams: The police and the poor in Paris 155 (1976) 2285-300

Thomas M. Adams: Charitable reform and the diffusion of economic ideas in eighteenth-century France 191 (1980) 858-66

Luigi Cajani: L'assistenza ai poveri nell'Italia del Settecento 191 (1980) 914-20

Prades, Jean-Martin de

Jean-Claude David: L'affaire de Prades en 1751-1752 d'après deux rapports de police 245 (1986) 359-71

prediction

Edward M. Jennings: The consequences of prediction 153 (1976) 1131-50

prejudice

Judith L. Schwartz: Cultural stereotypes and music in the eighteenth century 155 (1976) 1989-2013

preromanticism

Anna Ridehalgh: Preromantic attitudes and the birth of a legend: French pilgrimages to Ermenonville, 1778-1789 215 (1982) 231-52

Arthur H. Scouten: The Warton forgeries and the concept of Preromanticism 216 (1983) 465-66

press

Raymond Birn: *Livre et société* after ten years: formation of a discipline 151 (1976) 287-312

— Canada

C. Rouben: Propagande anti-philosophique dans les gazettes de Montréal et de Québec après la fin du régime français 216 (1983) 30-32

— England

Norma Perry: Voltaire and Felix Farley's *Bristol journal* 62 (1968) 137-50

Alberto Caracciolo et Rosa Maria Colombo: Public opinion and the development of modern society in England in the eighteenth century 193 (1980) 1812

A. J. Hanou: Anglo-Dutch relations: spectators and satire in the early eighteenth century 193 (1980) 1831-32

Peter V. Conroy: The *Spectators'* view of women 193 (1980) 1883-90

Calhoun Winton: Print culture and the developing audience in England: the periodicals 216 (1983) 265-66

— France

Raymond Birn: The French-language press and the *Encyclopédie*, 1750-1759 55 (1967) 263-86

Gary Bruce Rogers: *Diderot and the eighteenth-century French press* 107 (1973)

Paule Jansen: La presse de 1768: un inventaire et une analyse du contenu 153 (1976) 1113-29

Peter Lester Smith: The launching of the *Journal étranger* (1752-1754): the problem of audience 163 (1976) 117-27

R. Galliani: Voltaire en 1878: le premier centenaire d'après les journaux de l'époque 183 (1980) 91-115

Prévost, Antoine-François

Claire-Eliane Engel: L'abbé Prévost collaborateur d'une revue neuchâteloise 2 (1956) 225-32

Jean Sgard: Prévost: de l'ombre aux Lumières (1736-1746) 27 (1963) 1479-87

Robert S. Tate: *Petit de Bachaumont: his circle and the 'Mémoires secrets'* 65 (1968)

Jeanne R. Monty: *Les Romans de l'abbé Prévost: procédés littéraires et pensée morale* 78 (1970)

John Falvey: Psychological analysis and moral ambiguity in the narrative processes of Chasles, Prévost and Marivaux 94 (1972) 141-58

Steve Larkin: Voltaire and Prévost: a reappraisal 160 (1976) 7-135

Paul Winnack: Some English influences on the abbé Prévost 182 (1979) 285-302

Oscar A. Haac: Comedy in utopia: the literary imagination of Marivaux and the abbé Prévost 191 (1980) 684-85

Aurelio Principato: Rhétorique et technique narrative chez l'abbé Prévost 192 (1980) 1352-59

Jean-Paul Sermain: *Rhétorique et roman au dix-huitième siècle: l'exemple de Prévost et de Marivaux (1728-1742)* 233 (1985)

Steve Larkin: The abbé Prévost, a convert to the Church of England? 249 (1986) 197-225

— works: *Cleveland*

Philip Stewart: L'armature historique du *Cleveland* de Prévost 137 (1975) 121-39

James P. Gilroy: Peace and the pursuit of happiness in the French utopian novel: Fénelon's *Télémaque* and Prévost's *Cleveland* 176 (1979) 169-87

R. A. Francis: Prévost's *Cleveland* and Voltaire's *Candide* 191 (1980) 671-72

Steve Larkin: J.-J. Rousseau, the *Histoire de Cleveland* and the *Confessions* 192 (1980) 1295-97

R. A. Francis: Prévost's *Cleveland* and Voltaire's *Candide* 208 (1982) 295-303

B. L. H. Lewis: The influence of Chasles's *Illustres Françoises* on Prévost's *Cleveland* 219 (1983) 153-58

Alan J. Singerman: L'abbé Prévost et la quête du bonheur: lecture morale et philosophique de l'*Histoire de M. Cleveland* 228 (1984) 195-242

— — *Le Doyen de Killerine*

James P. Gilroy: Prévost's *Le Doyen de Killerine*: the career of an imperfect mentor 216 (1983) 452-53

James P. Gilroy: Prévost's *Le Doyen de Killerine*: the career of an imperfect mentor 228 (1984) 243-57

— — *Histoire d'une Grecque moderne*

Emita B. Hill: Virtue on trial: a defence of Prévost's Théophé 67 (1969) 191-209

Bernard Bray: Structures en série dans *Manon Lescaut* et *Histoire d'une Grecque moderne* de l'abbé Prévost 192 (1980) 1333-40

Peter V. Conroy: Image claire, image trouble dans l'*Histoire d'une Grecque moderne* de Prévost 217 (1983) 187-97

— — *Manon Lescaut*

Patrick Brady: *Manon Lescaut*: classical, romantic, or rococo? 53 (1967) 339-60

Diana Guiragossian: *Manon Lescaut* et la justice criminelle sous l'ancien régime 56 (1967) 679-91

Robert S. Tate: *Manon Lescaut* and the Enlightenment 70 (1970) 15-25

Robert M. E. De Rycke: Des Grieux's confession 84 (1971) 195-232

Manfred Kusch: *Manon Lescaut*, or voyage du chevalier Des Grieux dans la basse Romancie 143 (1975) 141-60

Lucette Desvignes: Vues de la terre promise: les visages de l'Amérique dans *Moll Flanders* et dans l'*Histoire de Manon Lescaut* 152 (1976) 543-57

Alan J. Singerman: L'abbé Prévost et la triple concupiscence: lecture augustinienne de *Manon Lescaut* 176 (1979) 189-229

Bernard Bray: Structures en série dans *Manon Lescaut* et *Histoire d'une Grecque moderne* de l'abbé Prévost 192 (1980) 1333-40

— — *Mémoires d'un honnête homme*

P. J. Tremewan: Narrative point of view in Prévost's *Mémoires d'un honnête homme* 205 (1982) 45-56

— — *Le Pour et contre*

Marie-Rose de Labriolle: '*Le Pour et contre*' et son temps 34-35 (1965)

Price, Richard

Henri Laboucheix: *Richard Price as moral philosopher and political theorist*, translated by Sylvia and David Raphael 207 (1982)

Priestley, Joseph

Henri Laboucheix: Chimie, matérialisme et théologie chez Joseph Priestley 153 (1976) 1219-44

printing

Betty Rizzo: 'Hail, printing!': the Commonwealthman's salute to the printed word in eighteenth-century England 216 (1983) 258-59

Jim Mitchell: The spread and fluctuation of eighteenth-century printing 230 (1985) 305-21

Prior, Matthew

Otis Fellows: Metaphysics and the *Bijoux indiscrets*: Diderot's debt to Prior 56 (1967) 509-40

privilege (publishing)

Anne Boës and Robert L. Dawson: The legitimation of *contrefaçons* and the police stamp of 1777 230 (1985) 461-84

Françoise Weil: Les libraires parisiens propriétaires d'éditions sans véritable privilège: l'exemple de Voltaire 249 (1986) 227-39

prize contests

Janis Spurlock: Essays in reform on the eve of revolution: the public essay contests of the Academy of Châlons-sur-Marne, France, 1776-1789 191 (1980) 885-86

Martin Staum: The prize contests in moral and political sciences 216 (1983) 437-39

progress

Norman Suckling: The Enlightenment and the idea of progress 58 (1967) 1461-80

Robert C. Elliott: The costs of utopia 152 (1976) 677-92

René Wellek: The price of progress in eighteenth-century reflections on literature 155 (1976) 2265-84

Dorothy Medlin: André Morellet and the idea of progress 189 (1980) 239-46

J. G. A. Pocock: Gibbon and the stages of society: progress, ambivalence and corruption in the *Decline and fall* 191 (1980) 537

Hiroshi Mizuta: Two Adams in the Scottish Enlightenment: Adam Smith and Adam Ferguson on progress 191 (1980) 812-19

Marie-Luise Spieckermann: The idea of teleology and the theory of scientific progress at the beginning of the eighteenth century 216 (1983) 328-29

Henry Lowood: Patriotism and progress: the role of the German patriotic and economic societies in the promotion of science and technology 216 (1983) 394-96

propaganda

R. S. Ridgway: *La Propagande philosophique dans les tragédies de Voltaire* 15 (1961)

J. H. Brumfitt: History and propaganda in Voltaire 24 (1963) 271-87

Robert Niklaus: La propagande philosophique au théâtre au siècle des Lumières 26 (1963) 1223-61

P. Laubriet: Les guides de voyages au début du XVIIIe siècle et la propagande philosophique 32 (1965) 269-325

André G. Bourassa: Polémique et propagande dans *Rome sauvée* et *Les Triumvirs* de Voltaire 60 (1968) 73-103

Gérard Luciani: L'œuvre de Carlo Gozzi et les polémiques théâtrales contre les Lumières 89 (1972) 939-74

J. P. de Beaumarchais: Beaumarchais, propagandiste de l'Amérique 151 (1976) 249-60

C. Rouben: Propagande anti-philosophique dans les gazettes de Montréal et de Québec après la fin du régime français 216 (1983) 30-32

Margarete G. Smith: J. H. S. Formey, assiduous journalist and discreet propagandist of new scientific discoveries and philosophical trends 216 (1983) 262-64

prostitution

D. A. Coward: Restif de La Bretonne and the reform of prostitution 176 (1979) 349-83

D. A. Coward: Eighteenth-century attitudes to prostitution 189 (1980) 363-99

Dennis Fletcher: 'The oldest profession': some eighteenth-century views 191 (1980) 1042-50

Magdy Gabriel Badir: Législation et définition de la prostitution au dix-huitième siècle 249 (1986) 447-66

Protestantism

Graham Gargett: *Voltaire and Protestantism* 188 (1980)

William H. Trapnell: *Voltaire and the eucharist* 198 (1981)

B. Soubeyran: De l'illuminisme cévenol aux réactions anti-philosophiques des protestants 216 (1983) 33-35

John D. Woodbridge: The reformed pastors of Languedoc face the movement of dechristianisation 1793-1794 216 (1983) 80-81

Steve Larkin: The abbé Prévost, a convert to the Church of England? 249 (1986) 197-225

Providence

Jerry L. Curtis: La providence: vicissitudes du dieu voltairien 118 (1974) 7-114

Marie-Hélène Cotoni: Dénigrement de la providence et défense des valeurs humaines dans les manuscrits clandestins de la première moitié du dix-huitième siècle 152 (1976) 497-513

Georges Gusdorf: Déclin de la providence? 153 (1976) 951-99

Henry F. May: The decline of providence? 154 (1976) 1401-16

psychology

Lester G. Crocker: L'analyse des rêves au XVIIIe siècle 23 (1963) 271-310

René Pomeau: Candide entre Marx et Freud 89 (1972) 1305-23

Philip Robinson: 'La conscience': a perceptual problem in Rousseau 90 (1972) 1377-94

John Falvey: Psychological analysis and moral ambiguity in the narrative processes of Chasles, Prévost and Marivaux 94 (1972) 141-58

James Maurice Kaplan: *'La Neuvaine de Cythère': une démarmontélisation de Marmontel* 113 (1973)

Carmelina Imbroscio: Recherches et réflexions de la médecine française du dix-huitième siècle sur les phénomènes psychosomatiques 190 (1980) 494-501

Sergio Moravia: Capturer l'invisible: pour une (pré-)histoire de la psychologie au 18e siècle 216 (1983) 318-20

public opinion

Jean Daniel Candaux: Charles Borde et la première crise d'antimilitarisme de l'opinion publique européenne 24 (1963) 315-44

Lester G. Crocker: Rousseau et l'"opinion' 55 (1967) 395-415

N. R. Johnson: Louis XIV devant l'opinion française contemporaine: ses dernières paroles au dauphin 88 (1972) 831-43

Alberto Caracciolo et Rosa Maria Colombo: Public opinion and the development of modern society in England in the eighteenth century 193 (1980) 1812

Puisieux, Madeleine d'Arsant, Mme de

Alice M. Laborde: Madame de Puisieux et Diderot: de l'égalité entre les sexes 216 (1983) 209

Quakers

William H. Barber: Voltaire and Quakerism: Enlightenment and the inner light 24 (1963) 81-109

Querelle des anciens et des modernes

Hans Kortum: Frugalité et luxe à travers la querelle des anciens et des modernes 56 (1967) 765-75

Kathleen Sonia Wilkins: *A study of the works of Claude Buffier* 66 (1969)

Michael Cardy: Discussion of the theory of climate in the *querelle des anciens et des modernes* 163 (1976) 73-88

Quesnay, François

Seizo Hotta: Quesnay or Hume: Beccaria between France and Britain 216 (1983) 281-83

Seizo Hotta: Quesnay or Hume: Beccaria between France and Britain 245 (1986) 457-65

Racine, Jean

Emilie P. Kostoroski: *The Eagle and the dove: Corneille and Racine in the literary criticism of eighteenth-century France* 95 (1972)

Richard Switzer: Racine, Sade, and the daisy chain 155 (1976) 2063-69

J. Peter Verdurmen: Varieties of determinism in Racine and Rowe: dramatic structure and the role of society 192 (1980) 1545-47

Racine, Louis

Edouard Guitton: Un thème 'philosophique': 'l'invention' des poètes de Louis Racine à Népomucène Lemercier 88 (1972) 677-709

Radichtchev, Alexandre

Igor Smirnov: Le problème de l'homme dans l'œuvre d'Alexandre Radichtchev 216 (1983) 324-26

Rameau, Jean-Philippe

Spire Pitou: Rameau's *Dardanus* at Fontainebleau in 1763 116 (1973) 281-305

Robert Wokler: Rameau, Rousseau, and the *Essai sur l'origine des langues* 117 (1974) 179-238

Howard Brofsky: Rameau and the Indians: the popularity of *Les Sauvages* 216 (1983) 99-100

Jean-Jacques Robrieux: Jean-Philippe Rameau et l'opinion philosophique en France au dix-huitième siècle 238 (1985) 269-395

Marie-Elisabeth Duchez: Valeur épistémologique de la théorie de la basse fondamental de Jean-Philippe Rameau: connaissance scientifique et représentation de la musique 245 (1986) 91-130

rationalism

Theodore Besterman: Reason and progress 24 (1963) 27-41

E. R. Briggs: Mysticism and rationalism in the debate upon eternal punishment 24 (1963) 241-54

Oscar A. Haac: Voltaire and Leibniz: two aspects of rationalism 25 (1963) 795-809

Elisabeth Labrousse: Obscurantisme et Lumières chez Pierre Bayle 26 (1963) 1037-48

J. Robert Loy: Nature, reason and enlightenment, Voltaire, Rousseau and Diderot 26 (1963) 1085-107

Henry Pettit: The limits of reason as literary theme in the English enlightenment 26 (1963) 1307-19

Sven Stelling-Michaud: Lumières et politique 27 (1963) 1519-43

Robert Voitle: The reason of the English Enlightenment 27 (1963) 1735-74

A. O. Aldridge: Apostles of reason: Camilo Henriquez and the French Enlightenment 55 (1967) 65-87

Claire McGlinchee: 'The smile of reason': its metamorphosis in late 18th-century architecture and literature 89 (1972) 993-1001

reform

Ronald Ian Boss: Linguet: the reformer as anti-*philosophe* 151 (1976) 333-51

Aldo Vallone: Aspetti dell'Illuminismo salentino 190 (1980) 214-17

William Doyle: Reforming the French criminal law at the end of the old regime: the example of president Dupaty 191 (1980) 866-72

Janis Spurlock: Essays in reform on the eve of revolution: the public essay contests of the Academy of Châlons-sur-Marne, France, 1776-1789 191 (1980) 885-86

Silvia Bordini Porretta: Tendenze riformatrici e città nuove nella Sicilia del Settecento 191 (1980) 907-14

Maria Rosa Saurin de La Iglesia: Riforma e reazione nella Galizia settecentesca (1764-1798) 191 (1980) 954-56

Alain Tichoux: Théorie et pratique du libéralisme réformateur: le paradoxe canadien (1760-1765) 191 (1980) 971-79

Marina Caffiero Trincia: Il problema della riforma della Chiesa e le istanze cattoliche de rinnovamento culturale in Italia nel XVIII secolo 192 (1980) 1135-41

Oscar A. Haac: A monstrous proposition: the Church stands in need of reform 216 (1983) 427-29

Regency

Mark Waddicor: An unpublished satire of the regency: *Les Devises de la cour* 124 (1974) 167-79

R. E. A. Waller: Voltaire and the regent 127 (1974) 7-39

Regnard, Jean-François

Annie Rivara: L'exotisme barbaresque dans *La Provençale*, fonction culturelle, pratiques éditoriales et de lecture 249 (1986) 157-74

Reid, Thomas

J. C. Stewart-Robertson: Reid's anatomy of culture: a Scottish response to the eloquent Jean-Jacques 205 (1982) 141-63

relativism

Charles Jacques Beyer: Montesquieu et le relativisme esthétique 24 (1963) 171-82

Isaiah Berlin: A note on alleged relativism in eighteenth-century European thought 191 (1980) 561-64

I. Gopnik: Universal language schemes and the linguistic relativity hypothesis 192 (1980) 1233-36

religion

J. H. Brumfitt: Voltaire and Warburton 18 (1961) 35-56

Jean H. Hagstrum: William Blake rejects the Enlightenment 25 (1963) 811-28

Marialuisa Lussu: Critica della religione e autonomia della morale in alcune figure dell'Illuminismo francese 192 (1980) 1085-93

Marie-Hélène Cotoni: L'image du Christ dans les courants déiste et matérialiste français du XVIIIe siècle 192 (1980) 1093-1100

Eduard Bene: La rénovation de l'abbaye des Prémontrés de Csorna à la fin du XVIIIe siècle 192 (1980) 1112-18

Bruno Morcavallo: Influenza del pensiero religioso di John Toland su David Hume 192 (1980) 1119-23

Elizabeth I. Nybakken: The Enlightenment and Calvinism: mutual support systems for the eighteenth-century American wilderness 192 (1980) 1126-35

Marina Caffiero Trincia: Il problema della riforma della Chiesa e le istanze cattoliche de rinnovamento culturale in Italia nel XVIII secolo 192 (1980) 1135-41

O. H. Bonnerot: L'Islam devant les Lumières: le marquis de Pastoret 192 (1980) 1142-43

David L. Anderson: Structures mythologiques et religieuses dans le roman épistolaire du XVIIIe siècle 192 (1980) 1273-75

William H. Trapnell: *Voltaire and the eucharist* 198 (1981)

Robert Challe: *Difficultés sur la religion proposées au père Malebranche*. Edition critique d'après un manuscrit inédit par Frédéric Deloffre et Melâhat Menemencioglu 209 (1982)

Jean-Claude David: Un théiste chez le baron d'Holbach: l'abbé Morellet 215 (1982) 253-72

Theodore E. D. Braun: Antiphilosophie dans les *Poésies sacrées* de Le Franc de Pompignan 216 (1983) 3-4

Maurice Colgan: Prophecy against reason: Ireland and the Apocalypse 216 (1983) 6-7

Carla Pellandra Cazzoli: La polémique antiphilosophique dans la prédication des ordres religieux de la seconde moitié du dix-huitième siècle en Italie du Nord 216 (1983) 28-29

Silvia Berti: César Chesneau Du Marsais entre gallicanisme et 'philosophie': l'*Exposition de la doctrine de l'Eglise gallicane par rapport aux prétentions de la cour de Rome* (1757) 216 (1983) 45-46

Michael Heyd: The reaction to enthusiasm and the secularisation of religious sensibilities in the early eighteenth century 216 (1983) 58-59

Bernard Plongeron: Echec a la sécularisation des Lumières: la religion comme lien social 216 (1983) 68-69

Stanley Tweyman: An 'inconvenience' of anthropomorphism 216 (1983) 79

John D. Woodbridge: The reformed pastors of Languedoc face the movement of dechristianisation 1793-1794 216 (1983) 80-81

Michel Bastiaensen: Mandéens et sabéens dans la pensée nouvelle 216 (1983) 89-91

Michael Cartwright: A curious attraction: missionary zeal and tribal androgyny in

Jesuit and American Indian relations during the Enlightenment 216 (1983) 100-102

Marie-Hélène Cotoni: *L'Exégèse du Nouveau Testament dans la philosophie française du dix-huitième siècle* 220 (1984)

Silvia Berti: César Chesneau Du Marsais entre gallicanisme et 'philosophie': l'*Exposition de la doctrine de l'Eglise gallicane, par rapport aux prétentions de la Cour de Rome* (1757) 241 (1986) 237-51

Renato G. Mazzolini and Shirley A. Roe: *Science against the unbelievers: the correspondence of Bonnet and Needham, 1760-1780* 243 (1986)

Jean-Claude David: L'affaire de Prades en 1751-1752 d'après deux rapports de police 245 (1986) 359-71

B. E. Schwarzbach and A. W. Fairbairn: The *Examen de la religion*: a bibliographical note 249 (1986) 91-156

— apologetics

B. Plongeron: Bonheur, et 'civilisation chrétienne': une nouvelle apologétique après 1760 154 (1976) 1637-55

— atheism

Jean Leduc: Les sources de l'athéisme et de l'immoralisme du marquis de Sade 68 (1969) 7-66

Marie Souviron: Les *Pensées philosophiques* de Diderot ou les 'Provinciales' de l'athéisme 238 (1985) 197-267

— deism

Günter Gawlick: Abraham's sacrifice of Isaac viewed by the English deists 56 (1967) 577-600

David Lévy: *Voltaire et son exégèse du Pentateuque: critique et polémique* 130 (1975)

Günter Gawlick: The English deists' contribution to the theory of toleration 152 (1976) 823-35

— dissent

Martin Fitzpatrick: Truth and tolerance in rational dissent in late eighteenth-century England 192 (1980) 1124-26

— dualism

Haydn T. Mason: Voltaire and Manichean dualism 26 (1963) 1143-60

— France

Colm Kiernan: *The Enlightenment and science in eighteenth-century France*. Second edition revised and enlarged 59A (1973)

— Jansenism

Robert Shackleton: Jansenism and the Enlightenment 57 (1967) 1387-97

Hélène Himelfarb: Saint Simon et le jansénisme des Lumières 88 (1972) 749-68

— Judaism

Bernard D. Weinryb: Enlightenment and German-Jewish *Haskalah* 27 (1963) 1817-47

Pierre Aubery: Montesquieu et les Juifs 87 (1972) 87-99

Dominique Bourel: La sécularisation dans le judaïsme prussien dans la période post-mendelssohnienne 216 (1983) 47-48

— mysticism

E. R. Briggs: Mysticism and rationalism in the debate upon eternal punishment 24 (1963) 241-54

— natural

Bertram Eugene Schwarzbach: Coincé entre Pluche et Lucrèce: Voltaire et la théologie naturelle 192 (1980) 1072-84

— Protestantism

Graham Gargett: *Voltaire and Protestantism* 188 (1980)

B. Soubeyran: De l'illuminisme cévenol aux réactions anti-philosophiques des protestants 216 (1983) 33-35

— providence

Pauline Kra: *Religion in Montesquieu's 'Lettres persanes'* 72 (1970)

Jerry L. Curtis: La providence: vicissitudes du dieu voltairien 118 (1974) 7-114

Georges Gusdorf: Déclin de la providence? 153 (1976) 951-99

Henry F. May: The decline of providence? 154 (1976) 1401-16

— Quakerism

W. H. Barber: Voltaire and Quakerism: Enlightenment and the inner light 24 (1963) 81-109

— Scotland

James K. Cameron: The Church of Scotland in the age of reason 58 (1967) 1939-51

— Socinianism

Zygmunt Jedryka: Le socinianisme et les Lumières 88 (1972) 809-29

R. E. Florida: *Voltaire and the socinians* 122 (1974)

Françoise Le Moal: Voltaire, Rousseau et le socinianisme 192 (1980) 1100

Zygmunt Jedryka: Le socinianisme entre Rousseau et Fichte 192 (1980) 1101

E. R. Briggs: English Socinianism around Newton and Whiston 216 (1983) 48-50

— Taoism

René Etiemble: Le mythe taoïste au XVIIIe siècle 25 (1963) 589-602

— toleration

Elisabeth Labrousse: Note à propos de la conception de la tolérance au XVIIIe siècle 56 (1967) 799-811

Ronald Ian Boss: Rousseau's civil religion and the meaning of belief: an answer to Bayle's paradox 84 (1971) 123-93

Günter Gawlick: The English deists' contribution to the theory of toleration 152 (1976) 823-35

W. Grossmann: Religious toleration in Germany, 1648-1750 192 (1980) 1103-1105

Martin Fitzpatrick: Truth and tolerance in rational dissent in late eighteenth-century England 192 (1980) 1124-26

Walter Grossmann: Religious toleration in Germany, 1648-1750 201 (1982) 115-41

Tolerance in four Dutch periodicals 1714-1771: *La Bibliothèque ancienne et moderne*, Amsterdam 1714-1726: H. Bots and J. de Vet; *Le Journal britannique*, The Hague 1750-1755: U. Janssens; *Nederlandsche Letter-courant*, Leyden 1759-1763: H. Stouten; *Vaderlandsche Letter-oefeningen*, Amsterdam 1761-1771: W. van den Berg 216 (1983) 73-77

Margaret D. Thomas: Michel de La Roche: a Huguenot critic of Calvin 238 (1985) 97-195

Rémond de Saint-Mard, Toussaint

Robert L. Myers: Fréron's critique of Rémond de Saint Mard 37 (1965) 147-64

Robert L. Myers: Rémond dialogues 60 (1968) 261-88

Robert L. Myers: *Rémond de Saint-Mard: a study of his major works followed by a modernised edition of 'Lucilie'* 74 (1970)

Renan, Ernest

Jean Balcou: Ernest Renan et l'héritage des Lumières 216 (1983) 418-19

Renout, Jean-Julien-Constantin

Spire Pitou: Renout's *La Mort d'Hercule*: text, sources, and structure 163 (1976) 129-53

republicanism

Alan T. McKenzie: Giuseppe Baretti and the 'republic of letters' in the eighteenth century 193 (1980) 1813-22

Restif de La Bretonne, Nicolas-Edme

Mark Poster: The concepts of sexual identity and life cycle in Restif's utopian thought 73 (1970) 241-71

Restoration

revolution

Charles G. Stricklen: The *philosophe*'s political mission: the creation of an idea, 1750-1789 86 (1971) 137-228

Alfred J. Bingham: Marie Joseph Chénier, ideologue and critic 94 (1972) 219-76

R. Galliani: Voltaire cité par les brochures de 1789 132 (1975) 17-54

Terence Murphy: Jean Baptiste René Robinet: the career of a man of letters 150 (1976) 183-250

R. R. Palmer: The Declaration of Independence in France 154 (1976) 1569-79

Jean Pierre Guicciardi: Tocqueville et les Lumières 163 (1976) 203-19

R. Galliani: La présence de Voltaire dans les brochures de 1790 169 (1977) 69-114

R. Galliani: Voltaire et les autres philosophes dans la Révolution: les brochures de 1791, 1792, 1793 174 (1978) 69-112

John Renwick: Chamfort, patriote en coulisses: réflexions sur une lettre inédite à Roland 183 (1980) 165-76

Graham E. Rodmell: Laclos, Brissot, and the petition of the Champ de Mars 183 (1980) 189-222

W. Schröder: La Révolution française de 1789 – une césure d'époque de l'histoire de la littérature? 190 (1980) 160-66

Henri Grange: Necker devant la Révolution française 190 (1980) 364-70

Girolamo Imbruglia et Paolo Viola: Sur le problème du pouvoir chez les républicains révolutionnaires 190 (1980) 370-77

Roger Barny: Un anti-philosophe dans la Révolution: Simon Nicolas Henri Linguet, de 1788 à 1794 190 (1980) 381-82

Paul LeClerc: The testing of a *philosophe*: André Morellet and the French Revolution 190 (1980) 382

Bronislaw Baczko: 'Former l'homme nouveau': utopie et pédagogie pendant la Révolution française 191 (1980) 643-45

Edna Hindie Lemay: Les modèles anglais et américain à l'Assemblée constituante 191 (1980) 872-84

Janis Spurlock: Essays in reform on the eve of revolution: the public essay contests of the Academy of Châlons-sur-Marne, France, 1776-1789 191 (1980) 885-86

Emmet Kennedy: The French Revolutionary catechisms: ruptures and continuities with Classical, Christian and Enlightenment moralities 191 (1980) 1031-33

Ruth Graham: The enlightened and revolutionary Oratorians of France 192 (1980) 1101-1103

Martin Staum: The Class of moral and political sciences, 1795-1803 192 (1980) 1183-89

James A. Leith: Space and revolution: public monuments and urban planning at the peak of the Terror 193 (1980) 1752-53

Emmet Kennedy: The French revolutionary catechisms: ruptures and continuities with Classical, Christian, and Enlightenment moralities 199 (1981) 353-62

Malcolm C. Cook: Politics in the fiction of the French Revolution, 1789-1794 201 (1982) 233-340

George Armstrong Kelly: War, revolution and terror: a public biography of Adam-Philippe de Custine 205 (1982) 211-95

Henri Coulet: Le roman anti-révolutionnaire en France à l'époque de la Révolution (1789-1800) 216 (1983) 7-9

László Ferenczi: Les ennemis hongrois des Lumières avant et après la Révolution 216 (1983) 12-13

David M. Klinck: An examination of the *notes de lecture* of Louis de Bonald: at the origins of the ideology of the radical right in France 216 (1983) 18-19

Jacques Lemaire: Un aspect de la pensée contre-révolutionnaire: la pensée antimaçonnique (1785-1805) 216 (1983) 20-21

John D. Woodbridge: The reformed pastors of Languedoc face the movement of dechristianisation 1793-1794 216 (1983) 80-81

James A. Leith: Symbolising a new era: some architectural projects under the Constituent and Legislative assemblies 216 (1983) 134-35

Luc Dhondt: La réaction nobiliaire et la révolution des notables de 1787-1789 en Flandre 216 (1983) 172-73

Vivian R. Gruder: From consensus to conflict: the élite, equality and representation, 1787-1788 216 (1983) 180-82

Florence Gauthier: De Mably a Robespierre: un programme économique égalitaire 1775-1793 216 (1983) 200-201

Horst Albert Glaser: Sade et la Révolution 216 (1983) 201-202

Eric Golay: Egalité populaire et égalité bourgeoise a Genève au temps de la Révolution 216 (1983) 203-204

Makoto Takahashi: François Boissel et ses principes de l'égalité en 1789 216 (1983) 220-21

Edna Hindie Lemay: Physiocratie et renouveau à l'Assemblée constituante 1789-1791 216 (1983) 285-87

Takaho Ando: Mme de Condorcet et la philosophie de la 'sympathie' 216 (1983) 335-36

Bronislaw Baczko: Civisme et vandalisme 216 (1983) 377-79

Joyce Seltzer: The French citizen's catechism: a *philosophe*'s moral vision in 1793 216 (1983) 406-407

Oscar A. Haac: A monstrous proposition: the Church stands in need of reform 216 (1983) 427-29

Luís Reis Torgal et Isabel Nobre Vargues: La réception des idées pédagogiques de la Révolution française par le premier libéralisme portugais (1820-1823) 216 (1983) 433-34

Rémy Saisselin: Le dix-huitième siècle de Paul Bourget 216 (1983) 436-37

Martin Staum: The prize contests in moral and political sciences 216 (1983) 437-39

Rey, Marc-Michel

Les Années de formation de F. H. Jacobi, d'après ses lettres inédites à M. M. Rey (1763-1771) avec Le Noble, de madame de Charrière, textes présentées par J. Th. de Booy et Roland Mortier 45 (1966)

Jeroom Vercruysse: Voltaire et Marc Michel Rey 58 (1967) 1707-63

rhetoric

R. Ginsberg: The argument of Voltaire's *L'Homme aux quarante écus*: a study in philosophic rhetoric 56 (1967) 611-57

Jeanne R. Monty: Voltaire's rhetoric: the use of written evidence in the alphabetical works 120 (1974) 41-77

Michel Delon: Les Lumières: travail d'un métaphore 152 (1976) 527-41

Jean Macary: Le dialogue de Diderot et l'anti-rhétorique 153 (1976) 1337-46

Ralph S. Pomeroy: Locke, Alembert, and the anti-rhetoric of the Enlightenment 154 (1976) 1657-75

Karlis Racevskis: Le discours philosophique à l'Académie française: une sémiotique de la démagogie et de l'arrivisme 190 (1980) 343-50

Aurelio Principato: Rhétorique et technique narrative chez l'abbé Prévost 192 (1980) 1352-59

Jean-Paul Sermain: *Rhétorique et roman au dix-huitième siècle: l'exemple de Prévost et de Marivaux (1728-1742)* 233 (1985)

Ricardo, David

Marco Guidi: State, society and the purposes of politics: David Ricardo's theory of economic policy and its origins 216 (1983) 425-26

Riccoboni, Marie-Jeanne Laboras de Mézières, Mme

Ronald C. Rosbottom: Parody and truth in Mme Riccoboni's continuation of *La Vie de Marianne* 81 (1971) 163-75

James C. Nicholls (ed.): *Mme Riccoboni's letters to David Hume, David Garrick and Sir Robert Liston, 1764-1783* 149 (1976)

Madelyn Gutwirth: Laclos and 'Le sexe': the rack of ambivalence 189 (1980) 247-96

Arlette André: Le féminisme chez madame Riccoboni 193 (1980) 1988-95

Richardson, Samuel

Colin Duckworth: Madame Denis's unpublished *Pamela*: a link between Richardson, Goldoni and Voltaire 76 (1970) 37-53

R. Niklaus: Crébillon fils et Richardson 89 (1972) 1169-85

Yvonne Noble: *Clarissa*: paradise irredeemably lost 154 (1976) 1529-45

rococo

Rémy G. Saisselin: The rococo muddle 47 (1966) 233-55

Patrick Brady: The *Lettres persanes*: rococo or neo-classical? 53 (1967) 47-77

Patrick Brady: *Manon Lescaut*: classical, romantic, or rococo? 53 (1967) 339-60

Patrick Brady: Why the rococo? The eighteenth century before the Enlightenment 190 (1980) 154-59

J. Robert Loy: Rococo and the novel as guide to periodisation in the eighteenth century 190 (1980) 166-76

Ilaria Magnani: Paradigma rococò in un'ode di L. Savioli 193 (1980) 1646-49

Patrick Brady: Rococo versus Enlightenment: a view from naturalism 216 (1983) 421

Roland, Jean-Marie

Gita May: Voltaire a-t-il fait une offre d'hospitalité à Rousseau? Un témoignage peu connu par Jean-Marie Roland 47 (1966) 93-113

Romania

Alexandru Dutu: National and European consciousness in the Romanian Enlightenment 55 (1967) 463-79

Adrian Marino: Aspects et idées politiques des Lumières roumaines 190 (1980) 356-64

Peter Horwath: Johann Friedel's Danubian journey along the Turkish border to 'Menschen wie aus dem Schoosse der lieben Mutter Natur' 191 (1980) 687-93

Irina Badescu: Une hypostase roumaine de la problématique des origines 192 (1980) 1199

Iacob Mârza: Horizon livresque des Lumières dans les bibliothèques roumaines de Transylvanie depuis le milieu du 18e siècle jusqu'aux premières décennies du 19e 216 (1983) 251-52

N. Liu: Les Lumières et l'orientation nationale de la culture Roumaine 216 (1983) 392-94

Romanticism

Dorothy B. Schlegel: Diderot as the transmitter of Shaftesbury's Romanticism 27 (1963) 1457-78

Patrick Brady: *Manon Lescaut*: classical, romantic, or rococo? 53 (1967) 339-60

G. Christie Wasberg: 'Transcendence' and 'immanence' in the philosophy of history from Enlightenment to Romanticism 58 (1967) 1829-38

Harold Orel: *English Romantic poets and the Enlightenment: nine essays on a literary relationship* 103 (1973)

Leslie F. Chard: Wordsworth and the Enlightenment: a reconsideration 152 (1976) 473-84

Rosicrucians

Mark Boulby: Enlightenment and Rosicrucianism 192 (1980) 1143-47

Roucher, Jean-Antoine

Edouard Guitton: L'architecture d'un nouveau monde dans *Les Mois* de Roucher 153 (1976) 937-49

Rousseau, Jean Baptiste

Henri Mydlarski: Vauvenargues, juge littéraire de son siècle 150 (1976) 149-81

Rousseau, Jean-Jacques

F. G. Healey: Rousseau, Voltaire and Corsica: some notes on an interesting enigma 10 (1959) 413-19

Virgil W. Topazio: Rousseau, man of contradictions 18 (1961) 77-93

Gita May: Voltaire a-t-il fait une offre d'hospitalité à Rousseau? Un témoignage peu connu par Jean Marie Roland 47 (1966) 93-113

L. Barclay: Louis de Bonald, prophet of the past? 55 (1967) 167-204

Virgil W. Topazio: Rousseau and Pirandello: a quest for identity and dignity 58 (1967) 1577-92

Rémy G. Saisselin: Rousseau and portraiture: from representation to fiction 60 (1968) 201-24

R. A. Leigh: Jean Jacques Rousseau and Mme de Warens: some recently recovered documents 67 (1969) 165-89

M. Molinier: Les relations de Deleyre et de Rousseau, 1753-1778, suivi de la correspondance inédite de Deleyre et du marquis de Girardin, août-décembre 1778 70 (1970) 43-176

Marie José Southworth: La notion de l'île chez Rousseau 70 (1970) 177-91

Michael Cardy: Rousseau's 'irréconciliable ennemi' Marmontel 87 (1972) 217-34

Richard A. Lebrun: Joseph de Maistre and Rousseau 88 (1972) 881-98

Jean A. Perkins: Justification and excuses in Rousseau 89 (1972) 1277-92

Richard Switzer: Voltaire, Rousseau et l'opéra 90 (1972) 1519-28

Christopher Thacker: Voltaire and Rousseau: eighteenth-century gardeners 90 (1972) 1595-614

R. A. Leigh: Rousseau, Voltaire and Saint-Péravy 94 (1972) 17-23

Carolyn Wilberger: Peter the Great: an 18th-century hero of our times? 96 (1972) 7-127

Blandine L. McLaughlin: *Diderot et l'amitié* 100 (1973)

Edward E. Malkin: Rousseau and Epictetus 106 (1973) 113-55

James F. Hamilton: Mme de Staël, partisan of Rousseau or Voltaire? 106 (1973) 253-65

Oscar A. Haac: Rousseau and Marivaux: action and interaction 124 (1974) 221-30

James F. Jones: Du Bos and Rousseau: a question of influence 127 (1974) 231-41

English Showalter: *Madame de Graffigny and Rousseau: between the two 'Discours'* 175 (1978)

Christiane Lanau: 'Je tiens Jean-Jacques Rousseau': un point de l'affaire Rousseau-Hume 182 (1979) 29-34

A.-M. Laborde: Rousseau, sémiotique d'une phtisie 182 (1979) 35-57

Jean-Pierre Le Bouler, Catherine Lafarge: Les emprunts de Mme Dupin à la Bibliothèque du roi dans les années 1748-1750 182 (1979) 107-85

Jean-Pierre Le Bouler et Robert Thiéry: Une partie retrouvée de l'*Ouvrage sur les femmes*, ou Mme Dupin dans la maison des 'Commères', avec un inventaire des papiers Dupin acquis à Monte Carlo le 8 octobre 1980 208 (1982) 373-403

Anna Ridehalgh: Preromantic attitudes and the birth of a legend: French pilgrimages to Ermenonville, 1778-1789 215 (1982) 231-52

Gita May: The Rousseauistic self and Stendhal's autobiographical dilemma 216 (1983) 429-30

J. Roussel: La célébrité des soupers d'Ermenonville 216 (1983) 435-36

Colette Piau-Gillot: La misogynie de J. J. Rousseau 219 (1983) 169-82

Jean-Jacques Robrieux: Jean-Philippe Rameau et l'opinion philosophique en France au dix-huitième siècle 238 (1985) 269-395

Jean-Pierre Le Bouler: Un chapitre inédit de l'*Ouvrage sur les femmes* de Mme Dupin 241 (1986) 253-69

R. Galliani: Rousseau, l'illumination de Vincennes et la critique moderne 245 (1986) 403-47

Aubrey Rosenberg: Three 'unknown' works relating to Jean-Jacques Rousseau 245 (1986) 449-55

R. Barny: *Rousseau dans la Révolution: le personnage de Jean-Jacques et les débuts du culte révolutionnaire (1787-1791)* 246 (1986)

R. A. Leigh: Wegelin's visit to Rousseau in 1763 249 (1986) 303-32

— bibliography

R. A. Leigh: Rousseau's letter to Voltaire on optimism (18 August 1756) 30 (1964) 247-309

George B. Watts: Charles Joseph Panckoucke, 'l'Atlas de la librairie française' 68 (1969) 67-205

— correspondence

Theodore Besterman: Rousseau, conseiller familial: deux lettres de John Albert Bentinck à Jean Jacques Rousseau 1 (1955) 175-81

R. A. Leigh: Rousseau's letter to Voltaire on optimism (18 August 1756) 30 (1964) 247-309

S. S. B. Taylor: Review: *Correspondance complète de Jean Jacques Rousseau*, éd. R. A. Leigh, vol i 41 (1966) 345-60

R. A. Leigh: Observations on the dating of certain Rousseau letters 47 (1966) 115-35

R. A. Leigh: Jean Jacques Rousseau and Mme de Warens: some recently recovered documents 67 (1969) 165-89

— criticism by

Monique Wagner: *Molière and the age of Enlightenment* 112 (1973)

— criticism of

John N. Pappas: *Berthier's 'Journal de Trévoux' and the philosophes* 3 (1957)

J. Vercruysse: C'est la faute à Rousseau, c'est la faute à Voltaire 23 (1963) 61-76

François Jost: La fortune de Rousseau aux Etats-Unis: esquisse d'une étude 25 (1963) 899-959

Samuel S. B. Taylor: Rousseau's contemporary reputation in France 27 (1963) 1545-74

Lionello Sozzi: Interprétations de Rousseau pendant la Révolution 64 (1968) 187-223

Anna Attridge: The reception of *La Nouvelle Héloïse* 120 (1974) 227-67

Peter France: Jean-Jacques Rousseau en Union Soviétique 182 (1979) 87-106

J. C. Stewart-Robertson: Reid's anatomy of culture: a Scottish response to the eloquent Jean-Jacques 205 (1982) 141-63

Tanguy L'Aminot: J.-J. Rousseau face à la droite française 1940-1944 242 (1985) 473-89

R. Galliani: Rousseau, l'illumination de Vincennes et la critique moderne 245 (1986) 403-47

R. Barny: *Rousseau dans la Révolution: le personnage de Jean-Jacques et les débuts du culte révolutionnaire (1787-1791)* 246 (1986)

— philosophy

J. Robert Loy: Nature, reason and enlightenment, Voltaire, Rousseau and Diderot 26 (1963) 1085-107

Lionel Gossman: Time and history in Rousseau 30 (1964) 311-49

P. D. Jimack: Rousseau and the primacy of self 32 (1965) 73-90

Merle L. Perkins: Rousseau on history, liberty and national survival 53 (1967) 79-169

Werner Bahner: Le Mot et la notion de 'peuple' dans l'œuvre de Rousseau 55 (1967) 113-27

Lester G. Crocker: Rousseau et l''opinion' 55 (1967) 395-415

John Pappas: Le rousseauisme de Voltaire 57 (1967) 1169-81

Corrado Rosso: Faut-il changer le monde ou le laisser tel qu'il est? Rousseau: de la *Lettre à Philopolis* à la *Lettre à Voltaire* 190 (1980) 390-95

F. M. Barnard: National culture and political legitimacy: Herder and Rousseau 216 (1983) 379-81

Lester G. Crocker: Rousseau's dilemma: man or citizen? 241 (1986) 271-84

— religion

Ronald Ian Boss: Rousseau's civil religion and the meaning of belief: an answer to Bayle's paradox 84 (1971) 123-93

Zygmunt Jedryka: Le socinianisme et les Lumières 88 (1972) 809-29

Françoise Le Moal: Voltaire, Rousseau et le socinianisme 192 (1980) 1100

Zygmunt Jedryka: Le socinianisme entre Rousseau et Fichte 192 (1980) 1101

Marie Souviron: Les *Pensées philosophiques* de Diderot ou les 'Provinciales' de l'athéisme 238 (1985) 197-267

— works

Theodore Besterman: Review: J.-J. Rousseau, *Œuvres complètes*, i 10 (1959) 519-21

David Scott: Rousseau and flowers: the poetry of botany 182 (1979) 73-86

Ingrid Kisliuk: Le symbolisme du jardin et l'imagination créatrice chez Rousseau, Bernardin de Saint-Pierre et Chateaubriand 185 (1980) 297-418

Jean-Pierre Le Bouler: Sur les écrits 'féministes' de Rousseau 193 (1980) 1891

Jean-Pierre Le Bouler: Sur les écrits 'féministes' de Rousseau 199 (1981) 225-36

Timothy Scanlan: Maxims in Rousseau's major autobiographical works 216 (1983) 364-65

Pierre Saint-Amand: Rousseau contre la science: l'exemple de la botanique dans les textes autobiographiques 219 (1983) 159-67

— — *Confessions*

Merle L. Perkins: Destiny, sentiment and time in the *Confessions* of Jean Jacques Rousseau 67 (1969) 133-64

Robert C. Carroll: Rousseau's bookish ontology 79 (1971) 103-52

M. B. Therrien: Rousseau: lucidité et sincérité 155 (1976) 2071-82

Steve Larkin: J.-J. Rousseau, the *Histoire de Cleveland* and the *Confessions* 192 (1980) 1295-97

Erdmann Waniek: Rousseau's *Confessions* and Moritz's *Anton Reiser*: narrative strategies for presenting the self 192 (1980) 1307-13

— — *Discours sur les sciences et les arts*

James F. Hamilton: A theory of art in Rousseau's first discourse 94 (1972) 73-87

James F. Hamilton: Virtue in Rousseau's first discourse 98 (1972) 119-29

R. Galliani: Rousseau, l'illumination de Vincennes et la critique moderne 245 (1986) 403-47

John Hope Mason: Reading Rousseau's First Discourse 249 (1986) 251-66

— — *Discours sur l'inégalité*

Merle L. Perkins: Liberty and the concept of legitimacy in the *Discours sur l'inégalité* 89 (1972) 1293-304

James F. Hamilton: Parallel interpretations, religious and political, of Rousseau's *Discours sur l'inégalité* 94 (1972) 7-16

Ch. Porset: Discours d'un anonyme sur l'inégalité 1754 182 (1979) 7-27

— — *Du contrat social*

Olivier Lutaud: D'*Areopagitica* à la *Lettre à un premier commis* et de l'*Agreement* au *Contrat social* 26 (1963) 1109-27

Suzanne Hélein-Koss: Albert Camus et le *Contrat social* 161 (1976) 165-204

Robert Ginsberg: Rousseau's *Contrat social* in current contexts 190 (1980) 252-58

Lajos Hopp: Fortune littéraire et politique du *Contrat social* en Hongrie et en Europe orientale 190 (1980) 320-26

— — *Emile*

Peter D. Jimack: *La Genèse et la rédaction de l'"Emile' de J.-J. Rousseau* 13 (1960)

P. D. Jimack: Rousseau misquoting Voltaire? 37 (1965) 77-79

Bronwen D. Sewall: The similarity between Rousseau's *Emile* and the early poetry of Wordsworth 106 (1973) 157-74

Godelieve Mercken-Spaas: The social anthropology of Rousseau's *Emile* 132 (1975) 137-81

R. J. P. Jordan: A new look at Rousseau as educator 182 (1979) 59-72

Timothy M. Scanlan: Patterns of imagery in Rousseau's *Emile* 192 (1980) 1381-87

R. J. Howells: Deux histoires, un discours: *La Nouvelle Héloïse* et le récit des amours d'Emile et Sophie dans l'*Emile* 249 (1986) 267-94

— — *Essai sur l'origine des langues*

Robert Wokler: Rameau, Rousseau, and the *Essai sur l'origine des langues* 117 (1974) 179-238

Charles Porset: L'inquiétante étrangeté de l'*Essai sur l'origine des langues*: Rousseau et ses exégètes 154 (1976) 1715-58

Antonio Verri: On the Porset edition of Rousseau's *Essai sur l'origine des langues* 155 (1976) 2167-71

G. A. Wells: Condillac, Rousseau and Herder on the origin of language 230 (1985) 233-46

— — *Lettre à Christophe de Beaumont*

R. A. Leigh: The first edition of the *Lettre à Christophe de Beaumont* 81 (1971) 207-19

—— *Lettres à Sara*

Robert C. Carroll: Muse and Narcissus: Rousseau's *Lettres à Sara* 137 (1975) 81-107

—— *Lettres de la montagne*

R. A. Leigh: New light on the genesis of the *Lettres de la montagne*: Rousseau's marginalia on Tronchin 94 (1972) 89-119

—— *Lettre sur la musique française*

Françoise Escal: L'esthétique musicale de Rousseau à travers la *Lettre sur la musique française* 193 (1980) 1741-43

—— *La Nouvelle Héloïse*

Lionel Gossman: The worlds of *La Nouvelle Héloïse* 41 (1966) 235-76

David L. Anderson: Abélard and Héloïse: eighteenth-century motif 84 (1971) 7-51

Peter Willis: Rousseau, Stowe and 'le jardin anglais': speculations on visual sources for *La Nouvelle Héloïse* 90 (1972) 1791-98

David L. Anderson: Aspects of motif in *La Nouvelle Héloïse* 94 (1972) 25-72

Christie Vance McDonald: *The Extravagant shepherd: a study of the pastoral vision in Rousseau's 'Nouvelle Héloïse'* 105 (1973)

Anna Attridge: The reception of *La Nouvelle Héloïse* 120 (1974) 227-67

Arnaud Tripet: La *Nouvelle Héloïse* et la rêverie fabulatrice 192 (1980) 1388-95

R. J. Howells: Désir et distance dans *La Nouvelle Héloïse* 230 (1985) 223-32

R. J. Howells: Deux histoires, un discours: *La Nouvelle Héloïse* et le récit des amours d'Emile et Sophie dans l'*Emile* 249 (1986) 267-94

Santo L. Arico: The arrangement of St Preux's first letter to Julie in *La Nouvelle Héloïse* 249 (1986) 295-301

—— *La Reine Fantasque*

Raymonde Robert: Rousseau et la féerie: *La Reine Fantasque* 192 (1980) 1370-81

—— *Rêveries du promeneur solitaire*

Francesco Gentile: Utopia e realismo nel gioco politico del viandante solitario 191 (1980) 678-84

Rousseau, Pierre

Raymond F. Birn: *Pierre Rousseau and the philosophes of Bouillon* 29 (1964)

Rowe, Nicholas

J. Peter Verdurmen: Varieties of determinism in Racine and Rowe: dramatic structure and the role of society 192 (1980) 1545-47

Royal Society of London

Xavier Coyer: L'élection de l'abbé Coyer à la Royal Society of London: deux lettres inédites de Voltaire et de d'Alembert 249 (1986) 379-80

Russia

Valerie A. Tumins: Voltaire and the rise of Russian drama 27 (1963) 1689-701

Valerie A. Tumins: Enlightenment and mysticism in eighteenth-century Russia 58 (1967) 1671-88

Carolyn Wilberger: Peter the Great: an 18th-century hero of our times? 96 (1972) 7-127

Barbara Widenor Maggs: Answers from eighteenth-century China to certain questions on Voltaire's sinology 120 (19) 179-98

Arnold Miller: Vera Zasulich's *Jean-Jacques Rousseau*: a Russian revolutionary's view of Rousseau's political thought 129 (1975) 67-114

Barbara Widenor Maggs: Eighteenth-century Russian reflections on the Lisbon earthquake, Voltaire and optimism 137 (1975) 7-29

J. Laurence Black: Nicholas Karamzin and the dilemma of luxury in eighteenth-century Russia 151 (1976) 313-22

Jacques Proust: Diderot et l'expérience russe: un exemple de pratique théorique au XVIIIe siècle 154 (1976) 1777-1800

C. H. Wilberger: *Voltaire's Russia: window on the east* 164 (1976)

J. Laurence Black: Citizenship training and moral regeneration as the mainstay of Russian schools 167 (1977) 427-51

Peter France: Jean-Jacques Rousseau en Union Soviétique 182 (1979) 87-106

J. Laurence Black: The Imperial educational society for noble girls in St Petersburg (1765-1796) 191 (1980) 1003

I. Serman: Kantemir et le problème du contexte dans le mouvement littéraire russe du XVIIIe siècle 193 (1980) 1644-46

Valerie A. Tumins: Secularisation of Russian literature in the eighteenth century 216 (1983) 77-78

Daniel L. Schlafly: Western Europe discovers Russia: foreign travellers in the reign of Catherine the Great 216 (1983) 115-17

Maurice Colin: Peut-on parler d'une idéologie nobiliaire en Russie? 216 (1983) 166-68

Kenneth Craven: Publish and languish: the fate of Nikolai Ivanovich Novikov (1743-1818), propagator of the Enlightenment under Catherine II 216 (1983) 238-39

Igor Smirnov: Le problème de l'homme dans l'œuvre d'Alexandre Radichtchev 216 (1983) 324-26

Giulia Cantarutti: Patriotisme et sentiment national dans les *Betrachtungen und Gedanken* (1803-1805) de F. M. Klinger, un représentant des Lumières allemandes à la cour russe 216 (1983) 383-85

Georges Festa: Images et réalités de la vie commerciale italienne à travers le *Voyage d'Italie* de Sade 217 (1983) 23-26

Robert F. O'Reilly: Desire in Sade's *Les 120 Journées de Sodome* 217 (1983) 249-56

Josué V. Harari: D'une raison à l'autre: le dispositif Sade 230 (1985) 273-82

Julie C. Hayes: Sophistry and displacement: the poetics of Sade's ciphers 242 (1986) 335-43

Robert F. O'Reilly: Language and the transcendent subject in three works of the marquis de Sade: *Les 120 journées de Sodome, La Philosophie dans le boudoir*, and *Justine* 249 (1986) 399-406

Saint-Evremond, Charles de Marguetel de Saint-Denis, seigneur de

Alberto Gil Novales: Vertu et morale: Saint-Evremond en Espagne: Jaime Sicre 216 (1983) 349-50

Saint-Hilaire, Isidore-Geoffroy

Franco Crispini: Mostri e mostruosità: un problema delle 'sciences de la vie' da Diderot a I. Geoffroy Saint-Hilaire 192 (1980) 1189-98

Saint-Hyacinthe, Thémiseul de

Elisabeth Carayol: *Thémiseul de Saint-Hyacinthe, 1684-1746* 221 (1984)

Saint-Lambert, Jean-François, marquis de

J. Robert Loy: Saint-Lambert, moralist: philosophy at second hand; Enlightenment among the titled 216 (1983) 353-54

Saint-Martin, Louis-Claude de

Léon Cellier: Saint-Martin et Voltaire 24 (1963) 355-68

Jean Roussel: Esotérisme et utopie: L.-C. de Saint-Martin 191 (1980) 723-29

Romano Baldi: Louis-Claude de Saint-Martin et la question de l'origine des langues 193 (1980) 1650-58

Saint-Péravy, Jean-Nicolas-Marcel Guérineau de

R. A. Leigh: Rousseau, Voltaire and Saint-Péravy 94 (1972) 17-23

Saint-Pierre, Charles-Irénée Castel de

Merle L. Perkins: Voltaire and the abbé de Saint-Pierre on world peace 18 (1961) 9-34

Merle L. Perkins: *Voltaire's concept of international order* 36 (1965)

Elspeth M. Horsman: The abbé de Saint-Pierre and domestic politics 190 (1980) 284-90

Michelangelo Ghio: I progetti di pace perpertua dell'abate di St Pierre nei giudizi di Rousseau, Leibniz e Voltaire 190 (1980) 307-18

Saint-Simon, Louis de Rouvroy, duc de

Hélène Himelfarb: Saint Simon et le jansénisme des Lumières 88 (1972) 749-68

Sanches, Antonio Nunes Ribeiro

Pierre van Bever: La religion du docteur Antonio Nunes Ribeiro Sanches 41 (1966) 277-83

Sand, Georges

Ute van Runset: Illuminisme et Lumières: impact sur les idées sociales de George Sand 216 (1983) 439-41

Sanson, Nicolas

Renée Simon: *Nicolas Fréret, académicien* 17 (1961)

Sardinia

G. Festa: Le voyage en Sardaigne au siècle des Lumières 249 (1986) 439-45

satire

Oscar A. Haac: L'amour dans les collèges jésuites: une satire anonyme du dix-huitième siècle 18 (1961) 95-111

Claude E. Jones: Satire and certain English satirists of the Enlightenment 25 (1963) 885-97

Jeanne R. Monty: *Etude sur le style polémique de Voltaire: le 'Dictionnaire philosophique'* 44 (1966)

Pierre Haffter: L'usage satirique des causales dans les contes de Voltaire 53 (1967) 7-28

Roy S. Wolper: Swift's enlightened gulls 58 (1967) 1915-37

Donna Isaacs Dalnekoff: Voltaire's *Le Monde comme il va*: a satire on satire 106 (1973) 85-102

Ahmad Gunny: Voltaire and the novel: Sterne 124 (1974) 149-61

Mark Waddicor: An unpublished satire of the regency: *Les Devises de la cour* 124 (1974) 167-79

Donna Isaacs Dalnekoff: The meaning of Eldorado: utopia and satire in *Candide* 127 (1974) 41-59

Vladimir R. Rossman: L'onomancie, exemple de satire dans l'*Encyclopédie* 127 (19) 223-30

Liliane Willens: *Voltaire's comic theatre: composition, conflict and critics* 136 (1975)

Ahmad Gunny: *Voltaire and English literature: a study of English literary influences on Voltaire* 177 (1979)

Edward A. Bloom: Eden betray'd: city motifs in satire 191 (1980) 956-62

C. J. Rawson: Satire, fiction, and extreme situations 192 (1980) 1286

A. J. Hanou: Anglo-Dutch relations: spectators and satire in the early eighteenth century 193 (1980) 1831-32

Lionel P. Honoré: The philosophical satire of La Mettrie 215 (1982) 175-222

Wayne H. Finke: José Gerardo de Hervás and his *Sátira contra los malos escritores de este siglo* 216 (1983) 13-14

Thomas R. Cleary: Illusion in late baroque painting and complex perspective in Enlightenment satire 216 (1983) 131

Lionel P. Honoré: The philosophical satire of La Mettrie: part II 241 (1986) 203-36

Saurin, Bernard-Joseph

G. Roth: Diderot 'renverse' *Le Siège de Calais* de Saurin 2 (1956) 233-40

savages

Lionello Sozzi: Bougainville e i selvaggi 192 (1980) 1181-83

Mathé Allain: The coloniser's viewpoint: Louisiana Indians as seen by the French 216 (1983) 87-88

Townsend W. Bowling: European man encounters the New World native in the French novel 1751-1800 216 (1983) 95-97

Howard Brofsky: Rameau and the Indians: the popularity of *Les Sauvages* 216 (1983) 99-100

Philip Stewart: Du sauvage au colon anglais: l'Américain au dix-huitième siècle 216 (1983) 120-21

Savioli, L.

Ilaria Magnani: Paradigma rococò in un'ode di L. Savioli 193 (1980) 1646-49

Scandinavia

G. C. Wasberg: The influence of the 'enlightened' philosophy of history on Scandinavian political thought 27 (1963) 1775-85

Theodore Besterman: A provisional bibliography of Scandinavian and Finnish editions and translations of Voltaire 47 (1966) 53-92

Carol Gold: Educational reform in Denmark, 1784-1814 167 (1977) 49-64

H. Aarnold Barton: Popular education in Sweden: theory and practice 167 (1977) 523-41 scepticism

Richard H. Popkin: Scepticism in the Enlightenment 26 (1963) 1321-45

Martin S. Staum: Newton and Voltaire: constructive sceptics 62 (1968) 29-56

Marie Souviron: Les *Pensées philosophiques* de Diderot ou les 'Provinciales' de l'athéisme 238 (1985) 197-267

Schall, J. E. F.

Mario A. Cattaneo: La discussione su Beccaria in Germania: K. F. Hommel e J. E. F. Schall 191 (1980) 935-43

Scheffer, Carl Fredrik

Gunnar von Proschwitz: Lettres inédites de madame Du Deffand, du président Hénault et du comte de Bulkeley au baron Carl Fredrik Scheffer 1751-1756 10 (1959) 267-412

Schiller, Friedrich

Erdmann Waniek: Pragmatic lesson and romantic tale: moral perspective in Schiller's *Der Verbrecher aus verlorener Ehre* (1786) and Tieck's *Der blonde Eckbert* (1797) 216 (1983) 369-70

science

Jean A. Perkins: Voltaire and the natural sciences 37 (1965) 61-76

Pierre M. Conlon: La Condamine the inquisitive 55 (1967) 361-93

Colm Kiernan: *The Enlightenment and science in eighteenth-century France*. Second edition revised and enlarged 59A (1973)

Denise Brahimi: Exotisme, science et idéologie 151 (1976) 363-84

Paolo Casini: La loi naturelle: réflexion politique et sciences exactes 151 (1976) 417-32

Donald M. Hassler: Erasmus Darwin and Enlightenment origins of science fiction 153 (1976) 1045-56

Gabrijela Vidan: Diderot: la construction scientifique et son relais par l'imagination 155 (1976) 2207-22

Jeanne Chenu: Littérature scientifique en Nouvelle Grenade à la veille de l'indépendance: du discours à la pratique 167 (1977) 313-36

Emmet Kennedy: Destutt de Tracy and the unity of the sciences 171 (1977) 223-39

Eugenio Lecaldano: Il metodo della 'scienza dell'uomo' nell'Illuminismo scozzese da Hutcheson a Smith 190 (1980) 457-67

Alberto Gil Novales: Il concetto di accademia delle scienze in Spagna, secolo XVIII 190 (1980) 470-71

Irina Badescu: Une hypostase roumaine de la problématique des origines 192 (1980) 1199

Antonio Verri: Antropologia e linguistica in Rousseau 192 (1980) 1205-18

Daniel Droixhe: Le cercle et le gland: linguistique et anthropologie chez Hamann 192 (1980) 1246-56

Ann Thomson: From 'l'histoire naturelle de l'homme' to the natural history of mankind 216 (1983) 121-22

— astronomy

Hélène Monod-Cassidy: Un astronome-philosophe, Jérôme de Lalande 56 (1967) 907-30

David Beeson (ed.): Maupertuis, *Lettre d'un horloger anglois à un astronome de Pékin* 230 (1985) 189-222

— biology

Miguel Benítez: Entre le mythe et la science: Benoît de Maillet et l'origine des êtres dans la mer 216 (1983) 307-309

— botany

David Scott: Rousseau and flowers: the poetry of botany 182 (1979) 73-86

Pierre Saint-Amand: Rousseau contre la science: l'exemple de la botanique dans les textes autobiographiques 219 (1983) 159-67

— chemistry

Maurice Crosland: The development of chemistry in the eighteenth century 24 (1963) 369-441

Robert L. Walters: Chemistry at Cirey 58 (1967) 1807-27

Louis S. Greenbaum: The humanitarianism of Antoine Laurent Lavoisier 88 (1972) 651-75

Arthur Donovan: Chemistry in the Scottish Enlightenment 152 (1976) 587-605

Karl Hofbauer: Chemistry's enlightened audience 153 (1976) 1069-86

Henri Laboucheix: Chimie, matérialisme et théologie chez Joseph Priestley 153 (1976) 1219-44

— cosmology

Alain-Marc Rieu: Kant: critique du 'Cosmologisme' et fin des Lumières 216 (1983) 324

— ethnology

Roger Mercier: Image de l'autre et image de soi-même dans le discours ethnologique au XVIIIe siècle 154 (1976) 1417-35

— geology

Marguerite Carozzi: Voltaire's geological observations in *Les Singularités de la nature* 215 (1982) 101-19

— journalism

Marie-Rose de Labriolle: *'Le Pour et contre' et son temps* 34-35 (1965)

— medicine

Jean Starobinski: La nostalgie: théories médicales et expression littéraire 27 (1963) 1505-18

Renée Waldinger: Voltaire and medicine 58 (1967) 1777-806

Carmelina Imbroscio: Recherches et réflexions de la médecine française du dix-huitième siècle sur les phénomènes psychosomatiques 190 (1980) 494-501

Paul Hoffmann: La théorie de l'homme dans la *Medicina rationalis systematica* de Friedrich Hoffmann 216 (1983) 314-15

— methodology

Maurice Crosland: 'Nature' and measurement in eighteenth-century France 87 (1972) 277-309

J. I. Biró: Description and explanation in Hume's science of man 190 (1980) 449-57

Maria Teresa Marcialis: Pirronismo e perfettibilità della scienza nell'*Histoire de l'Académie royale des sciences* (1676-1776) 190 (1980) 472-80

James L. Larson: Kant's principle of formal purposiveness 190 (1980) 507-508

Stefano Poggi: Le categorie dell'esperienza scientifica nella prima ricezione del kantismo 190 (1980) 513-17

Massimo Mugnai: Linguaggio e teoria nella concezione della scienza di J. Heinrich Lambert 190 (1980) 517

— natural history

Maurice Crosland: The development of chemistry in the eighteenth century 24 (1963) 369-441

Otis Fellows: Buffon's place in the Enlightenment 25 (1963) 603-29

Elizabeth Anderson: La collaboration de Sonnini de Manoncourt à l'*Histoire naturelle* de Buffon 120 (1974) 329-58

Krzysztof Pomian: Médailles/coquilles = érudition/philosophie 154 (1976) 1677-1703

Ann Thomson: From 'l'histoire naturelle de l'homme' to the natural history of mankind 216 (1983) 121-22

Giulio Barsanti: Linné et Buffon: deux images différentes de la nature et de l'histoire naturelle 216 (1983) 306-307

— physics

Linda Gardiner Janik: Searching for the metaphysics of science: the structure and composition of Mme Du Châtelet's *Institutions de physique, 1737-1740* 201 (1982) 85-113

— physiognomy

Marcia Allentuck: Fuseli and Lavater: physiognomical theory and the Enlightenment 55 (1967) 89-112

— physiology

François Azouvi: Quelques jalons dans la préhistoire de la cénesthésie 216 (1983) 303-305

John Neubauer: Albrecht von Haller's philosophy of physiology 216 (1983) 320-22

— progress

M. L. Dufrenoy: Maupertuis et le progrès scientifique 25 (1963) 519-87

— society

Roger Hahn: The application of science to society: the societies of arts 25 (1963) 829-36

Julian Huxley: A factor overlooked by the *philosophes*: the population explosion 25 (1963) 861-83

Agnes Raymond: Le problème de la population chez les encyclopédistes 26 (1963) 1379-88

— technology

F. G. Healey: The Enlightenment view of 'homo faber' 25 (1963) 837-59

science fiction

Donald M. Hassler: Erasmus Darwin and Enlightenment origins of science fiction 153 (1976) 1045-56

Scotland

Robert D. Thornton: Robert Burns and the Scottish Enlightenment 58 (1967) 1533-49

Clarence Tracy: Johnson's *Journey to the western islands of Scotland*: a reconsideration 58 (1967) 1593-606

Hugh Trevor-Roper: The Scottish Enlightenment 58 (1967) 1635-58

R. G. Cant: The Scottish universities in the eighteenth century 58 (1967) 1953-66

D. Young: Scotland and Edinburgh in the eighteenth century 58 (1967) 1967-90

Roger L. Emerson: The social composition of enlightened Scotland: the select society of Edinburgh, 1754-1764 114 (1973) 291-329

John Barker: A *rara avis in terris?*: Lord Forbes of Pitsligo as Enlightenment figure 151 (1976) 225-34

Paul Chamley: Sir James Steuart, économiste et philosophe, ses affinités avec la franc-maçonnerie et son influence sur l'idéalisme allemand 151 (1976) 433-47

Arthur Donovan: Chemistry in the Scottish Enlightenment 152 (1976) 587-605

Hiroshi Mizuta: Towards a definition of the Scottish Enlightenment 154 (1976) 1459-64

Roger L. Emerson: Scottish universities in the eighteenth century, 1690-1800 167 (1977) 453-74

Laurence L. Bongie: Voltaire's English, high treason and a manifesto for bonnie prince Charles 171 (1977) 7-29

F. J. McLynn: Voltaire and the Jacobite rising of 1745 185 (1980) 7-20

Eugenio Lecaldano: Il metodo della 'scienza dell'uomo' nell'Illuminismo scozzese da Hutcheson a Smith 190 (1980) 457-67

Peter Burke: Scottish historians and the feudal system: the conceptualisation of social change 191 (1980) 537-39

Nicholas Phillipson: Virtue, commerce, and the science of man in early eighteenth-century Scotland 191 (1980) 750-53

Hiroshi Mizuta: Two Adams in the Scottish Enlightenment: Adam Smith and Adam Ferguson on progress 191 (1980) 812-19

Istvan Hont: Equality and the structure of needs in eighteenth-century Scottish political economy 216 (1983) 204-207

Norbert Waszek: Bibliography of the Scottish Enlightenment in Germany 230 (1985) 283-303

Roger L. Emerson: Natural philosophy and the problem of the Scottish Enlightenment 242 (1986) 243-91

Anand C. Chitnis: Agricultural improvement, political management and civic virtue in enlightened Scotland: an historiographical critique 245 (1986) 475-88

— religion

James K. Cameron: The Church of Scotland in the age of reason 58 (1967) 1939-51

Scott, Geoffrey

C. P. Courtney: *The Portrait of Zélide*: Geoffrey Scott and Belle de Zuylen 219 (1983) 281-88

Scott, Walter

Harold Orel: *English Romantic poets and the Enlightenment: nine essays on a literary relationship* 103 (1973)

288

sculpture

Theodore Besterman: The terra-cotta statue of Voltaire made by Houdon for Beaumarchais 12 (1960) 21-27

David Irwin: The Italian Renaissance viewed by an 18th-century sculptor 193 (1980) 1664-67

Roberta Roani Villani: Lo scultore pistoiese Francesco Carradori 193 (1980) 1707-10

Gerhard Charles Rump: The so-called 'Charakterköpfe' (characteristic heads) of Franz Xaver Messerschmidt (1736-1783) 216 (1983) 143-45

G. Festa: Images du Bernin au dix-huitième siècle: l'œuvre du sculpteur jugée par les voyageurs français en Italie 241 (1986) 87-94

secularisation

Dominique Bourel: La sécularisation dans le judaïsme prussien dans la période post-mendelssohnienne 216 (1983) 47-48

J. W. Buisman: Quelques aspects sociologiques de la sécularisation dans les Pays-Bas septentrionaux pendant la seconde moitié du dix-huitième siècle: une approche singulière 216 (1983) 50-51

David Dowdey: Secularisation in Moses Mendelssohn's thinking: harmony between the world of Judaism and Enlightenment? 216 (1983) 52-53

Verena Ehrlich-Haefeli: Sécularisation, langue et structure familiale: la figure du père dans le théâtre de Lessing et de Diderot 216 (1983) 53-56

Michael Heyd: The reaction to enthusiasm and the secularisation of religious sensibilities in the early eighteenth century 216 (1983) 58-59

Edward M. Jennings: Changes in English law, learning and finance, 1650-1750: time and secularisation 216 (1983) 61-62

Daniel Ligou: La sécularisation des rituels maçonniques en France au dix-huitième siècle 216 (1983) 62-65

Henri Mydlarski: La sécularisation de la pensée chez les moralistes de dix-huitième siècle 216 (1983) 65-66

Bernard Plongeron: Echec a la sécularisation des Lumières: la religion comme lien social 216 (1983) 68-69

Manuel Augusto Rodrigues: La sécularisation au Portugal 216 (1983) 70

Valerie A. Tumins: Secularisation of Russian literature in the eighteenth century 216 (1983) 77-78

John D. Woodbridge: The reformed pastors of Languedoc face the movement of dechristianisation 1793-1794 216 (1983) 80-81

Sénac de Meilhan, Gabriel

M. G. Carroll: Sénac de Meilhan's *Les Deux cousins*: a monarchist paradox at the end of the *ancien régime* 171 (1977) 211-21

Senancour, Etienne-Jean-Baptiste-Pierre-Ignace Pivert de

Béatrice Didier: Senancour et les Lumières 87 (1972) 311-31

Seneca

Stephen Werner: Voltaire and Seneca 67 (1969) 29-44

William T. Conroy: *Diderot's 'Essai sur Sénèque'* 131 (1975)

William T. Conroy: Three neglected sources of Diderot's *Essai sur Sénèque*: Ponçol, Peyrilhe, L'Estoile 176 (1979) 259-71

sensationalism

Merle L. Perkins: The crisis of sensationalism in Diderot's *Lettre sur les aveugles* 174 (1978) 167-88

sensibility

D. A. Coward: Laclos et la sensibilité 87 (1972) 235-51

English Showalter: Sensibility at Cirey: Mme Du Châtelet, Mme de Graffigny, and the *Voltairomanie* 135 (1975) 181-92

Jean Garagnon: La sensibilité comme idéologie de substitution de la noblesse dans *Aline et Valcour* 216 (1983) 174-77

G. A. Starr: Egalitarian and elitist implications of sensibility 216 (1983) 218-20

sensualism

Walter Moser: De la signification d'une poésie insignifiante: examen de la poésie fugitive au XVIIIe siècle et de ses rapports avec la pensée sensualiste en France 94 (19) 277-415

sentiment

M. L. Perkins: Destiny, sentiment and time in the *Confessions* of Jean Jacques Rousseau 67 (1969) 133-64

David Williams: Voltaire on the sentimental novel 135 (1975) 115-34

sentimentality

Ferenc Biró: L'apparition de la mentalité sentimentale dans la vie littéraire de la Hongrie des Lumières 191 (1980) 997-1003

Wolf Wucherpfennig: 'Die unvergnügte Seele': mélancolie et idylle dans le siècle des Lumières 216 (1983) 372-73

Serbia

Barbara W. Maggs: Voltaire and the Balkans: aspects of the Enlightenment in 18th-century Croatia and Serbia 189 (1980) 81-118

shorthand

Joel J. Gold: Competitive British shorthand systems: or, the case of the battling brachygraphers 216 (1983) 246-48

Shuvalov (family)

Letters to the Shuvalovs, ed. Christopher Todd 108 (1973)

Sicily

Silvia Bordini Porretta: Tendenze riformatrici e città nuove nella Sicilia del Settecento 191 (1980) 907-14

Sicre, Jaime

Alberto Gil Novales: Vertu et morale: Saint-Evremond en Espagne: Jaime Sicre 216 (1983) 349-50

Silhouette, Etienne de

Richard Gilbert Knapp: *The Fortunes of Pope's 'Essay on man' in eighteenth-century France* 82 (1971)

Simon, Richard

Marie-Hélène Cotoni: *L'Exégèse du Nouveau Testament dans la philosophie française du dix-huitième siècle* 220 (1984)

sincerity

Emita B. Hill: Sincerity and self-awareness in the *Paysan parvenu* 88 (1972) 735-48

slavery

William R. Womack: Eighteenth-century themes in the *Histoire philosophique et politique des deux Indes* of Guillaume Raynal 96 (1972) 129-265

Emeka Abanime: Voltaire antiesclavagiste 182 (1979) 237-51

Colette Verger Michael: Condorcet and the inherent contradiction in the American affirmation of natural rights and slaveholding 191 (1980) 768-74

Marie-Thérèse Isaac: L'Européen à la rencontre du noir-esclave des Etats-Unis d'Amérique d'après les *Voyages* du marquis de Chastellux 216 (1983) 111-12

Liliane Willens: Lafayette's emancipation experiment in French Guiana 1786-1792 216 (1983) 222-24

Liliane Willens: Lafayette's emancipation experiment in French Guiana – 1786-1792 242 (1986) 345-62

Slovenia

Jože Koruza: L'éveil de la conscience nationale et les idées du siècle des Lumières dans la littérature slovène de la deuxième moitié du dix-huitième siècle 216 (1983) 390-92

Smith, Adam

Eugenio Lecaldano: Il metodo della 'scienza dell'uomo' nell'Illuminismo scozzese da Hutcheson a Smith 190 (1980) 457-67

Hiroshi Mizuta: Two Adams in the Scottish Enlightenment: Adam Smith and Adam Ferguson on progress 191 (1980) 812-19

Ian Ross: The physiocrats and Adam Smith 216 (1983) 292-93

Hiroshi Mizuta: Adam Smith and Benjamin Constant 216 (1983) 430-32

Smollett, Tobias

E. T. Helmick: Voltaire and *Humphry Clinker* 67 (1969) 59-64

Margarette Smith: Smollett and matrimonial bawdy 228 (1984) 39-46

socialism

Guy Besse: Marx, Engels et le XVIIIe siècle français 24 (1963) 155-70

Aaron Noland: Rousseau and nineteenth-century French socialism 57 (1967) 1097-122

René Pomeau: Candide entre Marx et Freud 89 (1972) 1305-23

societies, learned

Roger Hahn: The application of science to society: the societies of arts 25 (1963) 829-36

Henry Lowood: Patriotism and progress: the role of the German patriotic and economic societies in the promotion of science and technology 216 (1983) 394-96

society

Roger Hahn: The application of science to society: the societies of arts 25 (1963) 829-36

Ann Thomson: Le philosophe et la société 190 (1980) 273-84

Peter L. Smith: Natural order and social code in eighteenth-century French comedy 192 (1980) 1527

Bernard Plongeron: Echec a la sécularisation des Lumières: la religion comme lien social 216 (1983) 68-69

Paul H. Meyer: The breakdown of hierarchial concepts in 18th-century French society, literature, and art 216 (1983) 210-11

— social change

J. G. A. Pocock: Gibbon and the stages of society: progress, ambivalence and corruption in the *Decline and fall* 191 (1980) 537

Peter Burke: Scottish historians and the feudal system: the conceptualisation of social change 191 (1980) 537-39

— social criticism

John Van Eerde: Aspects of social criticism in eighteenth-century French comedy 37 (1965) 81-107

James S. Munro: Moral and social preoccupations in early eighteenth-century French comedy 57 (1967) 1031-54

D. J. Adams: Style and social ideas in *Jacques le fataliste* 124 (1974) 231-48

Godelieve Mercken-Spaas: The social anthropology of Rousseau's *Emile* 132 (1975) 137-81

David Y. Jacobson: Trial by jury and criticism of the old régime 153 (1976) 1099-111

S. F. Davies: Louvet as social critic: *Les Amours du Chevalier de Faublas* 183 (1980) 223-37

Irmgard A. Hartig: Réflexions sur la cellule familiale dans l'utopie sociale de Sylvain Maréchal 191 (1980) 685-87

L. Adams: Anson in Frivola: an exercise in social criticism: Coyer's *Découverte de l'île Frivole* (1751) 191 (1980) 851-58

Janis Spurlock: Essays in reform on the eve of revolution: the public essay contests of the Academy of Châlons-sur-Marne, France, 1776-1789 191 (1980) 885-86

Mona Scheuermann: Social protest in the eighteenth-century English novel 191 (1980) 962-65

— social history

Louis S. Greenbaum: Health-care and hospital-building in eighteenth-century France: reform proposals of Du Pont de Nemours and Condorcet 152 (1976) 895-930

Vilmos Gyenis: L'idéal du bonheur et la vie quotidienne dans l'Europe centrale et orientale au milieu du XVIIIe siècle: les rapports de la prose mineure 153 (1976) 1019-43

D. A. Coward: Eighteenth-century attitudes to prostitution 189 (1980) 363-99

Robert Shackleton: The Enlightenment and the artisan 190 (1980) 53-62

Peter Burke: Scottish historians and the feudal system: the conceptualisation of social change 191 (1980) 537-39

Vittorio E. Giuntella: La città dell'Illuminismo 191 (1980) 927-35

Robert Niklaus: Etude comparée de la situation de la femme en Angleterre et en France 193 (1980) 1909-18

— social problems

John Dunkley: *Gambling: a social and moral problem in France, 1685-1792* 235 (1985)

— sociology

R. J. Howells: The metaphysic of nature: basic values and their application in the social philosophy of Rousseau 60 (1968) 109-200

Darline Gay Levy: Simon Linguet's sociological system: an exhortation to patience and invitation to revolution 70 (1970) 219-93

Arnold Ages: The private Voltaire: three studies in the correspondence 81 (1971) 7-125

Raymond Birn: *Livre et société* after ten years: formation of a discipline 151 (1976) 287-312

Orest Ranum: D'Alembert, Tacitus and the political sociology of despotism 191 (1980) 547-58

Sergio Bartolommei: Analisi di una similitudine: 'età dell'uomo' ed 'età del genere umano' in Turgot 191 (1980) 747-49

Nicholas Phillipson: Virtue, commerce, and the science of man in early eighteenth-century Scotland 191 (1980) 750-53

Nadia Boccara Postigliola: Il 'craving for employment' nella scienza dell'uomo e della società di David Hume 191 (1980) 753-60

Darline Gay Levy: Despotism in Simon-Nicolas-Henri Linguet's science of society: theory and application 191 (1980) 761-68

Joyce Seltzer: Volney's science of political society: from observations to application 191 (1980) 774-81

Ida Cappiello: I Giacobini e le scienze sociali 191 (1980) 781-88

Carlo Bordini: Interpretazioni sul pensiero sociale di Gaetano Filangieri 191 (1980) 900-906

Henri Laboucheix: *Richard Price as moral philosopher and political theorist*, translated by Sylvia and David Raphael 207 (1982)

J. W. Buisman: Quelques aspects sociologiques de la sécularisation dans les Pays-Bas septentrionaux pendant la seconde moitié du dix-huitième siècle: une approche singulière 216 (1983) 50-51

Hernâni A. Resende: Sur l'étude des prémisses théoriques de la pensée dialectique au sein des doctrines sociales en France au siècle des Lumières: remarques de méthode 216 (1983) 69-70

Ute van Runset: Illuminisme et Lumières: impact sur les idées sociales de George Sand 216 (1983) 439-41

Socinianism

Zygmunt Jedryka: Le socinianisme et les Lumières 88 (1972) 809-29

R. E. Florida: *Voltaire and the socinians* 122 (1974)

Françoise Le Moal: Voltaire, Rousseau et le socinianisme 192 (1980) 1100

Zygmunt Jedryka: Le socinianisme entre Rousseau et Fichte 192 (1980) 1101

E. R. Briggs: English Socinianism around Newton and Whiston 216 (1983) 48-50

Socrates

Raymond Trousson: Grandeur et décadence de Socrate chez Jean Jacques Rousseau 58 (1967) 1659-69

Sonnenfels, Joseph von

B. Becker-Cantarino: Joseph von Sonnenfels and the development of secular education in eighteenth-century Austria 167 (1977) 29-47

Sonnini de Manoncourt, Charles-Nicolas-Sigisbert

Elizabeth Anderson: La collaboration de Sonnini de Manoncourt à l'*Histoire naturelle* de Buffon 120 (1974) 329-58

sorcery

Jacques Marx: L'abbé Fiard et ses sorciers 124 (1974) 253-69

soul

Paul Hoffmann: La controverse entre Leibniz et Stahl sur la nature de l'âme 190 (1980) 492-94

Paul Hoffmann: La controverse entre Leibniz et Stahl sur la nature de l'âme 199 (1981) 237-49

sovereignty

Ian M. Wilson: *The Influence of Hobbes and Locke in the shaping of the concept of sovereignty in eighteenth-century France* 101 (1973)

Spain

Daniel Henri Pageaux: La *Gaceta de Madrid* et les traductions espagnoles d'ouvrages français (1750- 1770) 57 (1967) 1147-68

Paul Ilie: Voltaire and Spain: the meaning of *Don Pèdre* 117 (1974) 153-78

Christopher Todd: A provisional bibliography of published Spanish translations of Voltaire 161 (1976) 43-136

George M. Addy: The first generation of academic reform in Spanish universities, 1760-1789 167 (1977) 475-89

Rinaldo Froldi: L'Illuminismo nella cultura spagnola: stato degli studi e prospettive della futura ricerca 190 (1980) 225-35

Danielle Johnson-Cousin: Les 'leçons de déclamation' de Germaine Necker: note sur le 'mystère Clairon' 183 (1980) 161-64

Maria Gaetana Salvatores Scarpa: L'idée de 'bonheur' chez madame de Staël 191 (1980) 1004-1009

Stahl, Georg Ernst

Maurice Crosland: The development of chemistry in the eighteenth century 24 (1963) 369-441

Paul Hoffmann: La controverse entre Leibniz et Stahl sur la nature de l'âme 190 (1980) 492-94

Paul Hoffmann: La controverse entre Leibniz et Stahl sur la nature de l'âme 199 (1981) 237-49

Steele, Richard

Calhoun Winton: Addison and Steele in the English Enlightenment 27 (1963) 1901-18

Stendhal

Arnold Ages: Stendhal and Voltaire: the *philosophe* as target 62 (1968) 83-99

Gita May: The Rousseauistic self and Stendhal's autobiographical dilemma 216 (1983) 429-30

Sterne, Laurence

Ahmad Gunny: Voltaire and the novel: Sterne 124 (1974) 149-61

Christie V. McDonald: L'œuvre du texte: fragmentation et système dans *Tristram Shandy* 192 (1980) 1395-1403

Ruth Perry: Women in *Tristram Shandy* 193 (1980) 1967-68

Emile Lizé: Voltaire et les *Sermons de M. Yorick* 215 (1982) 99-100

Steuart, James

Paul Chamley: Sir James Steuart, économiste et philosophe, ses affinités avec la franc-maçonnerie et son influence sur l'idéalisme allemand 151 (1976) 433-47

Stuart, Prince Charles Edward

Laurence L. Bongie: Voltaire's English, high treason and a manifesto for bonnie prince Charles 171 (1977) 7-29

Sturm und Drang

Janine Buenzod: De l'*Aufklärung* au *Sturm und Drang*: continuité ou rupture? 24 (1963) 289-313

style

Suard, Jean-Baptiste-Antoine

Sulzer, Johann Georg

supernatural

Switzerland

Claire-Eliane Engel: L'abbé Prévost collaborateur d'une revue neuchâteloise 2 (1956) 225-32

Jacques Marx: *Charles Bonnet contre les Lumières* 156-157 (1976)

Graham Gargett: *Voltaire and Protestantism* 188 (1980)

Madeleine Therrien: Situation de la littérature francophone en Suisse entre 1685 et 1789 216 (1983) 471-72

Tacitus

Orest Ranum: D'Alembert, Tacitus and the political sociology of despotism 191 (1980) 547-58

Catherine Volpilhac-Auger: *Tacite et Montesquieu* 232 (1985)

Tahiti

Paolo Casini: Tahiti, Diderot e l'utopia 191 (1980) 653-60

Urs Bitterli: Visiteurs du pacifique en Europe au siècle des Lumières 216 (1983) 93-95

taste

Rémy Gilbert Saisselin: Le passé, le goût, et l'histoire 27 (1963) 1445-55

technology

F. G. Healey: The Enlightenment view of 'homo faber' 25 (1963) 837-59

David Irwin: The industrial revolution and the dissemination of neoclassical taste 153 (1976) 1087-98

L. Versini: Un maître de forges au service des Lumières et de la révolution américaine: François Ignace de Wendel, 1741-1795 155 (1976) 2173-206

Pietro Giustini: Le 'machines arithmétiques' nella cultura illuministica 190 (1980) 518

Michael Cardy: Technology as play: the case of Vaucanson 216 (1983) 311-12

Henry Lowood: Patriotism and progress: the role of the German patriotic and economic societies in the promotion of science and technology 216 (1983) 394-96

Michael Cardy: Technology as play: the case of Vaucanson 241 (1986) 109-23

Teleki, Joseph

Dóra Csanak: L'*Essai sur la foiblesse des esprits-forts* du comte Joseph Teleki 216 (1983) 9-10

Terence

— criticism

Marie-Rose de Labriolle: *'Le Pour et contre' et son temps* 34-35 (1965)

Marquis d'Argenson: *Notices sur les œuvres de théâtre*, éd. H. Lagrave 42-43 (1966)

D. Williams: *Voltaire: literary critic* 48 (1966)

— dramatic structure

J. Peter Verdurmen: Varieties of determinism in Racine and Rowe: dramatic structure and the role of society 192 (1980) 1545-47

— *drame*

Theodore E. D. Braun: La conscience de la présence des spectateurs dans la comédie larmoyante et dans le drame 192 (1980) 1527-34

Monique Moser-Verrey: Le drame bourgeois ou l'édification du public 192 (1980) 1534-35

— England

J. Peter Verdurmen: Restoration tragedy and after: the theatre of trauma 216 (1983) 37-39

Shirley Strum Kenny: Print culture and the developing audience in England: dramatic literature 216 (1983) 267-69

Joan Hinde Stewart: *Le Nouveau Théâtre anglais* ou la 'liberté dans la diction' 216 (1983) 468-69

— France

Arnold Ages: The private Voltaire: three studies in the correspondence 81 (1971) 7-125

Katharine Whitman Carson: *Aspects of contemporary society in 'Gil Blas'* 110 (1973)

Monique Wagner: *Molière and the age of Enlightenment* 112 (1973)

Anne Lacombe: Du théâtre au roman: Sade 129 (1975) 115-43

Pierre Peyronnet: L'exotisme américain sur la scène française du XVIIIe siècle 154 (1976) 1617-27

W. D. Howarth: Tragedy into melodrama: the fortunes of the Calas affair on the stage 174 (1978) 121-50

Henri Lagrave: Les structures du théâtre dans la province française: le cas exemplaire de Bordeaux 192 (1980) 1425-31

Philip Koch: L'*Histoire de l'ancien Théâtre-Italien*: la part des frères Parfaict 192 (1980) 1460-63

Pierre Peyronnet: Un thème privilégié des Comédiens-Italiens à Paris: la jalousie 192 (1980) 1463-68

Stella Gargantini Rabbi: Le mythe d'Electre dans le théâtre français du XVIIIe siècle 192 (1980) 1547-55

Philip Koch: L'*Histoire de l'Ancien Théâtre-Italien*: la part des frères Parfaict 199 (1981) 25-46

James H. Davis: Morality, virtue, and children's theatre in eighteenth-century France 216 (1983) 343-44

— Germany

J. H. Tisch: Nature and function of historical reality in German early Enlightenment drama 58 (1967) 1551-75

— historical

Anne Boës: *La Lanterne magique de l'histoire: essai sur le théâtre historique en France de 1750 à 1789* 213 (1982)

— Italy

Gérard Luciani: L'œuvre de Carlo Gozzi et les polémiques théâtrales contre les Lumières 89 (1972) 939-74

Maria Ines Aliverti et Marco Alderigi: Théâtre et spectacle à Pise au temps de Léopold Ier (1765-1790) 192 (1980) 1432-40

Letizia Norci Cagiano de Azevedo: Elementi illuministici nelle scenografie fantastiche del primo Settecento italiano 193 (1980) 1670-80

Milena Montanile: Morale et vertu dans la tragédie jacobine en Italie (1796-1799) 216 (1983) 356-57

— parody

Jürgen von Stackelberg: La parodie dramatique au XVIIIe siècle: formes et fonctions 192 (1980) 1519-26

— Russia

V. A. Tumins: Voltaire and the rise of Russian drama 27 (1963) 1689-701

A. G. Cross: The eighteenth-century Russian theatre through British eyes 219 (1983) 225-40

— technique

Retta M. Taney: The effect of Brecht's techniques in the Berliner Ensemble's *Trumpets and drums* on the staging of *The Recruiting officer* by the National Theatre of Great Britain 192 (1980) 1440-46

Seymour Howard: The revival of ancient archaic art in the late eighteenth century and the use of archaising postures and modes in drama and living sculpture 192 (1980) 1453-60

— theory

Virginia Edith Swain: Diderot's *Paradoxe sur le comédien*: the paradox of reading 208 (1982) 1-71

— tragedy

R. S. Ridgway: *La Propagande philosophique dans les tragédies de Voltaire* 15 (1961)

John Van Eerde: The people in eighteenth-century tragedy from *Œdipe* to *Guillaume Tell* 27 (1963) 1703-13

W. P. Albrecht: John Dennis and the sublime pleasures of tragedy 87 (1972) 65-85

Emilie P. Kostoroski: *The Eagle and the dove: Corneille and Racine in the literary criticism of eighteenth-century France* 95 (1972)

Sylvia Vance: History as dramatic reinforcement: Voltaire's use of history in four tragedies set in the middle ages 150 (1976) 7-31

Lucette Perol: Diderot, les tragiques grecs et le père Brumoy 154 (1976) 1593-1616

Raymond Trousson: Le théâtre tragique grec au siècle des Lumières 155 (1976) 2113-36

W. D. Howarth: Tragedy into melodrama: the fortunes of the Calas affair on the stage 174 (1978) 121-50

Calhoun Winton: The tragic muse in enlightened England 192 (1980) 1535-37

J. Peter Verdurmen: Restoration tragedy and after: the theatre of trauma 216 (1983) 37-39

Milena Montanile: Morale et vertu dans la tragédie jacobine en Italie (1796-1799) 216 (1983) 356-57

Théâtre français

Samuel Taylor: La collaboration de Voltaire au *Théâtre français* (1767-1769) 18 (1961) 57-75

Théâtre-Italien

Philip Koch: L'*Histoire de l'ancien Théâtre-Italien*: la part des frères Parfaict 192 (1980) 1460-63

Pierre Peyronnet: Un thème privilégié des Comédiens-Italiens à Paris: la jalousie 192 (1980) 1463-68

Jack Richtman: Seven *canevas* for the Théâtre-Italien: early theatrical ventures by Charles-Antoine Coypel, court painter under Louis XV 192 (1980) 1469-77

Philip Koch: L'*Histoire de l'Ancien Théâtre-Italien*: la part des frères Parfaict 199 (1981) 25-46

Philip Koch: Nature et signification des *Sujets de plusieurs comédies italiennes* 216 (1983) 456-57

theology

Henri Laboucheix: Chimie, matérialisme et théologie chez Joseph Priestley 153 (1976) 1219-44

Bertram Eugene Schwarzbach: Coincé entre Pluche et Lucrèce: Voltaire et la théologie naturelle 192 (1980) 1072-84

Thomson, James

Ruth T. Murdoch: Voltaire, James Thomson, and a poem for the marquise Du Châtelet 6 (1958) 147-53

David R. Anderson: Thomson, natural evil, and the eighteenth-century sublime 245 (1986) 489-99

Thurot, François

Marie-Louise Barthel: Un aspect négligé de la linguistique des Lumières: Thurot et Harris 192 (1980) 1256-63

Tieck, Ludwig

Erdmann Waniek: Pragmatic lesson and romantic tale: moral perspective in Schiller's *Der Verbrecher aus verlorener Ehre* (1786) and Tieck's *Der blonde Eckbert* (1797) 216 (1983) 369-70

Tiepolo, Giambattista

William L. Barcham: Giambattista Tiepolo's *Translation of the holy house*: a sacred image in the Enlightenment 193 (1980) 1688-89

time

Lionel Gossman: Time and history in Rousseau 30 (1964) 311-49

Merle L. Perkins: Destiny, sentiment and time in the *Confessions* of Jean Jacques Rousseau 67 (1969) 133-64

Edward M. Jennings: The consequences of prediction 153 (1976) 1131-50

John Neubauer: Narrative uses of time in the eighteenth-century novel 192 (1980) 1284-86

Tocqueville, Alexis-Henri-Charles-Maurice Clérel, comte de

Jean Pierre Guicciardi: Tocqueville et les Lumières 163 (1976) 203-19

Toland, John

Bruno Morcavallo: Influenza del pensiero religioso di John Toland su David Hume 192 (1980) 1119-23

toleration

Elisabeth Labrousse: Note à propos de la conception de la tolérance au XVIIIe siècle 56 (1967) 799-811

Ronald Ian Boss: Rousseau's civil religion and the meaning of belief: an answer to Bayle's paradox 84 (1971) 123-93

Günter Gawlick: The English deists' contribution to the theory of toleration 152 (1976) 823-35

W. Grossmann: Religious toleration in Germany, 1648-1750 192 (1980) 1103-1105

Martin Fitzpatrick: Truth and tolerance in rational dissent in late eighteenth-century England 192 (1980) 1124-26

Walter Grossmann: Religious toleration in Germany, 1648-1750 201 (1982) 115-41

Tolerance in four Dutch periodicals 1714-1771: *La Bibliothèque ancienne et moderne*, Amsterdam 1714-1726: H. Bots and J. de Vet; *Le Journal britannique*, The Hague 1750-1755: U. Janssens; *Nederlandsche Letter-courant*, Leyden 1759-1763: H. Stouten; *Vaderlandsche Letter-oefeningen*, Amsterdam 1761-1771: W. van den Berg 216 (1983) 73-77

Margaret D. Thomas: Michel de La Roche: a Huguenot critic of Calvin 238 (1985) 97-195

translation

Judith Sloman: Dryden's preface to the *Fables*: translation as aesthetic experience 193 (1980) 1587-95

José Miguel Caso Gonzales: Traduction de livres dans l'Espagne du dix-huitième siècle 216 (1983) 237-38

travel

P. Laubriet: Les guides de voyages au début du XVIIIe siècle et la propagande philosophique 32 (1965) 269-325

René Pomeau: Voyage et Lumières dans la littérature française du XVIIIe siècle 57 (1967) 1269-89

Clarence Tracy: Johnson's *Journey to the western islands of Scotland*: a reconsideration 58 (1967) 1593-606

Alan Frost: The Pacific Ocean: the eighteenth century's 'new world' 152 (1976) 779-822

Maurice Roelens: L'expérience de l'espace américain dans les récits de voyage entre La Hontan et Charlevoix 155 (1976) 1861-95

Giuliana Toso Rodinis: Vivant Denon e le sue note al *Voyage di H. Swinburne dans les deux Siciles* 193 (1980) 1669

Peter Boerner: The great travel collections of the eighteenth century: their scope and purpose 193 (1980) 1798-1805

Jean Ducrocq: Relations de voyages et récits symboliques: *Robinson* et *Gulliver* 215 (1982) 1-0008

J. Chupeau: Le voyageur philosophe ou Robert Challe au miroir du *Journal d'un voyage aux Indes* 215 (1982) 45-61

Urs Bitterli: Visiteurs du pacifique en Europe au siècle des Lumières 216 (1983) 93-95

Merete Grevlund: Du bon usage du récit de voyage: l'exemple de la Chine 216 (1983) 106-107

Ahmad Gunny: European travellers' impressions of the Mascarenes and southern Africa in the eighteenth century 216 (1983) 107-108

C. P. Hanlon: Some observations on French contacts with aboriginal society (1801-1803) 216 (1983) 109-10

Marie-Thérèse Isaac: L'Européen à la rencontre du noir-esclave des Etats-Unis d'Amérique d'après les *Voyages* du marquis de Chastellux 216 (1983) 111-12

Leopoldo Jobim: A la découverte du Mato Grosso au siècle des Lumières 216 (1983) 112

J. G. Reish: France's children discover the other: Mme de Genlis's tales of travel and instruction 216 (1983) 113-15

Daniel L. Schlafly: Western Europe discovers Russia: foreign travellers in the reign of Catherine the Great 216 (1983) 115-17

Robert Toupin: Pierre Potier, jésuite belge chez les Hurons du Détroit (1744-1781): les chemins d'un espace nouveau à explorer 216 (1983) 122-24

Georges Festa: Images et réalités de la vie commerciale italienne à travers le *Voyage d'Italie* de Sade 217 (1983) 23-26

Mireille Gille: La 'Lettre d'Italie' au dix-huitième siècle: forme et signification 219 (1983) 257-72

G. Festa: Images du Bernin au dix-huitième siècle: l'œuvre du sculpteur jugée par les voyageurs français en Italie 241 (1986) 87-94

Jean-Michel Racault: Système de la toponymie et organisation de l'espace romanesque dans *Paul et Virginie* 242 (1986) 377-418

John Lough: Encounters between British travellers and eighteenth-century French writers 245 (1986) 1-90

G. Festa: Le voyage en Sardaigne au siècle des Lumières 249 (1986) 439-45

Trenchard, John

Enrico Nuzzo: The theme of equality in Trenchard's and Gordon's *Cato's letters* 216 (1983) 211-13

Tronchin, Jean-Robert

R. A. Leigh: New light on the genesis of the *Lettres de la montagne*: Rousseau's marginalia on Tronchin 94 (1972) 89-119

H. Nicholas Bakalar: An unpublished Voltaire letter 124 (1974) 133-35

Tronchin, Théodore

A. Magnan: Un épisode oublié de la lutte des médecins parisiens contre Théodore Tronchin: à propos de deux lettres de Voltaire 94 (1972) 417-29

troubador

Juliette Rigal: L'iconographie de la *Henriade* au XVIIIe siècle ou la naissance du style troubador 32 (1965) 23-71

James P. Gilroy: Peace and the pursuit of happiness in the French utopian novel: Fénelon's *Télémaque* and Prévost's *Cleveland* 176 (1979) 169-87

Raymond Trousson: Orientations et problèmes de l'utopie au siècle des Lumières (rapport de synthèse) 191 (1980) 613-36

Alberto Andreatta: Alle origini dell'anarchismo moderno: Dom Deschamps: la metafisica al servizio dell'utopia 191 (1980) 637-43

Bronislaw Baczko: 'Former l'homme nouveau': utopie et pédagogie pendant la Révolution française 191 (1980) 643-45

Alberto Beretta Anguissola: Désir et utopie chez Foigny, Rétif et Casanova 191 (1980) 645-47

Marialuisa Bignami: Utopian elements in Daniel Defoe's novels 191 (1980) 647-53

Paolo Casini: Tahiti, Diderot e l'utopia 191 (1980) 653-60

Roger Clark: Aliénation et utopie: fonctions du héros dans la littérature utopique française du XVIIIe siècle 191 (1980) 661-62

Alain Faudemay: L'utopie chez Voltaire: de la philosophie au conte 191 (1980) 663-64

Beatrice C. Fink: Utopian nurtures 191 (1980) 664-71

Byron Gassman: Alexander Pope as utopian: Arcadia to apocalypse 191 (1980) 672-78

Francesco Gentile: Utopia e realismo nel gioco politico del viandante solitario 191 (1980) 678-84

Oscar A. Haac: Comedy in utopia: the literary imagination of Marivaux and the abbé Prévost 191 (1980) 684-85

Irmgard A. Hartig: Réflexions sur la cellule familiale dans l'utopie sociale de Sylvain Maréchal 191 (1980) 685-87

Catherine Lafarge: Londres en 1781: une utopie inédite de L. S. Mercier 191 (1980) 693-94

Claudia-Anne Lopez: L'utopie americaine du dr Guillotin 191 (1980) 694-98

Maria Ludassy: Tendances autoritaires et tendances anarchiques dans les utopies du XVIIIe siècle 191 (1980) 699-701

Temple Maynard: Utopia and dystopia in the oriental genre in England in the eighteenth century 191 (1980) 706-11

Monique Mosser et Jean-Pierre Mouilleseaux: Architecture, politique et utopie: vers une *Foederapolis europeana*: les monuments à la paix de Louis Combes 191 (1980) 712-16

Antonio Paoluzzi: L'utopia dalla scienza politica alla letteratura 191 (1980) 717-22

Jean Roussel: Esotérisme et utopie: L.-C. de Saint-Martin 191 (1980) 723-29

Lois Ann Russell: A colonial utopia: the Acadia of Robert Challe 191 (1980) 729-31

N. Wagner: Utopie et littérature: la *Basiliade* de Morelly 191 (1980) 731-32

L. Adams: Anson in Frivola: an exercise in social criticism: Coyer's *Découverte de l'île Frivole* (1751) 191 (1980) 851-58

Jenny Mezciems: Utopia and 'the thing which is not': relationships between ideal and real in some utopian fictions 191 (1980) 711

Annette Bridgman: Heavenly cities on earth: urban planning and mass culture in 18th-century utopias 193 (1980) 1753-54

Charline Sacks: Le rôle de la femme dans la société utopique de Restif de La Bretonne 216 (1983) 216-18

Jean-Michel Racault: *Paul et Virginie* et l'utopie: de la 'petite société' au mythe collectif 242 (1986) 419-71

Vaines, Jean de

Michael Waters: Unpublished letters from Mlle Clairon to Jean de Vaines 137 (1975) 141-89

vandalism

Bronislaw Baczko: Civisme et vandalisme 216 (1983) 377-79

Van Effen, Justus

P. J. Buijnsters: The tutor/governess between nobility and bourgeoisie: some considerations with reference to an essay of 1734 by Justus van Effen 216 (1983) 164-66

Justus van Effen: *Le Misanthrope*, edited by James L. Schorr 248 (1986)

Vansommer, John

Joseph G. Fucilla: A letter from Voltaire to Cav. Vansommer 1 (1955) 111-13

Norma Perry: John Vansommer of Spitalfields: Huguenot, silk-designer, and correspondent of Voltaire 60 (1968) 289-310

Vaucanson, Jacques de

Michael Cardy: Technology as play: the case of Vaucanson 216 (1983) 311-12

Michael Cardy: Technology as play: the case of Vaucanson 241 (1986) 109-23

Vauvenargues, Luc de Clapiers, marquis de

Henri Mydlarski: Vauvenargues, juge littéraire de son siècle 150 (1976) 149-81

Jeroom Vercruysse: Vauvenargues trahi: pour une édition authentique de ses œuvres 170 (1977) 7-124

Henri Mydlarski: Vauvenargues, critique de Corneille 176 (1979) 231-58

Henri Mydlarski: Vauvenargues, ou le moraliste devant la nécessité d'une économie politique 191 (1980) 819-27

Yvon Belaval: L'esprit de Voltaire 24 (1963) 139-54

Jeroom Vercruysse: Les Provinces-Unies vues par Voltaire 27 (1963) 1715-21

Guy Périer de Féral: La descendance collatérale de Voltaire 41 (1966) 285-342

Jeroom Vercruysse: *Voltaire et la Hollande* 46 (1966)

Gavin de Beer and André-Michel Rousseau: *Voltaire's British visitors* 49 (1967)

Alfred J. Bingham: Voltaire and Marmontel 55 (1967) 205-62

Theodore E. D. Braun: Voltaire's perception of truth in quarrels with his enemies 55 (1967) 287-95

Renée Waldinger: Voltaire and medicine 58 (1967) 1777-806

Arnold Ages: Stendhal and Voltaire: the *philosophe* as target 62 (1968) 83-99

Emanuel Rostworowski: Voltaire et la Pologne 62 (1968) 101-21

Norma Perry: Voltaire and Felix Farley's *Bristol journal* 62 (1968) 137-50

Stephen Werner: Voltaire and Seneca 67 (1969) 29-44

Arnold Ages: The private Voltaire: three studies in the correspondence 81 (1971) 7-125

Jacqueline Marchand: De Voltaire à Bunuel 89 (1972) 1003-16

Richard Switzer: Voltaire, Rousseau et l'opéra 90 (1972) 1519-28

Christopher Thacker: Voltaire and Rousseau: eighteenth-century gardeners 90 (1972) 1595-614

Carolyn Wilberger: Peter the Great: an 18th-century hero of our times? 96 (1972) 7-127

Robert H. McDonald: A forgotten Voltairean poem: *Voltaire et le comte de Maistre* by Anne Bignan 102 (1973) 231-64

James F. Hamilton: Mme de Staël, partisan of Rousseau or Voltaire? 106 (1973) 253-65

Arnold Ages: Voltaire and Horace: the testimony of the correspondence 120 (1974) 199-221

R. E. Florida: *Voltaire and the socinians* 122 (1974)

R. Galliani: Voltaire cité par les brochures de 1789 132 (1975) 17-54

Norma Perry: *Sir Everard Fawkener, friend and correspondent of Voltaire* 133 (1975)

André Michel Rousseau: *L'Angleterre et Voltaire* 145-147 (1976)

David H. Jory: Voltaire and the Greeks 153 (1976) 1169-87

Jacques Wagner: Lisibilité et dénégation: propos sur un préambule voltairien 155 (1976) 2223-64

Th. Besterman: William Beckford's notes on a life of Voltaire 163 (1976) 53-55

C. H. Wilberger: *Voltaire's Russia: window on the east* 164 (1976)

R. Galliani: La présence de Voltaire dans les brochures de 1790 169 (1977) 69-114

Nelly H. Severin: Voltaire's campaign againts saints' days 171 (19) 55-69

R. Galliani: Voltaire et les autres philosophes dans la Révolution: les brochures de 1791, 1792, 1793 174 (1978) 69-112

G. Gargett: Voltaire, Richelieu and the problem of Huguenot emancipation in the reign of Louis XV 176 (1979) 97-132

Ahmad Gunny: *Voltaire and English literature: a study of English literary influences on Voltaire* 177 (1979)

William H. Barber: Voltaire and Samuel Clarke 179 (1979) 47-61

P. Casini: Briarée en miniature: Voltaire et Newton 179 (1979) 63-77

Samuel S. B. Taylor: Voltaire's humour 179 (1979) 101-16

William H. Barber: Voltaire et Newton 179 (1979) 193-202

Michèle Mat-Hasquin: L'image de Voltaire dans les *Mémoires secrets* 182 (1979) 319-29

R. Galliani: Voltaire en 1878: le premier centenaire d'après les journaux de l'époque 183 (1980) 91-115

Jacques Chouillet: 'Etre Voltaire ou rien': réflexions sur le voltairianisme de Diderot 185 (1980) 225-36

Barbara W. Maggs: Voltaire and the Balkans: aspects of the Enlightenment in 18th-century Croatia and Serbia 189 (1980) 81-118

Jean Mohsen Fahmy: *Voltaire et Paris* 195 (1981)

Michèle Mat-Hasquin: *Voltaire et l'antiquité grecque* 197 (1981)

W. D. Howarth: Voltaire, Ninon de L'Enclos and the evolution of a dramatic genre 199 (1981) 63-72

Jan Lavička: Voltaire et la Bohême 219 (1983) 105-15

Carol Kleiner Willen: From protégé to persona: the evolution of the Voltaire-Desmahis relationship 230 (1985) 127-36

H. A. Stavan: Landgraf Frederick II of Hesse-Kassel and Voltaire 241 (1986) 161-83

— and Frederick II

Voltaire's commentary on Frederick's *L'Art de la guerre*, ed. Theodore Besterman 2 (1956) 61-206

Frederick II: *L'Anti-Machiavel*, éd. Charles Fleischauer 5 (1958)

Norma Perry: A forged letter from Frederick to Voltaire 60 (1968) 225-27

Robert Kusch: Voltaire as symbol of the eighteenth century in Carlyle's *Frederick* 79 (1971) 61-72

Jeroom Vercruysse: *L'Elégant tableau de l'Europe* ou Voltaire édité 'de main de maître' 106 (1973) 103-11

Jeroom Vercruysse: L'œuvre de *Poéshie* corrigée: notes marginales de Voltaire sur les poésies de Frédéric II 176 (1979) 51-62

Christiane Mervaud: *Voltaire et Frédéric II: une dramaturgie des Lumières 1736-1778* 234 (1985)

Voltaire

David Williams: Voltaire's guardianship of Marie Corneille and the pursuit of Fréron 98 (1972) 27-46

Pierre B. Daprini: Le *Discours aux Welches* ou la France vue de Ferney 98 (1972) 47-60

Helen Hancock: Voltaire et l'affaire des mainmortables: un ultime combat 114 (1973) 79-98

John Renwick: *Marmontel, Voltaire and the Bélisaire affair* 121 (1974)

Emile Lizé: Une affaire de pommes à Ferney: Simon Bigex contre Antoine Adam 129 (1975) 19-26

G. Gargett: Voltaire, Gilbert de Voisins's *Mémoires* and the problem of Huguenot civil rights (1767-1768) 174 (1978) 7-57

Alexander Jovicevich: Voltaire and La Harpe - l'affaire des manuscrits: a reappraisal 176 (1979) 77-95

David Williams: Voltaire's war with England: the appeal to Europe 1760-1764 179 (1979) 79-100

H. A. Stavan: Voltaire et la duchesse de Gotha 185 (1980) 27-56

Jean-Claude David: Quelques actes notariés inédits concernant Voltaire 230 (1985) 145-65

Renato G. Mazzolini and Shirley A. Roe: *Science against the unbelievers: the correspondence of Bonnet and Needham, 1760-1780* 243 (1986)

— 1770-death

L. A. Boiteux: Voltaire et le ménage Suard 1 (1955) 19-109

Jean Daniel Candaux: Des documents nouveaux sur la mort de Voltaire? 20 (1962) 261-63

Léon Cellier: Saint-Martin et Voltaire 24 (1963) 355-68

Jeroom Vercruysse: Lettre de Henri Rieu sur les derniers jours de Voltaire 135 (1975) 193-98

Colin Duckworth: Voltaire at Ferney: an unpublished description 174 (1978) 61-67

John Renwick: *Voltaire et Morangiés 1772-1773, ou les Lumières l'ont échappé belle* 202 (1982)

R. Galliani: Quelques faits inédits sur la mort de Voltaire 217 (1983) 159-75

Jean-Claude David: Quelques actes notariés inédits concernant Voltaire 230 (1985) 145-65

— bibliography

Theodore Besterman: Note on the authorship of the *Connaissance des beautés* 4 (1957) 291-94

Hywel Berwyn Evans: A provisional bibliography of English editions and translations of Voltaire 8 (1959) 9-121

Theodore Besterman: Some eighteenth-century Voltaire editions unknown to Bengesco: second edition 8 (1959) 123-242

Voltaire

— — Kehl edition

— correspondence

Voltaire

Margaret Chenais: The 'man of the triangle' in Voltaire's correspondence with countess Bentinck 10 (1959) 421-24

Theodore Besterman: Voltaire's correspondence: additions V 10 (1959) 439-518

Theodore Besterman: Voltaire's correspondence: additions VI 12 (1960) 71-110

Marta Rezler: The Voltaire-d'Alembert correspondence: an historical and bibliographical re-appraisal 20 (1962) 9-139

Albert Gyergyai: Un correspondant hongrois de Voltaire: le comte Fekete de Galanta 25 (1963) 779-93

R. A. Leigh: Rousseau's letter to Voltaire on optimism (18 August 1756) 30 (1964) 247-309

Th. Braun: A forgotten letter from Voltaire to Le Franc de Pompignan 41 (1966) 231-34

James R. Knowlson and Harold T. Betteridge: The Voltaire-Hirschel dispute: unpublished letters and documents 47 (1966) 39-52

John Renwick: Reconstruction and interpretation of the genesis of the *Bélisaire* affaire, with an unpublished letter from Marmontel to Voltaire 53 (1967) 171-222

Arnold Ages: Voltaire and the Old testament: the testimony of his correspondence 55 (1967) 43-63

Norma Perry: A forged letter from Frederick to Voltaire 60 (1968) 225-27

Norma Perry: John Vansommer of Spitalfields: Huguenot, silk-designer, and correspondent of Voltaire 60 (1968) 289-310

John B. Shipley: Two Voltaire letters: to the third earl of Bute and to the duc de Richelieu 62 (1968) 7-11

T. J. Barling: Voltaire's correspondence with Lord Hervey: three new letters 62 (1968) 13-27

Christopher Thacker: M. A. D.: an editor of Voltaire's letters identified 62 (1968) 309-10

Enrico Straub: A propos d'une lettre inconnue de Voltaire 67 (1969) 21-27

Jeroom Vercruysse: Turgot et Vergennes contre la lettre de Voltaire à Boncerf 67 (1969) 65-71

Theodore Besterman: Additions and corrections to the definitive edition of Voltaire's correspondence, I: vols 1-10 (Voltaire 85-95) 79 (1971) 7-60

Arnold Ages: The private Voltaire: three studies in the correspondence 81 (1971) 7-125

A. Magnan: Un épisode oublié de la lutte des médecins parisiens contre Théodore Tronchin: à propos de deux lettres de Voltaire 94 (1972) 417-29

Theodore Besterman: Additions and corrections to the definitive edition of Voltaire's correspondence, II: vols 1-22 (Voltaire 85-106) 102 (1973) 7-52

Paul LeClerc: Unpublished letters from Morellet to Voltaire 106 (1973) 63-80

Edgar Mass: *Le Marquis d'Adhémar: la correspondance inédite d'un ami des philosophes à la cour de Bayreuth* 109 (1973)

David Williams: *Voltaire: literary critic* 48 (1966)

Voltaire on Shakespeare, ed. Theodore Besterman 54 (1967)

David Williams: Voltaire and the language of the gods 62 (1968) 57-81

Monique Wagner: *Molière and the age of Enlightenment* 112 (1973)

Ahmad Gunny: Voltaire and the novel: Sterne 124 (1974) 149-61

David Williams: Voltaire on the sentimental novel 135 (1975) 115-34

Ahmad Gunny: Voltaire's thoughts on prose fiction 140 (1975) 7-20

Theodore E. D. Braun and Gerald R. Culley: Aeschylus, Voltaire, and Le Franc de Pompignan's *Prométhée*: a critical edition 160 (1976) 137-226

Jerolyn Scull: Voltaire's reading of Pascal: his quotations compared to early texts 161 (1976) 19-41

R. Galliani (ed.): Quelques notes inédites de Voltaire à l'*Esprit des lois* 163 (1976) 7-18

— criticism of

Theodore Besterman: Voltaire jugé par Flaubert 1 (1955) 133-58

René Pomeau: Etat présent des études voltairiennes 1 (1955) 183-200

Jean Seznec: Falconet, Voltaire et Diderot 2 (1956) 43-59

John N. Pappas: *Berthier's 'Journal de Trévoux' and the philosophes* 3 (1957)

Max I. Baym: John Fiske and Voltaire 4 (1957) 171-84

Colin Duckworth: Flaubert and Voltaire's *Dictionnaire philosophique* 18 (1961) 141-167

Jeroom Vercruysse: C'est la faute à Rousseau, c'est la faute à Voltaire 23 (1963) 61-76

Alfred J. Bingham: The earliest criticism of Voltaire's *Dictionnaire philosophique* 47 (1966) 15-37

Gustave Flaubert: *Le Théâtre de Voltaire*, edited for the first time by Theodore Besterman 50-51 (1967)

J. Marx: Joseph de Maistre contre Voltaire 89 (1972) 1017-48

Robert J. Buyck: Chateaubriand juge de Voltaire 114 (1973) 141-272

Raymond Setbon: Voltaire jugé par Charles Nodier 137 (1975) 55-71

Henri Mydlarski: Vauvenargues, juge littéraire de son siècle 150 (1976) 149-81

R. Galliani: Voltaire en 1878: le premier centenaire d'après les journaux de l'époque 183 (1980) 91-115

Jean Sareil: Le massacre de Voltaire dans les manuels scolaires 212 (1982) 83-161

Theodore E. D. Braun: Voltaire and his *contes*: a review essay on interpretations offered by Roy S. Wolper 212 (1982) 312-17

Vivienne Mylne: Wolper's view of Voltaire's tales 212 (1982) 318-27

Theodore E. D. Braun: Theodore Braun replies [on Roy S. Wolper's reading of Voltaire's *contes*] 212 (1982) 328-30

Voltaire

— philosophy

R. Galliani: Voltaire, Porphyre et les animaux 199 (1981) 125-38

Charles Porset: Ambiguïtés de la philosophie de Voltaire: sa réception par Pierre Leroux 216 (1983) 433

Pierre Aubery: Voltaire and antisemitism: a reply to Hertzberg 217 (1983) 177-82

R. Galliani: Voltaire, Astruc, et la maladie vénérienne 219 (1983) 19-36

Maureen F. O'Meara: Linguistic power-play: Voltaire's considerations on the evolution, use, and abuse of language 219 (1983) 93-103

E. D. James: Voltaire and the 'Ethics' of Spinoza 228 (1984) 67-87

E. D. James: Voltaire on free will 249 (1986) 1-18

— politics

Eric Cahm: Review: Peter Gay, *Voltaire's politics: the poet as realist* 12 (1960) 111-16

Merle L. Perkins: Voltaire and the abbé de Saint-Pierre on world peace 18 (1961) 9-34

Merle L. Perkins: Voltaire on the source of national power 20 (1962) 141-73

J. H. Brumfitt: History and propaganda in Voltaire 24 (1963) 271-87

Francis J. Carmody: Voltaire et la renaissance indo-iranienne 24 (1963) 345-54

Merle L. Perkins: Voltaire's concept of international order 26 (1963) 1291-306

Theodore Besterman: Voltaire, absolute monarchy, and the enlightened monarch 32 (1965) 7-21

Merle L. Perkins: *Voltaire's concept of international order* 36 (1965)

Robert S. Tate: Voltaire and the *parlements*: a reconsideration 90 (1972) 1529-43

Andrew Hunwick: Le patriotisme de Voltaire 116 (1973) 7-18

Durand Echeverria: Some unknown eighteenth-century editions of Voltaire's political pamphlets of 1771 127 (1974) 61-64

Laurence L. Bongie: Voltaire's English, high treason and a manifesto for bonnie prince Charles 171 (1977) 7-29

Michelangelo Ghio: I progetti di pace perpetua dell'abate di St Pierre nei giudizi di Rousseau, Leibniz e Voltaire 190 (1980) 307-18

Corrado Rosso: Faut-il changer le monde ou le laisser tel qu'il est? Rousseau: de la *Lettre à Philopolis* à la *Lettre à Voltaire* 190 (1980) 390-95

Lester G. Crocker: Voltaire and the political philosophers 219 (1983) 1-17

Wanda Dzwigala: Voltaire's sources on the Polish dissident question 241 (1986) 187-202

— religion

Theodore Besterman: Review: R. Pomeau, *La Religion de Voltaire* 4 (1957) 295-301

J. H. Brumfitt: Voltaire and Warburton 18 (1961) 35-56

P. Aubery: Voltaire et les juifs: ironie et démystification 24 (1963) 67-79

William H. Barber: Voltaire and Quakerism: Enlightenment and the inner light 24 (1963) 81-109

Alfred J. Bingham: Voltaire and the New testament 24 (1963) 183-218

Haydn T. Mason: Voltaire and Manichean dualism 26 (1963) 1143-60

Arnold Ages: Voltaire's Biblical criticism: a study in thematic repetitions 30 (1964) 205-21

Arnold Ages: Voltaire, Calmet and the Old testament 41 (1966) 87-187

Theodore Besterman: Voltaire's god 55 (1967) 23-41

Arnold Ages: Voltaire and the Old testament: the testimony of his correspondence 55 (1967) 43-63

William H. Williams: Voltaire and the utility of the lower clergy 58 (1967) 1869-91

Ronald Ian Boss: Rousseau's civil religion and the meaning of belief: an answer to Bayle's paradox 84 (1971) 123-93

Jerry L. Curtis: La providence: vicissitudes du dieu voltairien 118 (1974) 7-114

Daniel S. Hawley: L'Inde de Voltaire 120 (1974) 139-78

R. E. Florida: *Voltaire and the socinians* 122 (1974)

Magdy Gabriel Badir: *Voltaire et l'Islam* 125 (1974)

David Lévy: *Voltaire et son exégèse du Pentateuque: critique et polémique* 130 (1975)

Nelly H. Severin: Voltaire's campaign againts saints' days 171 (19) 55-69

Graham Gargett: *Voltaire and Protestantism* 188 (1980)

Bertram Eugene Schwarzbach: Coincé entre Pluche et Lucrèce: Voltaire et la théologie naturelle 192 (1980) 1072-84

Françoise Le Moal: Voltaire, Rousseau et le socinianisme 192 (1980) 1100

William H. Trapnell: *Voltaire and the eucharist* 198 (1981)

Bertram Eugene Schwarzbach: The sacred genealogy of a Voltairean polemic: the development of critical hypotheses regarding the composition of the canonical and apocryphal gospels 216 (1983) 72-73

Marie-Hélène Cotoni: *L'Exégèse du Nouveau Testament dans la philosophie française du dix-huitième siècle* 220 (1984)

Christiane Mervaud: Voltaire, saint Augustin et le duc Du Maine aux sources de *Cosi-Sancta* 228 (1984) 89-96

Bertram Eugene Schwarzbach: The sacred genealogy of a Voltairean polemic: the development of critical hypotheses regarding the composition of the canonical and apocryphal gospels 245 (1986) 303-50

— science

Jean A. Perkins: Voltaire and the natural sciences 37 (1965) 61-76

— works

Jeroom Vercruysse: Quelques vers inédits de Voltaire 12 (1960) 55-61

R. S. Ridgway: *La Propagande philosophique dans les tragédies de Voltaire* 15 (1961)

Samuel Taylor: La collaboration de Voltaire au *Théâtre français* (1767-1769) 18 (1961) 57-75

H. A. Stavan: Are Voltaire's tales narrative fantasies? a reply to Wolper 215 (1982) 281-87

—— *Cosi-Sancta*

Christiane Mervaud: Voltaire, saint Augustin et le duc Du Maine aux sources de *Cosi-Sancta* 228 (1984) 89-96

—— *Le Crocheteur borgne*

Jacqueline Hellegouarc'h: Genèse d'un conte de Voltaire 176 (1979) 7-36

R. Galliani: La date de composition du *Crocheteur borgne* par Voltaire 217 (1983) 141-46

—— *Dictionnaire philosophique*

Colin Duckworth: Flaubert and Voltaire's *Dictionnaire philosophique* 18 (1961) 141-167

Jeanne R. Monty: Notes sur le vocabulaire du *Dictionnaire philosophique* 41 (1966) 71-86

Jeanne R. Monty: *Etude sur le style polémique de Voltaire: le 'Dictionnaire philosophique'* 44 (1966)

Alfred J. Bingham: The earliest criticism of Voltaire's *Dictionnaire philosophique* 47 (1966) 15-37

Spire Pitou: Voltaire, Linguet, and China 98 (1972) 61-68

R. Galliani (ed.): Les notes marginales de Voltaire au *Dictionnaire philosophique* 161 (1976) 7-18

Bertram Eugene Schwarzbach: The problem of the Kehl additions to the *Dictionnaire philosophique*: sources, dating and authenticity 201 (1982) 7-66

—— *Dieu et les hommes*

Bertram Eugene Schwarzbach: The sacred genealogy of a Voltairean polemic: the development of critical hypotheses regarding the composition of the canonical and apocryphal gospels 216 (1983) 72-73

—— *Discours au très illustre et très excellent seigneur*

Bernard Gagnebin: Le médiateur d'une petite querelle genevoise 1 (1955) 115-23

—— *Discours aux Welches*

Pierre B. Daprini: Le *Discours aux Welches* ou la France vue de Ferney 98 (1972) 47-60

H. Watzlawick: Casanova and Voltaire's *Discours aux Welches* 171 (1977) 71-75

—— *Don Pèdre*

Paul Ilie: Voltaire and Spain: the meaning of *Don Pèdre* 117 (1974) 153-78

Eugène J. Weinraub: Plays as pedagogical laboratories: *Mahomet* and Don Pèdre 140 (1975) 45-61

Voltaire

—— *L'Ecossaise*

Colin Duckworth: Voltaire's *L'Ecossaise* and Palissot's *Les Philosophes*: a strategic battle in a major war 87 (1972) 333-51

Jack Yashinsky: Voltaire's *L'Ecossaise*: background, structure, originality 182 (1979) 253-71

—— *L'Enfant prodigue*

Jack Yashinsky: Voltaire's *Enfant prodigue* 163 (1976) 31-51

—— *Epître à madame la marquise Du Châtelet*

Ruth T. Murdoch: Voltaire, James Thomson, and a poem for the marquise Du Châtelet 6 (1958) 147-53

—— *Eriphyle*

Anne Sanderson: Voltaire and the problem of dramatic structure: the evolution of the form of *Eriphyle* 228 (1984) 97-128

—— *Essai sur les mœurs*

Basil Guy: *The French image of China before and after Voltaire* 21 (1963)

Richard A. Brooks: Voltaire and Garcilaso de la Vega 30 (1964) 189-204

Daniel S. Hawley: L'Inde de Voltaire 120 (1974) 139-78

Barbara Widenor Maggs: Answers from eighteenth-century China to certain questions on Voltaire's sinology 120 (19) 179-98

—— *La Guerre civile de Genève*

John Renwick: Voltaire et les antécédents de la *Guerre civile de Genève* 185 (1980) 57-86

—— *La Henriade*

Juliette Rigal: L'iconographie de la *Henriade* au XVIIIe siècle ou la naissance du style troubador 32 (1965) 23-71

Voltaire: *La Henriade*, édition critique par O. R. Taylor 38-40 (1965)

O. R. Taylor: *La Henriade*: a complementary note 60 (1968) 105-107

Norma Perry: Voltaire's London agents for the *Henriade*: Simond and Bénézet, Huguenot merchants 102 (1973) 265-99

R. E. A. Waller: Voltaire and the regent 127 (1974) 7-39

Francisco Lafarga: Sur la fortune de la *Henriade* en Espagne 199 (1981) 139-53

Owen Taylor: Voltaire et *La Ligue*: le projet de souscription – note complémentaire 212 (1982) 1-0005

Geraldine Sheridan: Voltaire's *Henriade*: a history of the 'subscriber' edition, 1728-1741 215 (1982) 77-89

—— *Histoire de Charles XII*

Lionel Gossman: Voltaire's *Charles XII*, history into art 25 (1963) 691-720

—— *Histoire de Jenni*

René Démoris: Genèse et symbolique de l'*Histoire de Jenni, ou le sage et l'athée* de Voltaire 199 (1981) 87-123

—— *Histoire des voyages de Scarmentado*

Leif Nedergaard-Hansen: Sur la date de composition de l'*Histoire des voyages de Scarmentado* 2 (1956) 273-77

—— *Histoire du docteur Akakia*

L'*Akakia* de Voltaire, éd. Charles Fleischauer 30 (1964) 7-145

—— *Histoire du parlement de Paris*

Nuci Kotta: Voltaire's *Histoire du parlement de Paris* 41 (1966) 219-30

—— *L'Homme aux quarante écus*

R. Ginsberg: The argument of Voltaire's *L'Homme aux quarante écus*: a study in philosophic rhetoric 56 (1967) 611-57

Larissa L. Albina: Les sources du conte *L'Homme aux quarante écus* 216 (1983) 273-75

Larissa L. Albina: Les sources du conte antiphysiocratique *L'Homme aux quarante écus* d'après les données nouvelles provenant de la bibliothèque personnelle de Voltaire 242 (1986) 159-68

—— *Idées républicaines*

Peter Gay: Voltaire's *Idées républicaines*: a study in bibliography and interpretation 6 (1958) 67-105

—— *L'Ingénu*

M. Alcover: La casuistique du père Tout à tous et *Les Provinciales* 81 (1971) 127-32

David E. Highnam: *L'Ingénu*: flawed masterpiece or masterful innovation 143 (1975) 71-83

M. G. Carroll: Some implications of 'vraisemblance' in Voltaire's *L'Ingénu* 183 (1980) 35-44

Zvi Levy: *L'Ingénu* ou l'*Anti-Candide* 183 (1980) 45-67

—— *Irène*

Theodore Besterman: Voltaire's directions to the actors in *Irène* 12 (1960) 67-69

Liliane Willens: Voltaire's *Irène* and his illusion of theatrical success 185 (1980) 87-101

Anne Sanderson: In the playwright's workshop: Voltaire's corrections to *Irène* 228 (1984) 129-70

— —*Jeannot et Colin*

Roy S. Wolper: The toppling of Jeannot 183 (1980) 69-82

— —*Lettres de M. de Voltaire à ses amis du Parnasse*

Jeroom Vercruysse: Voltaire correcteur de ses *Lettres de m. de Voltaire à ses amis du Parnasse* (1766) 201 (1982) 67-79

— —*Lettres philosophiques*

T. J. Barling: The literary art of the *Lettres philosophiques* 41 (1966) 7-69

T. J. Barling: The problem of the poem in the 20th *Lettre philosophique* 64 (1968) 151-63

Dorothy R. Thelander: The oak and the thinking reed 102 (1973) 53-63

Hans Mattauch: A translator's hand in Voltaire's fifth 'Letter concerning the English nation'? 106 (1973) 81-84

Anne Lacombe: La lettre sur l'insertion de la petite vérole et les *Lettres philosophiques* 117 (1974) 113-31

René Pomeau: Les *Lettres philosophiques*: le projet de Voltaire 179 (1979) 11-24

A.-M. Rousseau: Naissance d'un livre et d'un texte: les *Letters concerning the English nation* 179 (1979) 25-46

Julia L. Epstein: Voltaire's ventriloquism: voices in the first *Lettre philosophique* 182 (1979) 219-35

— —*Mahomet*

Renzo de Felice: Trois prises de position italiennes à propos de *Mahomet* 10 (1959) 259-66

P. D. Jimack: Rousseau misquoting Voltaire? 37 (1965) 77-79

Magdy Gabriel Badir: *Voltaire et l'Islam* 125 (1974)

Keith Cameron: Aspects of Voltaire's style in *Mahomet* 129 (1975) 7-17

Eugène J. Weinraub: Plays as pedagogical laboratories: *Mahomet* and Don Pèdre 140 (1975) 45-61

Thomas M. Carr: Dramatic structure and philosophy in *Brutus*, *Alzire* and *Mahomet* 143 (1975) 7-48

— —*Mémoire* ('Le corps des natifs')

Bernard Gagnebin: Le médiateur d'une petite querelle genevoise 1 (1955) 115-23

— —*Micromégas*

David L. Gobert: Comic in *Micromégas* as expressive of theme 37 (1965) 53-60

Ahmad Gunny: A propos de la date de composition de *Micromégas* 140 (19) 73-83

Vic Nachtergaele: *Micromégas*, ou le disfonctionnement des procédés de la narration 199 (1981) 73-86

D. W. Smith: The publication of *Micromégas* 219 (1983) 63-91

— — *La Pucelle*

Virgil W. Topazio: Voltaire's *Pucelle*: a study in burlesque 2 (1956) 207-23

Margaret Chenais: New light on the publication of the *Pucelle* 12 (1960) 9-20

Gloria M. Russo: Sexual roles and religious images in Voltaire's *La Pucelle* 171 (1977) 31-53

— — *Questions sur l'Encyclopédie*

Jeroom Vercruysse: Joseph Marie Durey de Morsan chroniqueur de Ferney (1769-1772) et l'édition neuchâteloise des *Questions sur l'Encyclopédie* 230 (1985) 323-91

— — *Relation de Berthier*

D. W. Smith: The first edition of the *Relation de Berthier* 137 (1975) 47-54

— — *Rome sauvée*

André G. Bourassa: Polémique et propagande dans *Rome sauvée* et *Les Triumvirs* de Voltaire 60 (1968) 73-103

Philippe Teissier: Une lettre de madame Denis au comte d'Argental sur *Rome sauvée* 176 (1979) 41-50

— — *Le Siècle de Louis XIV*

Jeroom Vercruysse: *L'Elégant tableau de l'Europe* ou Voltaire édité 'de main de maître' 106 (1973) 103-11

— — *Les Singularités de la nature*

Marguerite Carozzi: Voltaire's geological observations in *Les Singularités de la nature* 215 (1982) 101-19

— — *Le Songe de Platon*

R. Galliani: La date de composition du *Songe de Platon* par Voltaire 219 (1983) 37-57

— — *Tancrède*

John S. Henderson: *Voltaire's Tancrède* 61 (1968)

— — *Le Taureau blanc*

Maureen F. O'Meara: *Le Taureau blanc* and the activity of language 148 (1976) 115-75

— — *Le Temple du Goût*

Owen Taylor: Voltaire iconoclast: an introduction to *Le Temple du Goût* 212 (1982) 7-81

— — *Tout en dieu*

Patrick Henry: A different view of Voltaire's controversial *Tout en dieu* 135 (1975) 143-50

—— *Le Triumvirat*

André G. Bourassa: Polémique et propagande dans *Rome sauvée* et *Les Triumvirs* de Voltaire 60 (1968) 73-103

—— *La Voix du sage et du peuple*

Robert Shackleton: Voltaire and Montesquieu: a false attribution 6 (1958) 155-56

—— *Zadig*

U. Schick: Voltaire's adaptation of a literary source in *Zadig* 57 (1967) 1377-86

Michael H. Gertner: Five comic devices in *Zadig* 117 (1974) 133-52

Jenny H. Batlay: Analyse d'un chapitre de *Zadig*: le nez, démystification et moralité 132 (1975) 7-15

Nancy Senior: The structure of *Zadig* 135 (1975) 135-41

George A. Perla: Zadig, hero of the absurd 143 (1975) 49-70

Jacqueline Hellegouarc'h: Encore la duchesse Du Maine: note sur les rubans jaunes de *Zadig* 176 (1979) 37-40

Richard Waller: Voltaire, Parnell and the hermit 191 (1980) 994-96

R. J. Howells: *Télémaque* et *Zadig*: apports et rapports 215 (1982) 63-75

—— *Zaïre*

Theodore E. D. Braun: Subject, substance and structure in *Zaïre* and *Alzire* 87 (19) 181-96

Voyage à Paphos

Robert F. O'Reilly: The spurious attribution of the *Voyage à Paphos* and an appreciation of Montesquieu's *Temple de Gnide* 189 (1980) 229-37

Wales

R. George Thomas: The Enlightenment and Wales in the 18th century 27 (1963) 1575-91

Walpole, Horace

Colin Duckworth: Louis XVI and English history: a French reaction to Walpole, Hume and Gibbon on Richard III 176 (1979) 385-401

war

Merle L. Perkins: Jean Jacques Rousseau, liberté et état de guerre 57 (1967) 1217-31

Adrienne D. Hytier: Les philosophes et le problème de la guerre 127 (1974) 243-58

Henry Meyer: Voltaire on war and peace 144 (1975)

George Armstrong Kelly: War, revolution and terror: a public biography of Adam-Philippe de Custine 205 (1982) 211-95

Hubert C. Johnson: The *philosophes* as militarists 216 (1983) 387-88

Robert E. Jones: Patriotism and the opposition to war and expansion among the Russian nobility during the second half of the eighteenth century 216 (1983) 388-90

Warburton, William

J. H. Brumfitt: Voltaire and Warburton 18 (1961) 35-56

Warens, Françoise-Louise-Eléonore de La Tour, baronne de

R. A. Leigh: Jean Jacques Rousseau and Mme de Warens: some recently recovered documents 67 (1969) 165-89

Warton, Thomas

Arthur H. Scouten: The Warton forgeries and the concept of Preromanticism 216 (1983) 465-66

Webb, Daniel

Wilbert D. Jerome: Poetry and music as observed by Daniel Webb 193 (1980) 1730-35

Wegelin, Jacob

R. A. Leigh: Wegelin's visit to Rousseau in 1763 249 (1986) 303-32

Weise, Christian

Wolf Wucherpfennig: 'Die unvergnügte Seele': mélancolie et idylle dans le siècle des Lumières 216 (1983) 372-73

Wendel, François-Ignace de

L. Versini: Un maître de forges au service des Lumières et de la révolution américaine: François Ignace de Wendel, 1741-1795 155 (1976) 2173-206

Whiston, William

E. R. Briggs: English Socinianism around Newton and Whiston 216 (1983) 48-50

widow

Roseann Runte: The widow in eighteenth-century French comedy 192 (1980) 1537-44

Wieland, Christoph Martin

Charlotte C. Prather: Liberation and domesticity: two feminine ideals in the works of C. M. Wieland 193 (1980) 2002-2009

Charlotte M. Craig: Patterns for a princely preparation: the duke Carl August's enlightened curriculum 216 (1983) 168-69

Wilhelmine de Bayreuth

Edgar Mass: *Le Marquis d'Adhémar: la correspondance inédite d'un ami des philosophes à la cour de Bayreuth* 109 (1973)

witchcraft

B. Robert Kreiser: Witchcraft and ecclesiastical politics in early eighteenth-century Provence: the Cadière-Girard affair 192 (1980) 1072

Wollstonecraft, Mary

Gary Kelly: Expressive style and 'the female mind': Mary Wollstonecraft's *Vindication of the rights of woman* 193 (1980) 1942-49

Janet Todd: The female text – edited 193 (1980) 1949-55

women

Marie Laure Swiderski: L'image de la femme dans le roman au début du XVIIIe siècle: les *Illustres Françaises* de Robert Challe 90 (1972) 1505-18

Ellen McNiven Hine: The woman question in early eighteenth-century French literature: the influence of François Poulain de La Barre 116 (1973) 65-79

Pauline Kra: The role of the harem in imitations of Montesquieu's *Lettres persanes* 182 (1979) 273-83

Madelyn Gutwirth: Laclos and 'Le sexe': the rack of ambivalence 189 (1980) 247-96

Maria A. Villareal: Women: their place in the sun as seen through Goldoni 192 (1980) 1517-19

Roseann Runte: The widow in eighteenth-century French comedy 192 (1980) 1537-44

Peter V. Conroy: The *Spectators'* view of women 193 (1980) 1883-90

Jeannette Geffriaud Rosso: La représentation encyclopédiste de la femme 193 (1980) 1892-93

Adriana Sfragaro: La représentation de la femme chez Diderot 193 (1980) 1893-99

David Williams: Boudier de Villemert: 'philosopher of the fair sex' 193 (1980) 1899-1901

Volker Hoffmann: Caraterizzazione dei sessi nei testi teoretici e letterari dell'epoca Goethiana 193 (1980) 1901-1908

Robert Niklaus: Etude comparée de la situation de la femme en Angleterre et en France 193 (1980) 1909-18

Sarah Simmons: Héroïne ou figurante? La femme dans le roman du XVIIIe siècle en France 193 (1980) 1918-24

Marie-Laure Girou-Swiderski: Fonctions de la femme du peuple dans le roman du XVIIIe siècle 193 (1980) 1925

P. L. M. Fein: The role of women in certain eighteenth-century French *libertin* novels 193 (1980) 1925-32

Gae Brack: English literary ladies and the booksellers 193 (1980) 1932-39

Gary Kelly: Expressive style and 'the female mind': Mary Wollstonecraft's *Vindication of the rights of woman* 193 (1980) 1942-49

Janet Todd: The female text – edited 193 (1980) 1949-55

Christine Battersby: An enquiry concerning the Humean woman 193 (1980) 1964-67

Ruth Perry: Women in *Tristram Shandy* 193 (1980) 1967-68

William James Murray: Robert Burns: the poet as liberationist 193 (1980) 1969-80

Béatrice Didier: La femme à la recherche de son image: Mme de Charrière et l'écriture féminine dans la seconde moitié du XVIIIe siècle 193 (1980) 1981-88

Christine Oertel Sjögren: Pietism, pathology, or pragmatism in Goethe's *Bekenntnisse einer schönen Seele* 193 (1980) 2009-15

Elizabeth Fox-Genovese: Female identity: symbol and structure of bourgeois domesticity 193 (1980) 2016

Vilmos Gyenis: Le changement du rôle des femmes dans la vie littéraire au milieu du XVIIIe siècle 193 (1980) 2016-27

Carmen Chaves McClendon: Idleness and the eighteenth-century Spanish woman 193 (1980) 2027-28

Carla Pellandra Cazzoli: Dames et sigisbées: un début d'émancipation féminine? 193 (1980) 2028-35

Vivienne Mylne: What Suzanne knew: lesbianism and *La Religieuse* 208 (1982) 167-73

Jean-Pierre Le Bouler et Robert Thiéry: Une partie retrouvée de l'*Ouvrage sur les femmes*, ou Mme Dupin dans la maison des 'Commères', avec un inventaire des papiers Dupin acquis à Monte Carlo le 8 octobre 1980 208 (1982) 373-403

Daniel Brewer: Diderot and the image of the other (woman) 216 (1983) 97-98

David G. John: Women and men as equals in German comedy of the Enlightenment 216 (1983) 208-209

Alice M. Laborde: Madame de Puisieux et Diderot: de l'égalité entre les sexes 216 (1983) 209

Charline Sacks: Le rôle de la femme dans la société utopique de Restif de La Bretonne 216 (1983) 216-18

Ruth P. Dawson: Women communicating: eighteenth-century German journals edited by women 216 (1983) 239-41

Zola, Emile

Index of authors

Abanime, Emeka: Voltaire as an anthropologist: the case of the albino 143 (1975) 85-104
— Voltaire antiesclavagiste 182 (1979) 237-51

Abbott, John L.: Samuel Johnson, John Hawkesworth, and the rise of the *Gentleman's magazine*, 1738-1773 151 (1976) 31-46

Adams, D. J.: Style and social ideas in *Jacques le fataliste* 124 (1974) 231-48
— Experiment and experience in *Les Bijoux indiscrets* 182 (1979) 303-17
— *Le Neveu de Rameau* since 1950 217 (1983) 371-87

Adams, Leonard: *Coyer and the Enlightenment* 123 (1974)
— Anson in Frivola: an exercise in social criticism: Coyer's *Découverte de l'île Frivole* (1751) 191 (1980) 851-58

Adams, Thomas M.: Mendicity and moral alchemy: work as rehabilitation 151 (1976) 47-76
— Charitable reform and the diffusion of economic ideas in eighteenth-century France 191 (1980) 858-66

Addy, George M.: The first generation of academic reform in Spanish universities, 1760-1789 167 (1977) 475-89

Ages, Arnold: Voltaire's Biblical criticism: a study in thematic repetitions 30 (1964) 205-21
— Voltaire, Calmet and the Old testament 41 (1966) 87-187
— Voltaire and the Old testament: the testimony of his correspondence 55 (1967) 43-63
— Stendhal and Voltaire: the *philosophe* as target 62 (1968) 83-99
— The private Voltaire: three studies in the correspondence 81 (1971) 7-125
— Hugo and the *philosophes* 87 (1972) 37-64
— Voltaire and Horace: the testimony of the correspondence 120 (1974) 199-221
— Merimée and the *philosophes* 161 (1976) 245-52

Agrimi, Mario: Quelques échos en France de la pensée d'Antonio Genovesi 216 (1983) 445-47

343

— 'Connaturalización' in two early nineteenth-century versions of Voltaire's *Alzire* 242 (1986) 145-58

Anderson, David L.: Abélard and Héloïse: eighteenth-century motif 84 (1971) 7-51
— Aspects of motif in *La Nouvelle Héloïse* 94 (1972) 25-72
— Structures mythologiques et religieuses dans le roman épistolaire du XVIIIe siècle 192 (1980) 1273-75

Anderson, David R.: Thomson, natural evil, and the eighteenth-century sublime 245 (1986) 489-99

Anderson, Elizabeth: La collaboration de Sonnini de Manoncourt à l'*Histoire naturelle* de Buffon 120 (1974) 329-58

Ando, Takaho: Mme de Condorcet et la philosophie de la 'sympathie' 216 (1983) 335-36

André, Arlette: Recherches sur l'épicurisme de Sade: *Florville et Courval* 151 (1976) 119-29
— Le féminisme chez madame Riccoboni 193 (1980) 1988-95

Andreatta, Alberto: Alle origini dell'anarchismo moderno: Dom Deschamps: la metafisica al servizio dell'utopia 191 (1980) 637-43

Andresen, Julie: L'image des langues américaines au dix-huitième siècle 216 (1983) 88-89

Andries, Lise: Le roman de colportage au 18e siècle: évolution et analyse de contenu 216 (1983) 229-31

Andrivet, P.: Jean-Jacques Rousseau: quelques aperçus de son discours politique sur l'antiquité romaine 151 (1976) 131-48

Anghelou, Alkis: L'Européen et la découverte du grec moderne 216 (1983) 85-87

Applewhite, Harriet Branson, and Darline Gay Levy: The concept of modernisation and the French Enlightenment 84 (1971) 53-98

Argenson, René-Louis de Voyer, marquis d': *Notices sur les œuvres de théâtre*, éd. H. Lagrave 42-43 (1966)

Argyropoulos, Roxane: Patriotisme et sentiment national en Grèce au temps des Lumières 216 (1983) 377

345

Bailey, Charles R.: Attempts to institute a 'system' of secular secondary education in France, 1762-1789 167 (1977) 105-24

Bajkó, Mátyás: The development of Hungarian formal education in the eighteenth century 167 (1977) 191-221

Bakalar, H. Nicholas: An unpublished Voltaire letter 124 (1974) 133-35
— Language and logic: Diderot and the *grammairiens-philosophes* 132 (1975) 113-35

Baker, Keith Michael: Scientism, elitism and liberalism: the case of Condorcet 55 (1967) 129-65
— Condorcet's notes for a revised edition of his reception speech to the Académie française 169 (1977) 7-68

Balaÿ, Christophe: François Pétis de La Croix et les *Mille et un jours* 215 (1982) 9-43

Balázs, Eva H.: Physiocrates et pseudophysiocrates dans la Hongrie des Lumières 216 (1983) 275-77

Balcou, Jean: Si *Candide* aussi nous était conté: de la littérature populaire au mythe personnel 192 (1980) 1314-15
— Ernest Renan et l'héritage des Lumières 216 (1983) 418-19

Baldi, Romano: Louis-Claude de Saint-Martin et la question de l'origine des langues 193 (1980) 1650-58

Barber, Giles: The Cramers of Geneva and their trade in Europe between 1755 and 1766 30 (1964) 377-413
— Books from the old world and for the new: the British international trade in books in the eighteenth century 151 (1976) 185-224
— Voltaire and the English: catalogue of an exhibition 179 (1979) 159-91

Barber, William H.: Voltaire and Quakerism: Enlightenment and the inner light 24 (1963) 81-109
— Voltaire and Samuel Clarke 179 (1979) 47-61
— Voltaire et Newton 179 (1979) 193-202
— Obituary: Theodore Besterman 179 (1979) 221-25
— On editing Voltaire 242 (1985) 491-502

Barbier, Frédéric: Quelques documents inédits sur l'abbé Delille 189 (1980) 211-28

Barcham, William L.: Giambattista Tiepolo's *Translation of the holy house*: a

354

356

Cahm, Eric: Review: Peter Gay, *Voltaire's politics: the poet as realist* 12 (1960) 111-16

Cajani, Luigi: L'assistenza ai poveri nell'Italia del Settecento 191 (1980) 914-20

Caldwell, Ruth L.: Structure de la *Lettre sur les sourds et muets* 84 (1971) 109-22

Cameron, James K.: The Church of Scotland in the age of reason 58 (1967) 1939-51

Cameron, Keith: Aspects of Voltaire's style in *Mahomet* 129 (1975) 7-17

Cammarrota, Robert M.: *Così fan tutte*: Mozart's rhetoric of love and reason 193 (1980) 1719-20

Campbell, Glen: The search for equality of Lesage's picaresque heroes 216 (1983) 195-96

Candaux, Jean-Daniel: Review: Ira O. Wade, *The Search for a new Voltaire* 8 (1959) 243-251
— La publication de *Candide* à Paris 18 (1961) 173-78
— Les débuts de François Grasset 18 (1961) 197-235
— Des documents nouveaux sur la mort de Voltaire? 20 (1962) 261-63
— Charles Borde et la première crise d'antimilitarisme de l'opinion publique européenne 24 (1963) 315-44
— L'annonce des livres nouveaux au 18e siècle 216 (1983) 234-37

Canfield, J. Douglas: The fate of the Fall in *An essay on man* 193 (1980) 1575-76

Cant, R. G.: The Scottish universities in the eighteenth century 58 (1967) 1953-66

Cantarutti, Giulia: Patriotisme et sentiment national dans les *Betrachtungen und Gedanken* (1803-1805) de F. M. Klinger, un représentant des Lumières allemandes à la cour russe 216 (1983) 383-85

Cappiello, Ida: I Giacobini e le scienze sociali 191 (1980) 781-88

Caracciolo, Alberto, and Rosa Maria Colombo: Public opinion and the development of modern society in England in the eighteenth century 193 (1980) 1812

Caramaschi, Enzo: Du Bos et Voltaire 10 (1959) 113-236

— Image claire, image trouble dans l'*Histoire d'une Grecque moderne* de Prévost 217 (1983) 187-97

Conroy, William Thomas: *Diderot's 'Essai sur Sénèque'* 131 (1975)
— Three neglected sources of Diderot's *Essai sur Sénèque*: Ponçol, Peyrilhe, L'Estoile 176 (1979) 259-71

Cook, Malcolm C.: Politics in the fiction of the French Revolution, 1789-1794 201 (1982) 233-340
— Laclos and the *Galeries des Etats-Généraux* 228 (1984) 313-19

Cornea, Paul: Polygenèse et pluralisme des 'Lumières' 190 (1980) 203-208

Corni, Gustavo: Federico II e la politica agraria dell'assolutismo 191 (1980) 943-45

Costa, Gustavo: German antiquities and Gothic art in the early Italian Enlightenment 191 (1980) 559-61
— The desert and the rock: G. B. Vico's *New science* vis-à-vis eighteenth-century European culture 216 (1983) 450-51

Cotoni, Marie-Hélène: Dénigrement de la providence et défense des valeurs humaines dans les manuscrits clandestins de la première moitié du dix-huitième siècle 152 (1976) 497-513
— L'image du Christ dans les courants déiste et matérialiste français du XVIIIe siècle 192 (1980) 1093-1100
— *L'Exégèse du Nouveau Testament dans la philosophie française du dix-huitième siècle* 220 (1984)

Coulaud, Micheline: Les *Mémoires sur la matière étymologique* de Charles de Brosses 199 (1981) 287-352

Coulet, Henri: Voltaire et le problème du changement 152 (1976) 515-26
— La vertu de Gaudet 192 (1980) 1368-69
— Le roman anti-révolutionnaire en France à l'époque de la Révolution (1789-1800) 216 (1983) 7-9

Courtney, Cecil: *A preliminary bibliography of Isabelle de Charrière (Belle de Zuylen)* 186 (1980)
— *The Portrait of Zélide*: Geoffrey Scott and Belle de Zuylen 219 (1983) 281-88
— *A guide to the published works of Benjamin Constant* 239 (1985)

Coward, David: Laclos et la sensibilité 87 (1972) 235-51
— Restif de La Bretonne and the reform of prostitution 176 (1979) 349-83

— Eighteenth-century attitudes to prostitution 189 (1980) 363-99
— Restif as a reader of books 205 (1982) 89-132
— Laclos studies, 1968-1982 219 (1983) 289-330
— The Revolutionary pamphlets of Restif de La Bretonne 242 (1986) 293-334

Cox, Iris: *Montesquieu and the history of French laws* 218 (1983)

Coyer, Xavier: L'élection de l'abbé Coyer à la Royal Society of London: deux lettres inédites de Voltaire et de d'Alembert 249 (1986) 379-80

Cragg, Olga: Les maximes dans *Le Paysan parvenu* 228 (1984) 293-312

Craig, Charlotte M.: Mind and method: Sophie La Roche – a 'praeceptra filiarum Germaniae' 193 (1980) 1996-2002
— Patterns for a princely preparation: the duke Carl August's enlightened curriculum 216 (1983) 168-69

Craven, Kenneth: Publish and languish: the fate of Nikolai Ivanovich Novikov (1743-1818), propagator of the Enlightenment under Catherine II 216 (1983) 238-39

Craveri, Benedetta: Mme Du Deffand e Mme de Choiseul: un'amicizia femminile 193 (1980) 1956-63

Crimmins, James E.: 'The study of true politics': John Brown on manners and liberty 241 (1986) 65-86

Crispini, Franco: Mostri e mostruosità: un problema delle 'sciences de la vie' da Diderot a I. Geoffroy Saint-Hilaire 192 (1980) 1189-98

Crocker, Lester G.: Voltaire's struggle for humanism 4 (1957) 137-69
— L'analyse des rêves au XVIIIe siècle 23 (1963) 271-310
— Rousseau et l'"opinion" 55 (1967) 395-415
— Portrait de l'homme dans le *Paysan parvenu* 87 (1972) 253-76
— When myths die 151 (1976) 19-29
— Hidden affinities: Nietzsche and Rousseau 190 (1980) 119-41
— Voltaire and the political philosophers 219 (1983) 1-17
— Rousseau's dilemma: man or citizen? 241 (1986) 271-84

Crosland, Maurice: The development of chemistry in the eighteenth century 24 (1963) 369-441
— 'Nature' and measurement in eighteenth-century France 87 (1972) 277-309

Diderot, Denis: *Est-il bon? est-il méchant?*, édition critique par J. Undank 16 (1961)
— *La Religieuse*, édition critique par J. Parrish 22 (1963)
— *Ecrits inconnus de jeunesse 1745*, identifiés et présentés par J. Th. de Booy 178 (1979)

Didier, Béatrice: Senancour et les Lumières 87 (1972) 311-31
— L'exotisme et la mise en question du système familial et moral dans le roman à la fin du XVIIIe siècle: Beckford, Sade, Potocki 152 (1976) 571-86
— La femme à la recherche de son image: Mme de Charrière et l'écriture féminine dans la seconde moitié du XVIIIe siècle 193 (1980) 1981-88
— Musique primitive et musique extra-européenne chez quelques écrivains du dix-huitième siècle 216 (1983) 102-104

Dieckmann, Herbert: Diderot's *Promenade du sceptique*: a study in the relationship of thought and form 55 (1967) 417-38

Dimaras, C. Th.: D. Catargi, 'philosophe' grec 25 (1963) 509-18
— Notes sur la présence de Voltaire en Grèce 55 (1967) 439-44

Dimoff, Paul, and René Duthil: Une lettre inédite de Baculard d'Arnaud à Duclos sur l'affaire de Berlin 6 (1958) 141-46

di Rienzo, Eugenio: Diffusione del libro, classe intellettuale e problemi istituzionali dell'editoria nel Settecento francese 193 (1980) 1772-79

Donohoe, Joseph I.: Marivaux: the comedy of Enlightenment 98 (1972) 169-81

Donovan, Arthur: Chemistry in the Scottish Enlightenment 152 (1976) 587-605

Dos Santos, José Augusto: Education in Portuguese America in the eighteenth century 167 (1977) 395-425

Douglas, Denis: Inchworm's antecedents: caricatures of the Enlightenment in the English novel of the eighteenth century 216 (1983) 11-12

Douxchamps-Lefèvre, Cécile: La correspondance politique secrète sur la cour de France: 1er juillet 1774 – 22 décembre 1779 216 (1983) 241-42

Dowdey, David: Secularisation in Moses Mendelssohn's thinking: harmony between the world of Judaism and Enlightenment? 216 (1983) 52-53

Dowling, John: Manuel Godoy and the Spanish *ilustrados* 190 (1980) 326-34

Doyle, William: Reforming the French criminal law at the end of the old regime:

— Quelques lettres inédites de Mably 98 (1972) 183-97
— Voltaire cité par les brochures de 1789 132 (1975) 17-54
— Le débat en France sur le luxe: Voltaire ou Rousseau? 161 (1976) 205-17
— La présence de Voltaire dans les brochures de 1790 169 (1977) 69-114
— Voltaire et les autres philosophes dans la Révolution: les brochures de 1791, 1792, 1793 174 (1978) 69-112
— Voltaire en 1878: le premier centenaire d'après les journaux de l'époque 183 (1980) 91-115
— A propos de Voltaire, de Leibniz et de la *Théodicée* 189 (1980) 7-17
— Trois lettres inédites de Buffon 189 (1980) 205-10
— Voltaire, Porphyre et les animaux 199 (1981) 125-38
— L'idéologie de la noblesse dans le débat sur le luxe (1699-1756) 216 (1983) 173-74
— La date de composition du *Crocheteur borgne* par Voltaire 217 (1983) 141-46
— Quelques faits inédits sur la mort de Voltaire 217 (1983) 159-75
— Voltaire, Astruc, et la maladie vénérienne 219 (1983) 19-36
— La date de composition du *Songe de Platon* par Voltaire 219 (1983) 37-57
— Rousseau, l'illumination de Vincennes et la critique moderne 245 (1986) 403-47

Galliani, R. (ed.): Les notes marginales de Voltaire au *Dictionnaire philosophique* 161 (1976) 7-18

— Quelques notes inédites de Voltaire à l'*Esprit des lois* 163 (1976) 7-18

Garagnon, Jean: La culture populaire dans *Le Neveu de Rameau* 190 (1980) 318-20
— La sensibilité comme idéologie de substitution de la noblesse dans *Aline et Valcour* 216 (1983) 174-77

Gargantini Rabbi, Stella: Le mythe d'Electre dans le théâtre français du XVIIIe siècle 192 (1980) 1547-55
— Les Lumières dans la presse milanaise du 19e siècle (*Il Conciliatore* 1818-1819, *Il Politecnico* 1839-1845, 1860-1865): réception et débat 216 (1983) 423-24

Gargett, Graham: Voltaire, Gilbert de Voisins's *Mémoires* and the problem of Huguenot civil rights (1767-1768) 174 (1978) 7-57
— Voltaire, Richelieu and the problem of Huguenot emancipation in the reign of Louis XV 176 (1979) 97-132
— *Voltaire and Protestantism* 188 (1980)

Garofalo, Silvano: Gianfrancesco Pivati's *Nuovo dizionario* 194 (1981) 197-219

Gascón-Vera, Elena: A feminist writer of the eighteenth century: Giacomo Casanova 193 (1980) 1995-96

Gassman, Byron: Alexander Pope as utopian: Arcadia to apocalypse 191 (1980) 672-78

Gatty, Janette: Les *Six époques* de Beaumarchais: chronique de l'histoire vue et vécue 191 (1980) 574-81

Gaulin, Michel: Montesquieu et l'attribution de la lettre XXXIV des *Lettres persanes* 79 (1971) 73-78

Gauthier, Florence: L'universalité du genre humain chez Robespierre 190 (1980) 377-80
— De Mably a Robespierre: un programme économique égalitaire 1775-1793 216 (1983) 200-201

Gawlick, Günter: Cicero and the Enlightenment 25 (1963) 657-82
— Abraham's sacrifice of Isaac viewed by the English deists 56 (1967) 577-600
— The English deists' contribution to the theory of toleration 152 (1976) 823-35

Gay, Peter: Voltaire's *Idées républicaines*: a study in bibliography and interpretation 6 (1958) 67-105
— Against the gravediggers 152 (1976) 837-50

Gearhart, Suzanne: Rationality and the text: a study of Voltaire's historiography 140 (1975) 21-43

Geffriaud Rosso, Jeannette: La représentation encyclopédiste de la femme 193 (1980) 1892-93
— Libertinage et 'surcompensation' dans les rapports entre les sexes au dix-huitième siècle', d'après Laclos, Diderot et Crébillon fils 216 (1983) 348-49

Geiringer, Karl: Joseph Haydn, protagonist of the Enlightenment 25 (1963) 683-90
— The impact of the Enlightenment on the artistic concepts of Johann Sebastian Bach 56 (1967) 601-10
— Concepts of the Enlightenment as reflected in Gluck's Italian reform opera 88 (1972) 567-76

379

Gyenis, Vilmos: L'idéal du bonheur et la vie quotidienne dans l'Europe centrale et orientale au milieu du XVIIIe siècle: les rapports de la prose mineure 153 (1976) 1019-43
— Le changement du rôle des femmes dans la vie littéraire au milieu du XVIIIe siècle 193 (1980) 2016-27

Gyergyai, Albert: Un correspondant hongrois de Voltaire: le comte Fekete de Galanta 25 (1963) 779-93

Haac, Oscar A.: L'amour dans les collèges jésuites: une satire anonyme du dix-huitième siècle 18 (1961) 95-111
— Voltaire and Leibniz: two aspects of rationalism 25 (1963) 795-809
— Paradox and levels of understanding in Marivaux 56 (1967) 693-706
— Theories of literary criticism and Marivaux 88 (1972) 711-34
— Rousseau and Marivaux: action and interaction 124 (1974) 221-30
— Comedy in utopia: the literary imagination of Marivaux and the abbé Prévost 191 (1980) 684-85
— A monstrous proposition: the Church stands in need of reform 216 (1983) 427-29

Hackel, Roberta, and Richard L. Frautschi: Le comportement verbal du narrateur dans *Gil Blas*: quelques observations quantitatives 192 (1980) 1340-52

Haffter, Pierre: L'usage satirique des causales dans les contes de Voltaire 53 (1967) 7-28
— Voltaire et les italiques 189 (1980) 45-80

Hagstrum, Jean H.: William Blake rejects the Enlightenment 25 (1963) 811-28

Hahn, Roger: The application of science to society: the societies of arts 25 (1963) 829-36
— New thoughts on the origin of the *Encyclopédie* 190 (1980) 469

Hall, A. Rupert: Galileo in the eighteenth century 190 (1980) 81-100

Hall, H. Gaston: From extravagant poet to the writer as hero: Piron's *La Métromanie* and Pierre Cerou's *L'Amant auteur et valet* 183 (1980) 117-32

Hall, Thadd E.: The development of Enlightenment interest in eighteenth-century Corsica 64 (1968) 165-85

Hamans, Camiel: Universal language and the Netherlands 192 (1980) 1218-27

Hopp, Lajos: Fortune littéraire et politique du *Contrat social* en Hongrie et en Europe orientale 190 (1980) 320-26

Horsman, Elspeth M.: The abbé de Saint-Pierre and domestic politics 190 (1980) 284-90

Horwath, Peter: Literature in the service of enlightened absolutism: the age of Joseph II (1780-1790) 56 (1967) 707-34
— Johann Friedel's Danubian journey along the Turkish border to 'Menschen wie aus dem Schoosse der lieben Mutter Natur' 191 (1980) 687-93
— *Austriacus perfectus*: the ideal man of the Austrian literature of the Enlightenment 216 (1983) 59-61

Hotta, Seizo: Quesnay or Hume: Beccaria between France and Britain 216 (1983) 281-83
— Quesnay or Hume: Beccaria between France and Britain 245 (1986) 457-65

Houmanidis, Lazaros: Introduzione [to a collection of papers on economics] 191 (1980) 793-804

Howard, Seymour: The antiquarian market in Rome and the use of neo-classicism: a basis for Canova's new classics 153 (1976) 1057-68
— The revival of ancient archaic art in the late eighteenth century and the use of archaising postures and modes in drama and living sculpture 192 (1980) 1453-60
— Blake, classicism, gothicism, and nationalism 216 (1983) 132

Howarth, W. D.: Tragedy into melodrama: the fortunes of the Calas affair on the stage 174 (1978) 121-50
— Voltaire, Ninon de L'Enclos and the evolution of a dramatic genre 199 (1981) 63-72

Howells, R. J.: The metaphysic of nature: basic values and their application in the social philosophy of Rousseau 60 (1968) 109-200
— Marivaux and the heroic 171 (1977) 115-53
— *Télémaque* et *Zadig*: apports et rapports 215 (1982) 63-75
— Désir et distance dans *La Nouvelle Héloïse* 230 (1985) 223-32
— Deux histoires, un discours: *La Nouvelle Héloïse* et le récit des amours d'Emile et Sophie dans l'*Emile* 249 (1986) 267-94

Hubert, J. D.: Note malicieuse sur le jardin de Candide 70 (1970) 11-13

Hunter, P.: Print culture and the developing audience in England: fiction 216 (1983) 266-67

393

Longo, Mario: Illuminismo e storiografia filosofica: Brucker e l'*Encyclopédie* 191 (1980) 581-87

Lopez, Claudia-Anne: L'utopie americaine du dr Guillotin 191 (1980) 694-98

Lough, John: Luneau de Boisjermain v. the publishers of the *Encyclopédie* 23 (1963) 115-77
— The contemporary influence of the *Encyclopédie* 26 (1963) 1071-83
— The problem of the unsigned articles in the *Encyclopédie* 32 (1965) 327-90
— The *Encyclopédie* and Chambers's *Cyclopaedia* 185 (1980) 221-24
— The contributors to the *Encyclopédie* 223 (1984) 479-568
— Encounters between British travellers and eighteenth-century French writers 245 (1986) 1-90

Lowood, Henry: Patriotism and progress: the role of the German patriotic and economic societies in the promotion of science and technology 216 (1983) 394-96

Loy, J. Robert: Nature, reason and enlightenment, Voltaire, Rousseau and Diderot 26 (1963) 1085-107
— Rococo and the novel as guide to periodisation in the eighteenth century 190 (1980) 166-76

— Saint-Lambert, moralist: philosophy at second hand; Enlightenment among the titled 216 (1983) 353-54

Luciani, Gérard: L'œuvre de Carlo Gozzi et les polémiques théâtrales contre les Lumières 89 (1972) 939-74

Ludassy, Maria: Tendances autoritaires et tendances anarchiques dans les utopies du XVIIIe siècle 191 (1980) 699-701

Ludlow, Gregory: Eighteenth-century literature and the French new criticism 190 (1980) 258-60

Lüsebrink, Hans-Jürgen: L'affaire Cléreaux (Rouen 1785-1790): affrontements idéologiques et tensions institutionnelles sur la scène judiciaire de la fin du XVIIIe siècle 191 (1980) 892-900
— *Mémoire pour la fille Cléreaux* (Rouen 1785) 208 (1982) 323-72

Lussu, Marialuisa: Critica della religione e autonomia della morale in alcune figure dell'Illuminismo francese 192 (1980) 1085-93

Lutaud, Olivier: D'*Areopagitica* à la *Lettre à un premier commis* et de l'*Agreement* au *Contrat social* 26 (1963) 1109-27

romanesque dans *Paul et Virginie* 242 (1986) 377-418
— *Paul et Virginie* et l'utopie: de la 'petite société' au mythe collectif 242 (1986) 419-71

Racevskis, Karlis: Le règne des philosophes à l'Académie française, vu par les historiens du dix-neuvième siècle 154 (1976) 1801-12
— Le discours philosophique à l'Académie française: une sémiotique de la démagogie et de l'arrivisme 190 (1980) 343-50

Radisich, Paula Rea: Hubert Robert's Paris: truth, artifice, and spectacle 245 (1986) 501-18

Ramsey, Warren: Voltaire et 'l'art de peindre' 26 (1963) 1365-77

Ranum, Orest: D'Alembert, Tacitus and the political sociology of despotism 191 (1980) 547-58

Ranzani, Bruna Ombretta: Représentation, étiologie et prophylaxie des catastrophes naturelles au dix-huitième siècle 191 (1980) 1033-40

Rao, Anna Maria: Riformismo napoletano e rivoluzione: Giuseppe Maria Galanti 190 (1980) 382-90

Ratermanis, J. B. (ed.): Pierre Augustin Caron de Beaumarchais, *La Folle journée ou le mariage de Figaro* 63 (1968)

Rawson, C. J.: Satire, fiction, and extreme situations 192 (1980) 1286

Raymond, Agnes G.: Le problème de la population chez les encyclopédistes 26 (1963) 1379-88
— L'infâme: superstition ou calomnie? 57 (1967) 1291-306
— Encore quelques réflexions sur la 'chaîne secrète' des *Lettres persanes* 89 (1972) 1337-47

Raynor, David: Hume's critique of Helvétius's *De l'esprit* 215 (1982) 223-29

Redman, Harry: Marivaux's reputation among his contemporaries 47 (1966) 137-55

Redshaw, Adrienne M.: Voltaire and Lucretius 189 (1980) 19-43

Reish, J. G.: France's children discover the other: Mme de Genlis's tales of travel and instruction 216 (1983) 113-15

Renaud, Jean: De la théorie à la fiction: les *Salons* de Diderot 201 (1982) 143-62

Renwick, John: Reconstruction and interpretation of the genesis of the *Bélisaire*

of Franz Xaver Messerschmidt (1736-1783) 216 (1983) 143-45

Runset, Ute van: Illuminisme et Lumières: impact sur les idées sociales de George Sand 216 (1983) 439-41

Runte, Roseann: The widow in eighteenth-century French comedy 192 (1980) 1537-44

Russell, Bertrand: Voltaire's influence on me 6 (1958) 157-62

Russell, Lois Ann: A colonial utopia: the Acadia of Robert Challe 191 (1980) 729-31

Russo, Gloria M.: Sexual roles and religious images in Voltaire's *La Pucelle* 171 (1977) 31-53

Rustin, J.: Les 'suites' de Candide au XVIIIe siècle 90 (1972) 1395-416

Rychner, Jacques: A l'ombre des Lumières: coup d'œil sur la main d'œuvre de quelques imprimeurs du XVIIIe siècle 155 (1976) 1925-55

Rzadkowska, Ewa: Essai de périodisation des Lumières polonaises en relation avec les 'temps forts' des Lumières françaises 190 (1980) 176-82
— A propos d'une traduction polonaise du *Temple de Gnide* 216 (1983) 462-63

Sacks, Charline: Le rôle de la femme dans la société utopique de Restif de La Bretonne 216 (1983) 216-18

Sadrin, Paul: *Nicolas-Antoine Boulanger (1722-1759) ou avant nous le déluge* 240 (1986)

Saint-Amand, Pierre: Rousseau contre la science: l'exemple de la botanique dans les textes autobiographiques 219 (1983) 159-67

Saisselin, Rémy G.: Le passé, le goût, et l'histoire 27 (1963) 1445-55
— The rococo muddle 47 (1966) 233-55
— Rousseau and portraiture: from representation to fiction 60 (1968) 201-24
— The transformation of art into culture: from Pascal to Diderot 70 (1970) 193-218
— Architecture in the age of Louis XVI: from private luxury to public power 155 (1976) 1957-70
— Langage et peinture: la dialectique du regard 193 (1980) 1735-36
— Le dix-huitième siècle de Paul Bourget 216 (1983) 436-37
— Painting, writing and primitive purity: from expression to sign in eighteenth-century French painting and architecture 217 (1983) 257-369